ABJECT performances

Dissident Acts   *A series edited by Macarena Gomez-Barris and Diana Taylor*

ABJECT performances

AESTHETIC STRATEGIES IN LATINO CULTURAL PRODUCTION

LETICIA ALVARADO

Duke University Press / Durham and London / 2018

© 2018 Duke University Press
All rights reserved
Printed in the United States of America on acid-free paper ∞
Designed by Heather Hensley
Typeset in Scala Pro by Copperline Book Services, Inc.

Library of Congress Cataloging-in-Publication Data
Names: Alvarado, Leticia, [date] author.
Title: Abject performances : aesthetic strategies in Latino
cultural production / Leticia Alvarado.
Description: Durham : Duke University Press, 2018. | Series:
Dissident acts | Includes bibliographical references and index.
Identifiers: LCCN 2017045246 (print) | LCCN 2017051045 (ebook)
ISBN 9780822371939 (ebook)
ISBN 9780822370635 (hardcover : alk. paper)
ISBN 9780822370789 (pbk. : alk. paper)
Subjects: LCSH: Hispanic American mass media—Social aspects. |
Hispanic American arts—Social aspects. | Hispanic Americans
and mass media. | Mass media and culture.
Classification: LCC P94.5.H58 (ebook) | LCC P94.5.H58 A48
2018 (print) | DDC 302.2308968/073—dc23
LC record available at https://lccn.loc.gov/2017045246

Cover art: Xandra Ibarra with Sophia Wang, *Untitled (skins)*,
2015–2016. Performance documentation. Photograph by
Robbie Sweeny.

For the only people I ever want to see on purpose:
Sydney, Lu, and Mika.

And also for JEM. Love, a Hologram.

Contents

Acknowledgments

I AM HUMBLED BY THE AMOUNT OF support that brought this book to fruition.

My own institution, Brown University, generously provided financial support to assist with publication costs and supported leave time supplemented by a Ford Foundation postdoctoral fellowship, providing invaluable manuscript revision time. I am thankful to Chon Noriega and the Chicano Studies Research Center at University of California, Los Angeles, for serving as my host during my fellowship year. At the dissertation stage, the support of a Smithsonian Institution Latino Studies dissertation fellowship, under the mentorship of Marvette Pérez and Liza Kirwin at the National Museum of American History and Smithsonian Archives of American Art respectively, allowed me dedicated time away from teaching to focus on archival research and the writing of the bulk of my dissertation. A temporary teaching appointment at Wesleyan provided the financial support to cover day care to finish the dissertation and go on the market while the Yale Law School welcomed me into their quiet library for long writing sessions and provided a spot for my then-toddler in their day care across the way. I am thankful to them both. I am indebted to the institutions at which I conducted research and their respective archivists and librarians for their patience and guidance with my questions, including the Smithsonian Institution Archives, Galerie Lelong, the Fales Library, and the Chicano Studies Research Center. A special thanks to those that provided permissions for images to appear in these pages: the Ana Mendieta Estate, the Adrian Piper Foundation, SPACES—Saving and Preserving Arts and Cultural Environments, Harry Gamboa Jr., the Chicano Studies Research Center, and Ken Brown. A special thanks to Nao Bustamante and Xandra Ibarra for their work and generosity with permissions.

I am thankful for engaged colleagues who have contributed in different ways to the writing process. At Brown, Matt Guterl, Ralph Rodriguez, and Monica Muñoz Martinez have all provided direct feedback on different parts of the manuscript. Albert Laguna and Dixa Ramirez joined Monica and me in workshops that resulted in useful edits and much-needed New England camaraderie. C. Ondine Chavoya, Ricky Rodríguez, Deb Vargas, and Macarena Gómez-Barris served, perhaps unknowingly, as Latino mentors during my first few years in the professorate—thank you. A previous version of chapter 1 appeared in the *Journal of Latin American Cultural Studies*. My thanks to the anonymous reviewers of this publication for helping to develop the arguments that would eventually find a home here. Thank you also to Maja Horn for the invitation to contribute a short piece to *Small Axe: A Caribbean Journal of Cultural Criticism* that would further the eventual shape of chapter 1. A previous version of chapter 2 appeared in *Aztlán: A Journal of Chicano Studies*. My thanks to the anonymous and not-so-anonymous reviewers there for their attention to detail and for pushing me to a level of specificity and analysis I endeavor to apply to other sites. My thanks to Katie Lofton for her unwarranted generosity and willingness to read and offer substantial comment on what would become chapter 4. My thanks to Ricardo Bracho for editorial suggestions and to my research assistants, Pier Dominguez and Lilian Mengesha, for their bibliographic, formatting, and editorial help. I am especially thankful to Lily for her care and sustained diligence with the manuscript.

I am most indebted to Elizabeth Mesok, without whose editorial suggestions, grammar assistance, marginalia humor, and terrible taste in television I would not have completed this manuscript or, really, the dissertation from which it grew. At New York University, where I wrote my dissertation, I had the tremendous honor of working under the guidance of scholars whose star status has never ceased to terrify and inspire. I am not sure where I would be without my cochairs, María Josefina Saldaña-Portillo—Josie—and José Esteban Muñoz. Josie, for your mentorship and guidance (delivered with scathing honesty and trimmed with humor), for being an unforgiving superego, for insisting that I make time for your writing group (as I was first learning to navigate life with a newborn)—thank you. Thank you also for teaching me that I am my best writer as a rewriter. José . . . your work means so much to me, has impacted so fully the way I think and approach cultural production. I remember the day you invited me to share my work with you, the day you handed me a compilation DVD of works by Bustamante that you thought I should consider given my interest in abjection, the day you let me sit in your office bad-mouthing the work of an artist you yourself were writing about and would later challenge me to take up. You called me out for being scared of you and encouraged me not to be, yet your work gave me constant reason to be in awe. I always joked you trained me to be a less good version of you—I still believe that. This book would not have happened without you. Thank you. The rest of my committee was an embarrassing arsenal of talent—in addition to dissertation edits, Gayatri Gopinath served as my primary model for pedagogy and professionalism (though she may not have known it, she kept me from leaving graduate school that one time I wasn't sure I should stay); Crystal Parikh labored through my qualifying exams and then agreed to labor some more for my dissertation—thank you both. Though an outside reader, Licia Fiol-Matta provided years of mentorship and enthusiasm. I like to think of myself as Chicana born but Boricua raised in her classrooms on the Upper West Side. Gracias, Licia.

I suspected but did not know the full extent to which NYU would serve as site for peer collegiality and sustained intellectual friendships: Albert, Roy, Ariana, Johana, Karen, Sandra, Marisol, Carmen, and Joshua—thank you for harnessing brown feelings; Ariana (again) and Dacia for the unofficial SCA mamas support group; and Ronak, Lena, and Lezlie for cohort camaraderie.

At Duke, Ken Wissoker has been an engaging interlocutor from our first meeting, pairing enthusiasm with probing questions and, eventually, editorial requests and suggestions. Thank you for your patience and guidance.

Thank you also for your careful selection of readers whose requested re-visions helped me strengthen and clarify the arguments of the book. Any remaining weaknesses are entirely my own fault. Thank you too to Olivia Polk (and Jade Brooks and Nicole Campbell before her) for logistical help and being available to answer my incessant questions.

Thank you, *familia*, for your love, distractions, and dramas, but mostly for your pictures of cute nieces and nephews—a girl's gotta look up from her books. I love you.

Lu, this book is in many ways your twin. You shared your time so generously with it and helped remind me when I needed to pause and take five deep breaths (you are five, so this number organizes your life). Thank you, young child, for draining and sustaining me. Mika, you grew inside me as I worked on final revisions for this book and shared your first months with lingering revisions and publication logistics. Thank you for quietly sleeping in the carrier so that I could write these final words. I promise to make you another sibling book to grow with.

Sydney, there aren't enough thank yous. There aren't. I love you.

Sublime Abjection

On July 22, 2013, a group of nine transnational immigration activists approached the U.S. border severing Nogales, Sonora, Mexico, from Nogales, Arizona, United States to reenter a country they had been brought to as young children and then left—three voluntarily for this particular activist event, three on their own before the event to reunite with family, and three through federal deportation.[1] Resplendent in the synthetic iridescence of graduation caps and gowns, the Dream 9—as they've come to be known—locked arms and proceeded toward the national border to the cadence of their supporters' chants, who bridged the Nogales of here and there. Against the throng of these same chants, the Dream 9 were immediately taken into custody by Immigration and Customs Enforcement. They were released a month later into the limbo of the asylum process with the promise of a hearing date. Their release from custody marked the end of the first #BringThemHome campaign, orchestrated and staged by the

National Immigrant Youth Alliance. The activist protest event mobilized social media (Twitter, Facebook, and various video streaming sites) and a transnational base to integrate grassroots support as part of a large media performance event resonant to many of the political and aesthetic strategies of famed civil rights mobilizations of the 1960s and 1970s.

The group has been rightfully lauded for their bold challenge to border agents and to the larger American public to acknowledge them as subjects worthy of entry and sanctioned residency. Special note has been made of the three that chose to leave the United States to meet those in Mexico for a staged return, volunteering their own deportation after a life lived in fear of one. While self-deporting or attrition through enforcement was the ultimate goal of an aggressive conservative political agenda that created an increasingly hostile environment for the undocumented, on the rise since the 1990s, here it set the stage for insistence on admission, with the brandished signs of their supporters reading "undocumented unafraid" providing rich background scenery.[2] The participants were very purposefully attired and then christened to create a direct connection to the undocumented student activists known as DREAMers but also to the student activists of prior decades who were central to the institutionalization of Chicano and ethnic studies broadly, as well as gender and sexuality studies, among other forms of civic representation.[3]

Given these past successes, it is no surprise that the representative figure selected as part of a strategy to achieve concrete small victories with potentially large implications was that of the student. The political border performance mobilized familiar affects—pride over shame, bravery over fear—throughout its strategic staging along with a well-recognized aesthetic vocabulary. The Dream 9 both embraced a subject position that has served to demarcate the boundaries of American belonging through the distinction between sanctioned and unsanctioned residents—that of undocumented—while at the same time seeking to expunge the status and category of undocumented of its shameful associations through the figure of the student. To do so, they borrowed a strategy from LGBTQ coming-out narratives that perform the prideful revelation of a true self, an enactment of a performative calculus that equates revelation of status and inhabitation of the category of student as redeeming truth.[4] Focusing on the performative component of their action, its aesthetic gesture, the figure of the student is vital for a transformative equation that dissolves the patina of criminality that clings to the undocumented subject in favor of the sheen of the garbed graduate, the successful student at the cusp of potentiality and civic contribution.

In the face of very material consequences—incarceration and sustained separation from loved ones to name just a few—the activists mobilized a strategy that put on display their cultural citizenship, leveraging the ideological promise of meritocracy at the core of education to signal belonging and the right to civic participation.[5] In their caps and gowns they literalized the vision of eligibility for Deferred Action for Childhood Arrivals (DACA), which went into effect just a month before their publicized border crossing, surely in part due to the pressure exerted by DREAMers for over a decade. The aesthetic gesture of the event ultimately offers a performative argument for incorporation through assimilative potential. As immigration activists celebrated DACA while continuing to apply pressure and insist that this policy fails to assist many undocumented individuals, even after revisions to the policy in 2015, I watched coverage of this incredible intervention with ambivalence as once again, the revered, respectable, and protected figure of the student was mobilized despite its lack of applicability across the undocumented community and its limited implications for a diverse group identifiable under the umbrella of Latinidad.[6]

I want to linger in the folds of polyester on display to reflect on what they occlude and whom they obscure, to grapple with Latino performative strategies and the political possibilities they illuminate as well as the limits of a recourse to assimilationist appeals for respectability, to ultimately highlight and center strategies alternate to those on display in this border-crossing event. While the majority of the individual participants that constitute the Dream 9 were in their twenties, it was unclear from media coverage which of them were concurrently enrolled as students or were seeking return in order to enroll in institutions of higher education. I mention this to underscore the strategic representational deployment of the figure of the student as opposed to an adherence to an educational reality for the participants. We do know that one participant was a mother in her late thirties who had been brought to the United States as a child but left for Mexico when her husband was deported, bringing their U.S.-born child with her. Imagine her as a central performative figure—the reproducing foreign-born mother with her anchor baby.

With her demographic-growing capabilities, the woman of Latin American descent has long figured in the dominant U.S. imaginary as a particularly virulent threat, able to anchor in the nation with her resource-consuming offspring.[7] Represented as overly fertile, irresponsible, lazy, and manipulative, she is the ultimate figure to expunge if not relegate to the periphery of the nation. Stigmatized by a "moralized maternity," the abject mother is a figure that, along with cognate women of color archetypes, has been represented as in a state of perpetual sexual availability—impure yet desirable—against which proper white womanhood is forged.[8] Long a subject of legal and moral discourses, she shores up a normative national body organized around the responsible citizen-subject within a respectable family unit.[9] A central target of contemporary anti-immigrant legislation, what would it have meant to deploy the abject mother with her anchor baby, figuratively if not materially, at the performative center of this activist effort—not a mother within the romanticized family unit, the vessel for the propagation of a people and its culture, but rather an abject figure grappling with and deciding on separation within a mixed-status family of loved ones across the expanse of the border?[10] Herein lies an invitation to envision how strategies that center abjection might unfold, by gazing back as well as forward, to privilege the nonassimilative irreverence with which this pathologized mother might call forth new strategies, and indeed new politics, through abject performances.

The deployment of abjection as an irreverent aesthetic strategy unites the artists, performers, and cultural producers profiled in *Abject Performances*, as does their challenge to a bounded understanding of Latinidad. As a group, they are often active and informed, if marginal/ized, participants of political movements—Chicano nationalist, liberal feminist, immigration rights—who prioritize strategies and affects distinct from those long recognized as effective and elaborate them across a number of different terrains. Instead of the pride, bravery, and redemption on display by the Dream 9 that linked them to a politicized aesthetic history, these cultural producers cohere their aesthetic gestures around negative affects—uncertainty, disgust, unbelonging—capturing what lies far outside mainstream, inspirational Latino-centered social justice struggles. Collectively, they depict the structures of feeling of a contrapuntal affective terrain that demarcates a complex periphery of political projects as well as the incoherence and instability of interpellative identitarian categories (including "Latino," the very category that brings them together in these pages). Latinidad emerges here as a performative utterance that gestures at once to an affective state shared by a diverse community of individuals of Latin American dissent and the challenges of finite denotation.[11] As the work of cultural theorist José Esteban Muñoz has shown us, centering affect provides a narrative alternative to "standard stories of identity politics," especially those that place a premium on cultural/biological essence, community unity, and racial uplift.[12] The four principal chapters in this book take up these narrative alternatives, rooting in abjection, not merely to revisit well-trodden historical terrain but also to attend to the undertheorized relationship between performative and embodied nonrepresentative aesthetics and political movements.

Throughout, I rely on the unifying heuristic of affect, particularly negative affect as shaped by queer theory. An expansive body of scholarship has theorized the complexity and nuances of affect, underscoring its value for the analysis and politicized instrumentalization of collective feelings.[13] Building on this scholarship, I position affect as having prime importance for a study of aesthetics that seeks to understand and expand the collectivity we call Latinidad. The negative affect I invoke here is not of the nihilistic vein that has come to characterize the antirelational, "no future" camp of gay theory propelled by Lee Edelman.[14] Instead, I invoke the affective heuristic that avoids foreclosure of utopian longing for the future, the same heuristic proffered by a Muñozian camp of queer theory that privileges a nonhierarchical commons, a being-with defined by a logic not-yet-here Muñoz called queerness.[15] This not-yet-here, Muñoz argued, following the work of Marxist cultural theorist Ernst Bloch, was glimpsed often through minoritarian aesthetics.[16] I thus direct our attention to modes of community formation and social critique rooted in minoritarian abject performances as well as a refusal of identitarian coherence, a root and refusal that nonetheless coalesce into Latino affiliation and possibility theorized by a growing cadre of scholars as "brownness."[17] The depathologizing of negative affects glimpsed in the aesthetic renders them "resources for political action rather than as its antithesis," lending a predictive value to the aesthetic, opening up possible futures for our close interrogation.[18]

In *Abject Performances*, I both indicate the continued relevance and impact of aesthetic theory and advocate for its robust engagement in Latino studies in order to shift, within the ideologies it proffers, what we are able to imagine and demand of our political practices. Given scholarship that has shown us the centrality and indeed mutual constitutiveness of cultures of taste and distinction to those that regulate the strictures of race, classical aesthetic theory, specifically Immanuel Kant's offerings on the beautiful and sublime, must be engaged to make sense of dominant structuring logics of aesthetics and its effects but also contemporary elaborations of race.[19] With its rich history of the romantic embellishment of emotion, the Kantian structure of the sublime, specifically, serves as a necessary conduit if centering affect when thinking through the political workings of aesthetics. Instead of a desire for and focus on recuperative beauty—the other category of judgment in the Kantian dyad—the sublime is a complicated and vexed category that, as I show below and throughout, reveals the limits and fissures within the dominant organizing logic for aesthetic engagement derived from the famed enlightenment philosopher. My own theorization of the abject within the frame of the category of the sublime shows how an aesthetic of abjection can indicate a point beyond the horizon of what is currently known, provoked, or arrived at through negative affect. In doing so, the abject propels the sublime to simultaneously undermine the very logic of its framing.

Departing from Kant's foundational work, I designate the aesthetic as a collision with the sensate—the activation of the sensorial realm—and the political world within which it is bound, honing in on the subjectivities that might emerge from this collision.[20] The aesthetic here is a decidedly political and historically constituted terrain, an Althusserian apparatus that enables us to explore the subject that is hailed by aesthetic engagement as performatively construed and constructed while also querying the limited conventions through which individuals matter as subjects in and of (or denied) modernity. Foregrounding a performative understanding of the subject, *Abject Performances*, then, explores aesthetics as a site for the doing of a Latinidad predicated on a shared sense of being and a way of performing the self often in negative relation to majoritarian publics, a dynamic we might call intrinsically abject.

It then follows that within aesthetics, performance—broadly understood —and the challenges it poses to spectators is particularly generative in my analyses. Throughout I center practitioners that generate sustained cultural encounters within both the expected confines of art performance and installation but also the commercial endeavors of television and the religious stage. Durationality of audience engagement comes to be a key component of performance as I understand it, especially as it provides an affective link to the sublime within which I root abjection as an aesthetic practice. Theorized as boundless and without form, the sublime is evoked by performance's resistance to restrictive formal parameters in favor of the temporal drag of performance events that provide the sustained occasion to be accosted by an aesthetic against beauty.

Below I elaborate the two principal strands of theory on which *Abject Performances* builds: theories on the abject, opened up by the figure of the mother—occluded in the scene with which I opened—and Kantian aesthetic theory, whose structuring logic urgently requires our attention given its continued cultural impact. Both have long scholarly histories, especially in postmodern cultural criticism. I bring together these genealogies, unable to dislodge the modern subject forged through imperial and colonial projects that they rely on, to posit abjection as a fissure capable of reorienting our aesthetic engagement and therefore the politicized subjects we can imagine, relevant both within and beyond Latino studies.

Abject Mother Matters

Abjection, as an aesthetic strategy that reverberates in the social realm, emerges from an engagement with the scholarship of feminist and queer theorists who grapple with the legacies of psychoanalysis to reflect on projects of subjectivation as well as critical race scholars and their writing on abjection and specifically racialized minoritarian populations. A significant point of reference for these scholars, and for my own study, is Julia Kristeva's influential *Powers of Horror: An Essay on Abjection*, a Lacanian psychoanalytic tome that reflects on abjection as tied to the process of subject formation in part through literary analysis. For Kristeva, the abject is distinguished as something other than subject or object, sharing with the object its opposition to the speaking "I."[21] The abject coheres the subject through its exclusion as an in-between, ambiguous, and composite intermediary entity, yet threatens the constitution of the subject who is invested in the myth of wholeness and completeness lest he acknowledge the process by which he becomes subject. As Karen Shimakawa explains in her work on Asian American abjection, the abject in Kristeva refers to both an ontological state—the entity opposed to the subject, "the condition/ position of that which is deemed loathsome"—and a continual process "by which that appraisal is made," involving the jettisoning that confirms but also repeatedly determines the status of that which "disturbs identity, system, order [and] does not respect borders, positions, rules."[22] In other words, the subject is perpetually differentiating itself from the not-quite-subject, relying on an expulsion of what Darieck Scott calls "objects-to-be" to establish a relationship with the abject of simultaneous "attraction and repulsion."[23]

This theorization of subject formation lends itself well to thinking through the composition of Latinidad, a category already under duress by discourses on race and ethnicity that conjures diverse and unstable subjectivities. Dominant U.S. relationships to Latinos can be characterized by the above-mentioned attraction/repulsion dynamic. At times we are called into the life of the nation, invited to provide labor and to vote with our strong family values, while at other times we are central to xenophobic discourses that seek to expel or remove Latino traces from the national body. What is clear in this dynamic is the failure to account for the diversity of Latinidad within and across the national groups understood as Latino that, in some places, have become the demographic majority.[24] Some Latino national/ist groups were already present as conglomerations of different empires with their own enduring legacies of racial stratification when the U.S. was expanding its own borders; others were welcomed during specific historical moments as symbolic of reigning political ideologies; still others are part of the United States' colonial present. This is part of a dynamic Antonio Viego identifies as the queerness of Latinidad that "disturbs the logic by which ethnicity/race can be posed as a binary pair," concepts readily, if problematically, applicable to other minoritarian groups.[25] Latinidad's queerness as defined above is at the core of how I read and understand the political possibilities of Latino abject performances. Understood in this way, Latinidad signals an inherent incoherence whose queerness is shared by the figure of the pathologized mother eschewed in the political performance with which I began, herself outside normative prescriptions, primed to make use of abjection as a politicized strategy.

Turning to Kristeva allows us to understand why the abject mother, a significant figure in the history of representations of Latinidad, matters. In her *Powers of Horror*, Kristeva suggests that the maternal figure is central for the negative process of subject formation described above.[26] If we read Kristeva's "mother" not as an actual empirical mother but rather as a symbolic mother within a discursive order where heteropatriarchy is dominant, entering proper subjecthood entails abasement and expulsion of the feminine.[27] The subject must cast out the beloved symbol of that which is weak and despised in a patriarchal order in order to acquire social power, indeed, to cohere as subject. Further application of abjection to the social material realm allows us to reflect on the formation of a normative national identity cohered by the casting out of other undesirable bodies whose own interiority is diminished.

In her *Bodies That Matter*, Judith Butler facilitates precisely an application of the symbolic to the social, providing a model of subjectivity forged through performative enactment that has served as a touchstone for scholars who elaborate a theorization of the abject through minoritized populations. Butler argues that the status of "subject" is guaranteed through an "unlivable" domain—the uninhabitable zones variously and "densely" populated by minoritized communities, significantly always "'inside' the subject as its own founding repudiation."[28] Described as a foundational part of a system by both Butler and Kristeva, the resistive possibilities of the concept of the abject has been questioned. It is instead perceived as a reifying element of the social order.[29] But like Butler's now-famous offerings on gender's performative operation, an aesthetics of abjection makes visible the continuous labor required to cohere a dominant majority but also the dangers of desires for normative inclusion that will require repudiation of other abjects if seeking out proper subject status. Given Latinidad's instability as a performative site for the doing of racialized subjectivity, the elaboration of abjection in this book capitalizes on the lack of a proper singular subject that centers the antinormative sensibility at the core of brownness.

Those who do not desire to move from abject to subject but instead perform an abject collision that threatens to reveal the inequalities of a national body insistent on a legacy of freedom and equality propel my argument. While the figure of the pathologized Latina mother may serve to cohere national structures for the citizen subjects for whom the normatively structured home serves as principal site of patriotic indoctrination, she also has the ability to threaten the dignity of those normative structures, especially when she performs a critique and lack of aspiration to belong. In other words, the pathologized mother may indeed reify an existing order through a refusal of what the abject figure signifies, but threatens the nation's organizing myths when she insists on an alternate ethical barometer for understanding justice across national borders. What does it mean, then, that while included she is occluded from the stage of Latino national protests, such as the one with which I opened this book, unless she is recast as respectable through the ideological protection of normative family formations or the sheen of student robes? What might it mean to embrace her symbolic abjection and the strategies that could offer?

With this figure in sight, a focus on Latino abjection does not posit Latinidad as an exemplary site. Rather, following the important work of those who name the denizens of the abject realm, Latino abject aesthetic strategies expand the pantheon of available contestatory subjectivities while augmenting possible approaches to politicized aesthetics. Previous scholarship has elaborated the abject realm as composed of a largely minoritized populace providing a model to think about collectivity through negative affect as well as ways to think about abjection as a resistant engagement with identity politics writ large.[30] Few works center abjection in conjunction with Latinidad. It is no surprise that those that do share a deployment of queerness as an analytic to highlight the disruptive potential of abjection against dominant master narratives but also against those identity-reifying and exclusionary ones that organize minoritarian populations.[31] In her writing on recovering pleasure from our shameful desires as captured by a pornographic archive, for example, Juana María Rodríguez offers a counterintuitive proposition: "Rather than proposing a decolonial project aimed at wiping away the taint of racialized abjection," she states, "I want to consider the possibility of seizing our sexual imaginations to activate abjection as a resource for a reclamation of erotic-self-determination and world-making."[32] In her argument for entanglement with the complex affects that surely accompany an appeal to the abject, we are entreated to consider what might be useful about abjection. Instead of a rejection of abjection or working in opposition to its ethos—for instance, producing uplifting subject positions shored up by positive figures—given diversity successes and demands for national incorporation, an embrace of abjection as an aesthetic strategy allows us to center different goals and possibilities that, for myself as for Rodríguez, has "world-making" potential. I analyze a range of performative enunciations that show us how abjection becomes a powerful aesthetic mode to highlight the limits of assimilation that reinforce hegemonic norms by underscoring their desirability, simultaneously revealing and mobilizing the always abject root of difference. In doing so, abjection builds on women of color feminist approaches—architected in those Lordeian houses of difference—to coalition building and imagining futurity.[33]

Engaging abjection specifically as a heuristic additionally highlights the performative strategies of a Latinidad that makes its way within existing and minoritizing logics. Again, while not an exemplary site, the case studies explored in each of the chapters of this book reveal Latinidad as a promising rubric within which to explore the offerings of abjection. The works of the profiled cultural producers significantly gesture toward a mode of being beyond respectability politics of proper minority comportment in a postracial era.[34] To be clear, I am not centering here on a dynamic of ontological desire—a desire to be abject—but one of recognition of a social location and strategies to propel this recognition into a destabilizing force. While recent bombastic neonativist utterances on the national stage may seem to call for a counterstrategy of creating distance between abjection and minoritized communities through respectability, conservative performances of racism only underscore what we in communities of color have long known about the structure of nationalist fervor. It is against the politics of respectability and its seemingly successful dynamic of incorporation that I instead seek to parse out strategies for continued demands and expansion of what we understand as justice and freedom.

Latino abject performances reveal abjection not as a resource for empowerment fueled by a desire for normative inclusion but as a resource geared toward an ungraspable alternative social organization, a not-yet-here illuminated by the aesthetic. Mine is an elaboration of abjection aware of potential disappointments—a Blochian hope distinct from unhinged utopian dreaming that is tethered and reserved in its hope for the not-yet-here—but that is nonetheless insistent on an engagement with negative affect.[35] Led by the abject mother out of Kristeva and through Butler, abject performative strategies reveal a way beyond the entrenchment of respectability politics to which the robed student gestures. Centering the performative through the aesthetic requires that we take up one of its dominant organizing theories in productive critique in order to transform our understanding of an influential site often regarded as peripheral to political concerns despite its ability to structure our everyday. Namely, Immanuel Kant's aesthetic philosophy.

Kant on Cable

When performance artist Nao Bustamante—one of two performers under consideration in chapter 3—was asked to explain her abject performance *Barely Standing* (2010), she instead engaged her judges in a conversation about process, an elaboration of where she was trying to arrive and what wasn't supposed to, but ended up being, read by her audience. Echoes of an earlier proclamation—"I'm not responsible for your experience of my work"—lingered in the air between artist and judges. Bustamante refused to provide a coherent narrative to explain what her judges perceived as masturbatory fecal play, a reading Bustamante would neither confirm nor reject. The visibly distraught collective of judges found a representative voice in Jerry Saltz, the resident art critic, who summarized the discussion and provided what would later serve as the logic for Bustamante's dismissal, as follows: "So you don't really know what this piece is, we don't know what the piece is and it comes off, therefore, as incredibly familiar kind of adolescent mixed with shock-your-grandmother performance."[36] Bustamante's was the fourth elimination of the televised competition *Work of Art: The Next Great Artist,* which premiered during the summer of 2010 on the cable television network Bravo. Modeled after its successful sibling antecedents, *Project Runway* and *Top Chef,* all of Magical Elves Productions lineage, *Work of Art* elaborated a caricature of Kantian aesthetic judgment that informs broad approaches to the creation, reception, and judgment of cultural production. Its presence here, on cable, underlines the importance of a rigorous engagement with the theoretical apparatus that has informed the formation of art history as a field and process and that now seeps into the everyday and widely accessible format of television, especially for the consideration of the visual field within which Latinidad is signified. It is for this reason that I turn directly to Kant and his seminal work on aesthetics.

Kant's third critique, *The Critique of Judgment,* presents a disjointed, often tangentially constructed theory on beauty and the sublime, pure aesthetic judgment, the valuation of taste, and the figure of the genius—issues central to the discipline of art history and its project of canon formation as well as its culture of experts. For Kant the artist bears the status of genius, with innate aptitude guided by the rules of nature. This genius-artist's production of fine art is operationally concerned with attaining beauty through similitude or representational authenticity. Though limited by the form of the object itself, its subjective purposiveness, beauty is nonetheless predominantly concerned with quality; its judgment spurred by positive pleasure distinct from emotion, which Kant considers foreign to beauty. This absence of emotion or affect comes to be of prime importance. Indeed, Kant explains that the beautiful "is the symbol of the morally good, and only in this light (a point of view natural to every one, and one which every one exacts from others as a duty) does it give us pleasure with an attendant claim to the agreement of every one else, whereupon the mind becomes conscious of a certain ennoblement and elevation above mere sensibility to pleasure from impressions of sense, and also appraises the worth of others on the score of a like maxim of their judgment."[37] By establishing the beautiful as something naturally agreeable, through the repetition of "every one," and by way of a pleasure that simultaneously makes those enacting a judgment of beauty aware of an "ennoblement and elevation" among "every one else," Kant draws a connection between the moral and the aesthetic that pretends universality. The judgment of beauty, then, is determined by feelings of pleasure that provide a standard of universal validity. To achieve universality, declarations of beauty must be derived strictly from representation and must not be concerned with the real existence of the object, its material life or economy. For Kant, the ideal spectator, or judge of taste, therefore, must be disinterested. Pure aesthetic judgment cannot be tainted by empirical delight.

While Kant's organizing logic continues to inform cultures of spectatorship and especially judgment, the cultural and visual turn that can be said to constitute cultural studies has insisted on a study of the visual and aesthetics that is more broadly alive to relationships of power, placing cultural production squarely within social relations and in relation to capital, while expanding possible objects of study.[38] This scholarship insists that cultural products participate in ideological projects with the ability to hail spectators into specific subject positions and that aesthetic judgments partake in this dynamic. While aesthetic judgment, this scholarship helps us see, is "historically and socially conditioned," what the Kantian system "demanded was the discrete suppression of the vicissitudes of interpretive desire—social investment, particular identifications, and personal biases—under the imperatives of critical rigor."[39] Framed as such, it is no surprise then when we read that to serve as an appropriate judge, Kant stipulates that "[only] when men have got all they want can we tell who among the crowd has taste or not" and that taste "has not yet emerged from barbarism."[40] For this overbearing system of aesthetic judgment, the supposed "every one" that is capable of exerting fair judgment cited in Kant's earlier passage has a classed and gendered position that is absent from want and thus necessarily excludes those who don't participate in the plentitude required for disinterest, despite pretensions of universality—the poor, women, and racialized peoples. I emphasize these passages to show how race and class, among other vectors, are built into the foundation of Kantian aesthetic theory and the ideas of taste, judgment, and distinction, which structure contemporary cultural apparatuses.[41]

The Enlightenment project of modernity (of which Kant is a preeminent poster boy) instituted a tripartite division of knowledge wherein a culture of experts developed treatises on morals, science, and aesthetic theory.[42] The expert subject at the core of this development and division of modern knowledge systems needs to be thought of alongside those denied the category of subject. Through Kristeva, who amplifies our understanding of those that don't partake in the prerequisite plentitude described above, we can understand these individuals denied subjecthood as Enlightenment's abject. In his study of the concurrent emergence of cultures of taste and slavery, Simon Gikandi calls forth the abject ghostly presence of those "excluded from the domain of modern reason, aesthetic judgment, and the culture of taste" who are yet integral to its formation.[43] Indeed, Enlightenment's abject individuals emerge as a consequence of the relationship between aesthetics, among other cultural discourses, and structured racial and gender dominance and its economies—the selling of black bodies and the dispossession and displacement of native peoples—even when these were "structurally construed to be radical opposites."[44] These dynamics, Gikandi underscores, forge a dialectical relationship that serves as a condition for modernity, showing us the relevance for the application of Kristeva's theory of abjection on the aesthetic in order to understand constitutively hierarchized subject formations as integral to cultural apparatuses and built into the practices of spectatorship seeking beauty as the ideal.[45] If the subject is reified through its judgment of beauty, through representational simulacrum, what are the effects of cultural practices that avoid representation or Kantian purposiveness?

Kant brackets a much more interesting, though less elaborated, set of affective reactions as having to do with the sublime: an aesthetic judgment, triggered more by displeasure than pleasure, which captures precisely the limits of the imaginable. Described as about "negative experience[s] of *limits*," the category of the sublime has enjoyed contemporary critical attention.[46] Theorists of the sublime have argued that this is because the category of beauty "seems inadequate to account for the most recent contemporary arts, which have been interpreted as disruptive of classical and especially formalist form," or, as Sianne Ngai has argued, in order to meet "the twentieth-century avant-garde's attempt to separate the concepts of art and beauty."[47] It is precisely in its designation of the limits of the imaginable where I find promising misfires in the apparatus of the aesthetic.

Kant describes sublimity as directly connected to emotion, as opposed to the specifically articulated un-emotion-like pleasure of beauty. In distinction to the form-boundedness of beauty, a judgment of the sublime can be triggered by objects without form, producing what Kant describes as "negative pleasure." Within philosophy, the sublime has been theorized as the emotive site that frustrates reason—it is at once pleasurable and repulsive. The sublime is precisely about this seemingly unrepresentable paradox; it is "to be found, for its part, in an 'object without form' and the 'without-limit' is 'represented' in it or on the occasion of it, and yet gives the totality of the without-limit to be *thought*."[48] In other words, the sublime is most beckoned by the formally permeable or unbounded while providing the "occasion" to contemplate its own "without-limitness." Additionally, its affective proximity to unknowing, "awe" and "wonder," can "blur into terror."[49] This dissolution and formlessness has marked the sublime, in a way similar to abjection, as affiliated with queerness, despite its association with nature and religious transcendence; a queerness capable of magnifying the possibilities of Latinidad as a useful rubric.[50]

Bustamante's appearance on *Work of Art* was an extension of her televisual and popular culture interventions, dating back at least to the early 1990s.[51] Her grandmother-shocking performance suggests the type of abject failure around which this book is organized. Failing to create shocking art in line with commercial cable network standards, Bustamante instead challenged her judges to grapple with what Jennifer Doyle calls "difficult feelings," to excavate the affective terrain provoked by aesthetics beyond beauty, a terrain shared with the sublime's awe and wonder, as well as its queerness.[52] As Doyle explains, a difficult cultural text "addresses the political and historical dimension of our personal selves; it also expands the sphere of the intimate."[53] The abject as genre is characterized by difficulty— narratively and temporally—leaving spectators uncertain of their experience, a consequence of which is a self that ruminates, as Doyle suggests, on the political and historical as funneled through the personal, a deeply feminist intervention. Further, lingering or residual aftershocks of feeling returns the spectator to the performance into the indefinite future. The performance's boundaries extend beyond the knowable. They are both difficult to dismiss and difficult to sustain. They provoke the sublime and its attendant ambivalence and ambiguity. They unsettle spectators, constructed as cool and disinterested in the Kantian schema, affectively drawing them in to the disrupting parameters of the work.

For some, the sublime is necessarily emotionally disinterested and transcendent, much like the judgment of beauty, arguing that the sublime is sublime precisely because of "its emphatic affective resolution."[54] In my reading of Kant, however, his attempts to narrate resolution are tinged with uncertainty and anxiety, revealing attempts to grapple with the changing world. Bringing abjection as a concept to bear on aesthetic theory, the sublime is rendered vulnerable, especially when we consider its fruition as also reflecting a collision with racial and cultural difference and the incorporation of this difference through exhibitionary practices, recasting the awe and terror of racial difference into consumable and graspable beauty through truthful representation. In Kant's sublime, I read a fissure of possibility from which we can mine challenges to the very political apparatus it constructs in tandem with the beautiful. This possibility is activated through the use of the abject precisely by those cultural producers interested in provoking the spectator into the realm of the "indiscernible or unnameable, undecidable, indeterminate and unrepresentable," especially in relationship to racialized difference and identity formation.[55] At its most basic level, this book argues that abject performances produce a generative affective vortex within which a politics is elaborated by irreverently tapping the sublime. Traced back to and alongside the historic mobilizations of the late 1960s and early '70s that we now credit for effecting social change, the questions at the center of this book revolve around the alternative worldscapes illuminated by abject performances.

Abjection Performed

As is illuminated by the case studies that follow, the cultural producers of this study resist, play with, and frustrate their reinscription into hegemonic logics, pushing the sublime to rend asunder the dominant aesthetic apparatus through the abject, such that we might glimpse other possible arrangements of politicized collectivity. Latino studies scholars have long engaged in recuperative art historical excavations and canon reformation, seeking participation, indeed representation, in a broadly Eurocentric field. I take seriously the investment in identity formation and recuperation displayed in aesthetic practices from the hegemonic iterations of the Latino and feminist movements focused on creating empowered minority identities through biologizing and essentializing rhetoric. However, like Butler, I "despair over public politics when identity becomes its own policy," with boundaries policed and shored up at the expense of those whose visibility disrupts the uplifting image of a respectable population but who nonetheless deserve inclusion in the public life of the nation.[56] Consequently, in the case studies that follow, I seek to broaden critical perspectives on the relationship between politics and aesthetics by challenging the limited conventions upon which political art rests within the field of Latino studies, namely community building and ego reinforcement through recuperative identity formation. Through a politicized engagement with aesthetic theory rooted in the sublime, a disruptive, abject aesthetic practice can provide a site to shift "away from a hermeneutic that is primarily attuned to the epistemological"—to center a hermeneutic of doing as opposed to a known identity—when thinking about Latinidad.[57]

Abject Performances elaborates this disruptive aesthetic practice through a series of case studies on the abject aesthetic strategies of those Latino artists and cultural producers who shunned the standards of respectability used to conjure concrete minority identities by the most widely recognized political actors within activist communities since the late 1960s. Collectively they privilege the negative affect that most often becomes a target for elimination in recuperative identitarian projects. I draw from a diverse expressive archive ranging from the early performances of Cuban exile Ana Mendieta and the East Los Angeles collective Asco to the popular culture interventions of Chicana artist Nao Bustamante, as well as from the mass cultural production of ugliness on prime-time television's *Ugly Betty*, to the performative testimonies of personal subjection of Latino Mormons. This archive not only illustrates the broad performative cultural texts that help us think about abjection across different sites but also decenters the organization of Latino studies focused on a particular U.S. national coast, border, or national grouping and resists offering a teleological progress narrative. While temporally I shift from the late 1960s and early '70s, with performers engaged in productive critique of dominant movement politics within the liberal feminist and Chicano nationalist movements, to contemporary cultural producers negotiating the legacies of these movements—their successes and failures—I do so to show the parallel existence and persistence of abject strategies to those that are much more recognized and celebrated as politically efficacious. Geographically, I move across the nation from California to the Midwest and New York, with transnational gestures out to the Caribbean and Mexico, attentive to regional particularity while nonetheless emphasizing affective collectivity.

The first half of *Abject Performances* uses performance artists Mendieta (chapter 1) and the collective Asco (chapter 2) to reflect on and augment the art practices of the liberal feminist movement and Chicano nationalism, respectively. As the best-known artists with the largest amount of scholarship on their work, the first two chapters modify art historical narratives while making aggressive political claims about the offerings of these artists and abjection more broadly. Chapter 1, "Other Desires: Ana Mendieta's Abject Imaginings," seeks out an alternative framing of the Cuban-born artist long lauded for her Silueta Series (1973–1980), an earth-body works series that occupies a large expanse of the artist's working life and serves as the principal focal point that orients scholarship on her reception. This chapter, on the other hand, looks to Mendieta's engagement with alterity, the racial and gender vectors approached through the unsettling aesthetic force of her early abject performances from the 1970s. These performances have been historically relegated to a cursory status in the art historical canon and sometimes dismissed as inconsequential juvenilia in favor of her long-sustained Siluetas, with only recent shifts in scholarly focus. Art historical narratives into which Mendieta has been conscripted seek to interject her and her influence into a continuum of modern, minimalist, postmodern, and contemporary artists, sometimes drawing on this early work for their mapping. Instead, I am interested in situating Mendieta squarely within a theoretical genealogy of women of color feminisms and queer of color critique, an epistemological project that enlivens the political import of Mendieta's avant-gardism. I focus on abjection as a politicized aesthetic strategy, linking her early performances to her curatorial work in the early 1980s. These then bookend and reframe the more-recognized earth-body works in order to revise their critical interpretations. This frame requires a tracing of Mendieta's transnational currents and her negotiation of a racialized self through the racial stratifications of multiple locations—including Cuba, the U.S. Midwest, and Mexico—theorized comparatively alongside blackness. While not a redemptive reading of Mendieta's Siluetas, nor a dismissal of their aesthetic possibilities, I reflect on their epistemological contours, brought into focus anew when bookmarked by the abject and oppositional aesthetic practices that precede and exceed the Silueta Series. Ultimately, I argue Mendieta's recourse to the abject brings into focus analogous and shared relations to dominance by minoritized subjects beyond Cuban or even Latino particularity, and certainly beyond the essentialist feminist camp to which her Siluetas are often relegated, allowing us to think expansively about Mendieta's contributions specifically to the field of Latino studies, but also more broadly for American and ethnic studies to insist on comparative frameworks and expanded boundaries for the field.

Chapter 2, "Phantom Assholes: Asco's Affective Vortex," shifts our focus to California's East Los Angeles via the art collective Asco, rough contemporaries of Mendieta's. Just as Mendieta broadened a liberal feminist movement's understanding and deployment of the gendered body, Asco broadens Chicano nationalist understandings of community. A surge in Asco scholarship and exhibition, galvanized predominantly by two Los Angeles County Museum of Art (LACMA) exhibits—*Phantom Sightings: Art after the Chicano Movement* (2008) and *Asco: Elite of the Obscure, a Retrospective, 1972–1987* (2011)—has significantly expanded the accessibility of the Asco archive, including an extended network of Asco collaborators. Together, these contributions extend an invitation to rethink Asco's artistic and political contributions.[58] Accepting that invitation, this chapter renarrativizes existing accounts of Asco's formation and unifying ethos to show how the group's abject aesthetic strategies offer an alternative political vision of national belonging predicated on uncivic participation. Foregrounding a queer discordant site of genesis and recruitment that recasts Asco not as a concrete group but as an abject structure of feeling in Chicano East Los Angeles, I show how Asco's abject play uniquely highlights and challenges Chicano nationalist heteronormativity and its connection to representative presence as the grounds for enfranchisement in order to problematize sedimented models for minority national inclusion. By harnessing negative affect, Asco instead reveals a vulnerable collectivity that coheres around and validates feelings of disenchantment and dis-ease while resisting a reparative move toward coherent minority subjectivity and unified communities.

Together, these chapters intervene in prescribed modes of political engagement for Latinos. They entreat us to expand our bounds of study but also to be attuned to the local. They offer insight across multiple fields—critical race theory, queer theory, and gender and sexuality studies. They offer us ways to think about collectivity differently, to think through racialization comparatively by centering affect to arrive at, not unity, but a dynamic desire to work together for a world not-yet-here. Though these artists were sympathetic and shared political desires with those movements they traversed alongside, they chose abjection as a strategy not to belong to a hegemonic order but to critique it. They offer us a model for the doing of a Latinidad that is contestatory and heterogeneous.

The second half of *Abject Performances* shifts to consider contemporary cultural producers negotiating the legacies of the Chicano and liberal feminist movements. During what Ralph Rodriguez has called the postnationalist moment of the 1980s to the early 2000s, Latinos have been brought into and pushed out of the national body, sometimes at concurrent historical moments.[59] The third and fourth chapters cover the same terrain, taking us from the 1980s, dubbed "the decade of the Hispanic," through the liberal multiculturalism of the 1990s, peppered as it was with xenophobic backlash, and into the neoliberal present. Given the incorporation of difference in the contemporary political arena in what some have called neoliberal multiculturalism,[60] in chapter 3, "Of Betties Decorous and Abject: *Ugly Betty*'s America la fea and Nao Bustamante's America la bella," I pair an analysis of America Ferrera's mainstream performance of "Betty" in the prime-time television series *Ugly Betty* (2006–2010) and the abject performances of femininity throughout performance artist Nao Bustamante's repertoire, but especially her *America, the Beautiful* (1995–1998, 2002) and her appearance on Bravo's *Work of Art* (2010), in order to make sense of work that challenges the beautiful as linked to a politics of tolerance and diversity.

Throughout *Abject Performances*, different cultural producers are shown to use performance to bring disparate spaces into dialogue. For Mendieta and Asco, these spaces were the urban and rural landscape, the space of the museum or gallery, and that of quotidian thoroughfare. Their performances engaged a general public beyond the art world, whether through the accidental encounter—as in the case of Mendieta's bloody installations— or by performing down the middle of a busy street—as in the case of Asco's promenades. Thus, these first two chapters engage and expand the sites of art. The second two chapters further expand these sites, an action facilitated by the seemingly unlikely pairing of Bustamante and Ferrera in chapter 3. Like Mendieta and Asco, Bustamante engages political movements and a broader non-art-specific public but does so through her presence on television. Because Bustamante's performative brand has us approach performance art and television differently, in chapter 3 she is put in dialogue with another key performance of Latinidad on prime-time television, Ferrera's ugly Betty.

Both performers elaborate a gendered and racialized subjectivity, legible by reference to traditional standards of normative beauty. I argue that Ferrera's camp ugliness reifies this standard, functioning as the necessary complement to its white binary opposite and, by the show's end, coming to elaborate what we might call a mimetic minority beauty, providing popular aesthetic support for political strategies of racial uplift and decorum. Meanwhile, Bustamante's contemplation of the beautiful performs abject negotiations, deploying queer tactics that highlight the uncontainable excesses that seep through the mechanisms for beautifying the Latina body, as well as the rigid categorizations of proper normative minority identity, through an embrace of failure. Against the backdrop of multiple surges in anti-immigrant legislation and, counterintuitively, minority political representation, the juxtaposition of these two performers provides insight on the gendered incorporation of difference as structured by popular cultural apparatuses and explores queer abject aesthetics as a political strategy of identitarian refusal.

Where chapter 3 expands my fields of analysis beyond fine art performance to include popular television, the final chapter, "Arriving at Apostasy: Performative Testimonies of Ambivalent Belonging," opens out to yet a different terrain of cultural expression, the stage of religious conviction, and offers a sort of author performance for religious studies. Chapter 4 analyzes the performative testimonies of Latino members of the Church of Jesus Christ of Latter-Day Saints—popularly known as the Mormons—as well as a personal testimony of apostasy, an abject position that marks a willful departure from the organized church. The performative testimonies are augmented by a consideration of Mormon visual culture. The paintings contained within the central doctrinal text of the faith, the Book of Mormon, provide a visual entry point for my analysis. I argue that together with scripture they issue an interpellative call to several communities (Native American, Polynesian, Latin American, and Latino) through the protagonists they narrate as pre-Columbian denizens of the American continent, foremost among them the iniquitous Lamanites and righteous Nephites. In this chapter, I focus on Latino citation of Lamanite heritage and their affective oscillation between an embrace of abjection and cultural nationalist celebration as they navigate their seemingly contradictory status within the church—they are of unique spiritual import yet are abject subjects within its hierarchy. A focus on testimony allows me to center the aesthetic sensuousness of religious experience as testimonies often narrate the individual's sublime encounter with the divine. I do so to explore the sublime revelry of religiosity, read against the grain of a Kantian aesthetic register, and expand my consideration of the politics of an aesthetic of abjection beyond the realm of the cultural sector. Following María Josefina Saldaña-Portillo's insistence that "the act of testifying . . . issues an interpellative call to form a community of action," I analyze self-identified testimonies and testimonial enunciations both written and spoken as a performative genre in order to map the subjects and communities hailed by testimony.[61] From the first Latino bishop's 1978 "Mormonism and the Chicano" to the published proclamations of members who have recently migrated and joined the church, necessarily abject Lamanite identification seems to facilitate a sense of ambivalent belonging. This closing chapter also facilitates a reflection on my own investment in abjection as a former member of the church, the ways abjection offered a way out of what felt like a position full of promise, one left wanting in its abdication to normative desires for respectability.

These two final chapters allow us to meditate on the prevalence of aesthetic structures in the quotidian realm. Further, they compel us to question the success of visibility and belonging through existing political, cultural, and social models. At a contemporary moment demarcated by the postracial incorporation of difference across representative forums, *Abject Performances* offers timely intervention. The assumption that visibility, or what Cristina Beltrán calls racial presence, "is quickly presumed to signify not only racial progress but racial justice" guides this book's desire to seek out a set of politicized aesthetic strategies alternative to those of the Latino cultural renaissance that often accompanied and supported those movements now punctuated by institutional successes.[62] In these movements, the goals of civic representation were literalized in representational or realist aesthetic codes. The political effects of aesthetics have long been theorized, with more recent scholarship highlighting its racial, sexual, and gendered implications.[63] I owe a genealogical debt to this scholarship when I stress the centrality of aesthetics and a critical engagement with aesthetic theory for our political imaginings, centering cultural production situated beyond the representational in style, composition, and political aspirations. My own study hopes to add to this body as well as to scholarship organized under the rubrics of American and ethnic studies, performance and religious studies, as well as Latino studies, visual culture, and gender and sexuality studies.

The cultural producers profiled in this book offer us an incremental expansion of performance as a heuristic: from Mendieta's intergallery critique at A.I.R. to Asco's community engagement on neighborhood streets, to Bustamante and Ferrera's televisual invocations, and finally to the corporeal gestures signaling a heavenly beyond.

Collectively, they also tell us something about the difficulty of sustaining abject performances, the precariousness of staying with abjection as a strategy, but also, I hope, the difficulty in turning away from the possibilities it offers. Abject performances offer us a terrifyingly moving glimpse of a dynamism worth the risk of unfurling the polyester iridescence that cloaks respectability politics so that we might engage with the difficulty and promise of Latinidad's abject otherness.

Other Desires
Ana Mendieta's Abject Imaginings

Artist Ana Mendieta ends her curatorial statement for *Dialectics of Isolation: An Exhibition of Third World Women Artists* with a willful expression of ontological alterity:

> Do we exist? . . . To question our culture is to question our own existence, our human reality. To confront this fact means to acquire an awareness of ourselves. This in turn becomes a search, a questioning of who we are and how we will realize ourselves. . . .
>
> This exhibition points not necessarily to the injustice or incapacity of a society that has not been willing to include us, but more towards a personal will to continue being "other."[1]

The 1980 exhibit, co-organized with artists Kazuko and Zarina, filled the Artists in Residence (A.I.R.) Gallery with a range of multimedia works, from video to installation, interpreted through what one reviewer termed

Mendieta's "passion."[2] *Dialectics of Isolation* brought together "Third World Women here in America" through a curatorial gesture planted in the liberal mandate of the New York City cooperative's devotion to "advancing the status of women artists."[3] But a different impulse organized this group's rumination on collective isolation. As Mendieta's curatorial statement would reveal, *Dialectics of Isolation* cohered as a structure of feeling—what Raymond Williams theorized as an affective formation that acknowledges the lived and felt as well as "feeling as thought"—of burgeoning 1980s women of color feminist critiques.[4] Indeed this curatorial statement articulated the women of color feminist heuristic defined by Grace K. Hong and Roderick A. Ferguson as comparative and "fundamentally organized around difference" in "attempts to do the vexed work of forging coalitional politics through these differences."[5] In what follows, I trace Mendieta's intersectional feminist impulse to her early 1970s performances executed while pursuing her MFA at the University of Iowa's Intermedia program. It is here that Mendieta begins to elaborate a complex engagement with alterity, approaching its racialized and gendered vectors through the unsettling aesthetic force of her abject performances.

Mendieta's oeuvre is marked by shifts in media and aesthetic strategies from painting to performance, to earth-body work. Critically, she is most recognized for the latter—the ephemeral, figural markings she etched into and out of the earth and nature in her Silueta Series (1973–1980). Forcefully universalizing with their iconographic contours, different iterations of the Silueta in mud, ice, or fire, formed out of flowers, leaves, or rocks, present an essential yonic figure with arms outstretched or alongside the body proportional to Mendieta's nearly five-foot frame. Mendieta's sustained use of a simplified human form has generally been interpreted in three ways: first, by feminist art historians to codify her as an essentialist artist representing both the essence of woman and a primitive exoticism; second, to read Mendieta as an exilic subject whose work reflects her longing to ground herself, literally, through interment, with her Siluetas as representative of the indentation of this desire; and the third as a prescient practice saturated with blood that foreshadows Mendieta's violent and spectacular art-world-celebrity death.[6] Her biography and work have been held up by what Miwon Kwon has identified as contrasting "camps" in which the body, Mendieta's constant medium, is regarded as "a transparent signifier of identity and self" in the service of essentialist arguments, against social constructivists who cite "the body as a nexus of arbitrary conventions of meaning, the body as signature or sign."[7] More recent theoretical excavations have moved away from thinking of Mendieta's work from within these binary logics, focusing instead on suspended states of unknowing—pursuing the "path not taken" of the "what if"; embarking on the search of traces in a cave or in the psyche of the "what still"; and pondering, after loss, of the "what now" of vitalism's afterburn.[8] With few exceptions, Mendieta's Siluetas are still used as the principal vehicle to approach her theoretical and artistic contributions.[9]

I propose an alternate framing for the artist, one that centers an aesthetics of abjection as a politicized strategy and decenters the focus on her Silueta Series by linking her early performances to the curatorial work bookending the more-recognized earth-body work—a frame that can then be used to revise critical interpretations of these latter works. Mendieta's abject performances provide a site to reflect on embodied alternatives to weak multiculturalism's reification of identity that alter not only the way we think about the artist's oeuvre but also terms of inclusion for minoritized populations. Following Hong and Ferguson and their theorization of women of color feminism and queer of color critique, I read Mendieta's performances as "[refusing] to maintain that objects of comparison are static, unchanging, and empirically observable, and [refusing] to render illegible the shifting configurations of power that define such objects in the first place" while offering a "clear-eyed appraisal of the dividing line between valued and devalued, which can cut within, as well as across, racial groupings."[10] Throughout this book, abject performances serve as a rubric through which to rethink political strategies. Here, Mendieta's abjection expands the deployment of intersectionality as a concept. Critiques of intersectionality have outlined its limits as metaphor, but understanding its parameters as always in flux, when engaged through abjection, intersectionality is less a metaphor and more a sign of the failure of language to approximate shifting and ambivalent dynamics.[11] Its emergence signals an attempt developed by women of color to try to name this dynamic. Mendieta's recourse to the abject brings into focus analogous and shared relations to dominance by minoritized subjects, not only appraising the "dividing line" that delimits the abject from the nonabject, but also the ways these positions are mutually constituted beyond Cuban or even Latino particularity, allowing us to think expansively about Mendieta's contributions specifically for the field of Latino studies but also ethnic studies and American studies more broadly.

Given the multifarious scholarship on Mendieta's Siluetas, I turn only briefly to this work, using her abject performances as a frame to reimagine the promise of the work as a heuristic with signposts for caution. For José Esteban Muñoz, the Silueta form, evocative of the absent body, was a "deeply symbolic indention in the world," an "after-[burn] of mimetically generated intensity" imbued with a vitalism he called brownness.[12] These contours of the sensate demarcate a utopian methodology, by which to imagine, following Kandice Chuh, a subjectless critique for Latino studies while bringing into focus some of the notable silences in Mendieta scholarship, particularly regarding Mendieta's problematic appropriative gestures, most often used to signal the "primitive" or Other.[13] My aim is not to discount the theoretical contributions of her cultural production nor to discount the art historical cartographies into which she has been drafted, but to show her as also participating in a theoretical genealogy that explores the complicated negotiation of different ways of being and belonging, what Muñoz might describe as feeling brown "in a world painted white, organized by cultural mandates to 'feel white'" that tells us something about the political promise of abjection.[14]

Life Portrait

Any treatment of Mendieta's work must situate her as a child of the Cuban diaspora, one of Operación Pedro Pan's young, lost to the United States until a hoped-for end to Castro's godless regime.[15] The Catholic Church and CIA–cosponsored initiative delivered a pubescent Ana, months from her thirteenth birthday, and her *quinceañera* sister, Raquelín, to the Midwest's Iowa and its holding spaces for lost youth: other Pedro Panes but also orphans and young people with emotional and behavioral problems, many of whom had been in trouble with the law or came from dysfunctional homes—young abject subjects. Although descended from a Cuban family with a long legacy of political and cultural leaders, in the United States the Mendieta sisters were placed within a new social and racial apparatus distinct from the one they were accustomed to on the island, one in which their elite position was reversed. Instead of the affluence they experienced in Cuba, particularly in Havana's El Vedado, where they were looked after by black servants and educated in private schools, or the weekends and holidays spent with extended family in Cárdenas and Varadero, they were now at the mercy of Catholic Charities and their boarding institutions. From St. Mary's Home to the temporary foster homes the sisters were sent to, they were at times separated (despite promises to the contrary), assigned cleaning duties, accused of theft, and discouraged or prohibited from using their native language.[16] Despite Quiroga's reminder that "hers was a conscious aesthetic and political decision to inscribe within the work of art the life story of the artist who produced it," I do not rehearse this information believing her practice to be reducible to her biography.[17] I do so, rather, because her biography and her own citation of it highlight the need to consider multiple national and racial ideological frameworks, relationally and comparatively, to make sense of the project illuminated by Mendieta's work.

In exploration of the discursive formation of "bodies that matter," Judith Butler theorizes a social matrix with an abject realm that is useful to invoke here for making evident the Mendieta sisters' new social location. Butler argues that the abject, "those who are not yet 'subject,' but who form the constitutive outside to the domain of subject," create a discursive realm against whom the "subject" is constructed, shored up through the performative repetition of the repudiation of those they cast out.[18] Applied here, abjection signals a social location for minoritized populations against whom dominance is achieved by repeatedly casting out those subjects who threaten to reveal the inequalities of a national body insistent on framing its very foundation through a legacy of freedom and equality. Despite the privileged access to the United States that they received as Cold War exceptions, the Mendietas' very presence in institutions dedicated to the nonnormative, unclaimed, and unwanted signifies just how they mattered in the United States: they were abject subjects—criminal, service providers, performing racially coded symbolic labor. The Mendieta sisters, and the other youths they found themselves among, helped to define both U.S. Catholic Charities and their Iowan hosts as American: righteous and benevolent saviors delivering the young from Castro and other evils, but also superior to and deserving of domestic labor from their rescuees. While they were members of an elite back home, in the United States, the Mendieta sisters were abject creatures against whom white subjects forged their Americanness.

Consequently, it was in Iowa that Mendieta first began thinking of herself as something other than white: "It's then that I realized that I lived in a little world inside my head. It wasn't that being different was bad, it's that I had never realized that people were different."[19] From Raquelín, we know that "it never entered [their] minds that [they] were colored" until high school, when Ana would receive "anonymous phone calls in which she was called 'nigger' and told, 'Go back to Cuba, you whore!' . . . [She] later reported to Cuban television that, 'since I look Latin, I was always 'la putica,' the little whore, to them.'"[20] In the Midwest, the Mendieta sisters entered a matrix where they were marked by their Cubanness, an illegitimate otherness within a racialized society. This difference was measured against other racialized bodies that were beginning to threaten the hierarchized order of the 1960s United States. Interestingly, in the sisters' account above, they were othered through a punitive invocation of black bodies, forcing an abrupt renegotiation of their understanding of themselves as racialized subjects in relation to blackness. This significant shift in Mendieta's consideration of her racial identity, her developing sense of what we might call a U.S. Latinidad, invites a multisited and comparative approach to fully understand her future performative gestures. She prompts us to move from Cuba to the United States, not through the more common sites of analysis—such as coasts and borders—but taking us instead to the Midwest to consider her alongside other racialized populations.

In her aesthetic choices, we can see Mendieta exploring this complex racial matrix illuminated by her displacement from Cuba, beginning with her work on canvas—a body of production often overlooked or passed over for an emphasis on the Intermedia performances and installations that links her to a European avant-garde.[21] The rich work of her Intermedia performances, particularly as they explore racialization, however, is informed by the ways Mendieta activates the two-dimensional plane in painting. In the paintings created between 1969 and 1971, Mendieta is clearly a student of art history.[22] Her color blocking reflects knowledge of the vibrancy of Fauvism while elaborating her own muted and earthy palette; her rendering style invokes Gaugin and Matisse with touches of Picasso's "africanesque" markings and de Kooning's *Woman* series. Though Mendieta showed the ability to render the figure in a naturalistic way, she chose to alter her models through expressionistic gestures. The paintings also reflect Mendieta's interest in the sacred iconography of various cultures she was concurrently studying. Most of her largely figurative paintings were executed in bold broad contours, not unlike those that would etch out a Silueta, and are noteworthy as experiments in a visual register that moves beyond conventional standards of beauty.[23]

When Mendieta abandoned painting, she requested that any remaining canvases be destroyed, telling her mother, who stored them in her home, that they were no longer of use to her.[24] Because her mother ignored Mendieta's request, a significant number of paintings survived her desires.[25] One such painting is an untitled 1969 portrait for which Mendieta's mother sat as model (plate 1). Mendieta's portrait is framed as a bust. Its subject bears a deeply saturated countenance, rich in red ochers and defined with burnt umber, while the hair is a dark cinnamon that appears plaited through the striations created by electric cobalt and emerald. The dark color palette, with occasional highlights in chartreuse and cadmium yellow in heavy brush strokes, flattens the surface of the canvas, as do the expressionistic linear markings drawn over the entire surface of its subject. The linear patterning additionally differentiates the adorned neck and bust from the smooth planes of the face in the style of Picasso's primitivism or, as art historian Julia Herzberg suggests, perhaps directly referencing the markings on African masks she was studying in art history courses.[26] In this portrait, Mendieta significantly darkened, or browned, her mother's countenance, which is predominantly characterized by what Herzberg—one of the few Mendieta scholars to address this work—referred to as an "Africanizing air."[27]

In this work, we can read Mendieta as straddling two different racial ideologies, both haunted by the specter of blackness. As her teenage self told us above, Mendieta had "never realized that people were different" in Cuba—a privilege of her phenotypic "whiteness" and class. Once in the United States, Mendieta was drafted into a different racializing schema in which she was suddenly marked. On a visual register, she was now perceived as dark skinned, no longer white or protected from a racializing gaze. Mendieta's portrait indicates an engagement with this new racial schema, ruminating on its implications for her in the United States and for the way she considered her legacy and family abroad. While not unproblematic and framed through her privileged position as phenotypically whiter than she is black, Mendieta's use of what we might read as two-dimensional minstrelsy can also be understood as beginning an investigation of the comparative racialization implied when the epithet "nigger" was hurled at her as a teenager. Literally darkening the skin of her mother references the long history of blackface in Cuba, exploring a familial and national connection to blackness.

Jill Lane has argued that, historically, Cuban blackface or racial impersonation was central in the production of a form of Cubanity that "[enabled] the continued production and maintenance of racial difference itself" even while it nurtured notions of utopic *mestizaje*.[28] Though scholars exploring the incorporation of blackness by white Cuban Americans note its rearticulation of "Cuban-American whiteness in its conditions of privilege," Mendieta's diasporic frame invites us to think more expansively about the practice in performance as she explores the affective register of blackness in the United States.[29]

In her reading of Dominican performer Rita Indiana Hernandez's montra excess, Karen Jaime, following Eric Lott, interprets the performer's use of blackface as a generative recodification that brings into focus colonial legacies of race and religion, providing new ways of imagining collectivity.[30] This alternate engagement with racial difference is much closer to what Mendieta is performing, and it is in this spirit that I read her browning. In her brown-faced untitled portrait, she performs, through her mother, recognition of inhabiting a shared abjection with those marked by skin color as well as a nascent exploration of a politicized aesthetic strategy. In this way, we can consider Mendieta's work as contributing to what Miriam Jiménez Román and Juan Flores have identified as the Afro-Latin@ project, which seeks to highlight "racial, cultural, and socioeconomic contradictions within the overly vague idea of 'Latin@'" while it also "calls attention to the anti-Black racism within the Latin@ communities themselves."[31] While Mendieta's work can be seen as building on this project, she nonetheless remained distinct from her contemporaries in New York City who were exploring the nexus of blackness and Puerto Ricanness around which most Afro-Latin@ scholarship revolves. In addition to her midwestern locale, Mendieta's recourse to abject aesthetic strategies in her early pieces conjure an affective project that, as I will show, focuses on shared relationships to a dominant order, those structures of feeling, without carving out a specific linguistic identity and in fact denying easily mapped recognition.[32]

With the untitled painted portrait and the abject performances that follow, Mendieta's work performs what Muñoz would call a productive presentiment, providing a forward-facing glance into the project of women of color theorizing.[33] Along with *All the Women Are White, All the Blacks Are Men, but Some of Us Are Brave—Black Women's Studies, This Bridge Called My Back: Writings by Radical Women of Color,* coedited by Cherríe Moraga and Gloria Anzaldúa, is widely recognized as a germinal collection for women of color feminist theorizing and queer of color critique.[34] In addition to their editorial introductions, Moraga and Anzaldúa stage a dialogue on the racial dynamics within their Chicano households that involves expansive gestures out to the Latino community and beyond. Moraga's "La Guera" and Anzaldúa's "La Prieta" reflect on, respectively, phenotypic privilege and white passing, and otherized darkness that underscores hierarchies within their communities. Indeed, in "La Prieta," Anzaldúa writes, "I was terrified because in this writing I must be hard on people of color who are the oppressed victims. I am still afraid because I will have to call us on a lot of shit like our own racism, our fear of women and sexuality. . . . But above all, I am terrified of making my mother the villain in my life rather than showing how she has been a victim."[35] Like Anzaldúa's work in print, Mendieta's contemplation of darkness, *prietud*, demands a comparative and relational approach that beckons conversation on the forging of racialized communities where women of color understand their positioning in relation and response to white male domination and white feminist exclusion, as well as in relation to each other, by questioning preexisting and internalized beliefs, ideologies, and racial hierarchies of home, represented in the figure of the mother (here literalized in Mendieta's mother).

Mendieta's desire for a more palpable energy from her work, which she referred to as "magic," corresponded with a shift in her graduate training and her turn to new modes of mediation. Mendieta began working with performance in 1971, spurred by the director of the university's new Intermedia program, Hans Breder, also her then-lover. The Intermedia program, along with the Center for New Performing Arts, an interdisciplinary experimental collective also founded by Breder, established an environment that eschewed the fixity of any specific medium. Instead, as Breder explains, "Intermedia engages the spectator as participant. It is collaborative, conceptually grounded, performative, ritualistic, site-specific. It exists in liminal space where the interplay of two or more media propagate new ideas, new forms, new ways of seeing and being."[36] Inspired by a new aesthetic methodology, Mendieta's Intermedia performance would explore different vectors of oppression as they come to bear on her own body and its abject avatars in a midwestern community. Amelia Jones has argued that in performance art, "the artist (as the first 'viewer' of the work) and subsequent viewers/interpreters are caught up within the complex and fraught operations of representation—entangled in intersubjective spaces of desire, projection, and identification."[37] Mendieta's portrait of her mother begins to reveal this entanglement between art subject and viewer through the performative engagement of the two-dimensional plane. Intermedia performance will deepen the engagement with and challenge to Kantian aesthetic contemplation that Mendieta issues.

Embodied Abjection

Mendieta's 1972 *Untitled* (Glass on Body Imprints) presents a tableau of thirty-six exposures showing the artist's flesh pressed up against a sheet of Plexiglas; the soft skin of the face, breasts, thighs, and other body parts appears violently distorted behind the vertical clear plane held between Mendieta's hands. Of the thirty-six images, thirteen were printed as tightly cropped black-and-white photographs, all of the artist's face (figures 1.1–1.13). Mendieta's hair is casually parted down the middle, pulled back and up, providing a dark anchor for the flesh suspended in motion. The portraits beckon us to imagine a force capable of upturning a pout, or flattening a woman's face from jawline through cheekbone to brow. The viewer's gaze is placed at the axis of motion, parallel to the glass plane responsible for the magic of the captured gestures. It is uncertain whether the action is initiated or came to stop at the moment it meets the glass, but the clear plane and its positioning of the viewing subject makes the audience recipients of the moment of collision, making spectatorship an act between material and representational violence.

Mendieta's portrait-framed images in *Untitled* (Glass on Body Imprints) create a spectrum of states of abjection. In her influential *Powers of Horror: An Essay on Abjection*, Kristeva tells us, "There looms, within abjection, one of those violent, obscure, revolts of being, directed against a threat that seems to emanate from an exorbitant outside or inside, hurled beyond the scope of the possible, the tolerable, the thinkable."[38] The violent revolt of being that Mendieta captures here provides the opportunity to reflect on instability, mutability, and process. Mendieta as subject in each frame differs from pane to pane, a subject in the midst of transition. Mendieta's dark hair serves as anchor, yet her countenance is repeatedly disturbed by the violence established at the viewer's gaze. *Untitled* (Glass on Body Imprints) deploys violence not only in protest of gendered violence, as has been suggested by other critics, but also to elaborate an exploration of portrait states of racialization as linked to abjection.[39] The different vignettes make us imagine violence, as Kristeva might say, beyond the tolerable, that kind of unthinkable violence that is all too common a part of the lives of people of color; but they also begin to taunt the judging spectator to imagine "beyond

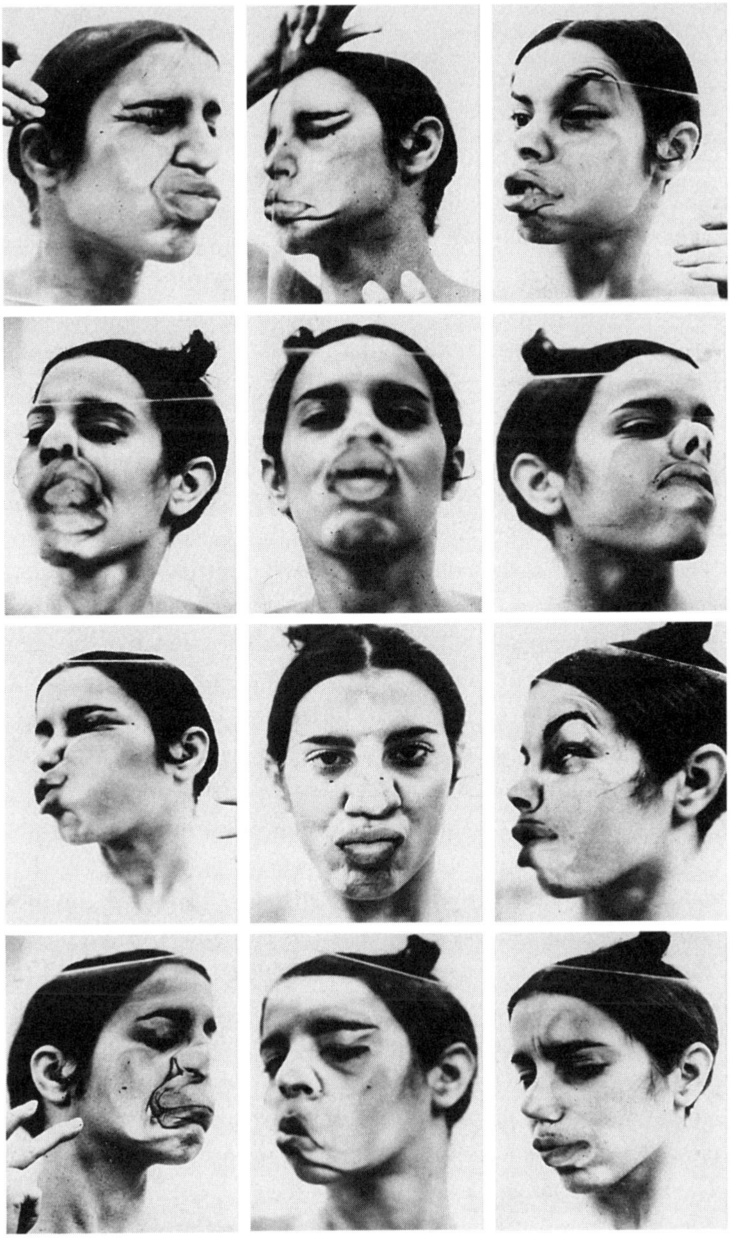

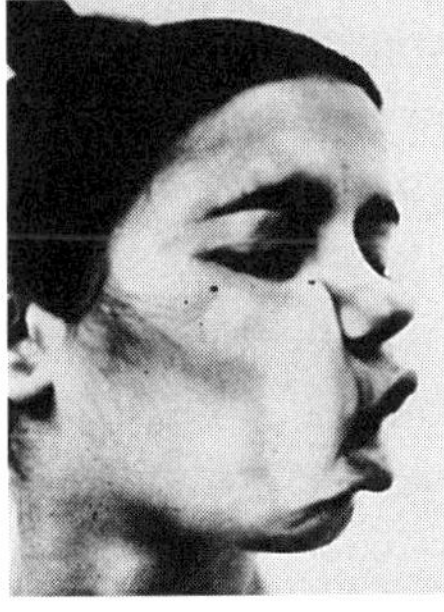

FIGURES 1.1–1.13 Ana Mendieta, *Untitled* (Glass on Body Imprints), 1972. Unique suite of thirteen lifetime black-and-white photographs, 10 × 8 inches (25.4 × 20.3 cm) each, Collection Princeton University Art Museum, Princeton, New Jersey. Copyright The Estate of Ana Mendieta Collection, L.L.C. Courtesy Galerie Lelong, New York.

the scope of the possible," the knowable ways of identifying individuals through a U.S. racial schema.

Tracing states of abjection, the female body, as Mendieta performs it, is manipulated beyond recognition, but along this spectrum there are flashes of familiar yet unstable countenances. In one particular image, Mendieta's gaze meets that of the audience. In this closely cropped portrait, the glass pane is pressed firmly against Mendieta's face, the swirling motion of the other portraits comes to a centered pause and creates an image of plump lips, broad nose, and a spectator-meeting gaze (figure 1.14). Here Mendieta activates what Matthew Pratt Guterl calls racial sightlines—popularly produced and accessible visual tropes through which we believe we see evidence of race.[40] Considered alongside Adrian Piper's *Self-Portrait Exaggerating My Negroid Features* (1981) from almost a decade later (figure 1.15), we can read Mendieta's portrait as a purposely hyperracialized façade that draws on popular notions of what being a person of color in the United States looks like. Given the predominance of the black/white binary, it is not surprising that Mendieta would reference blackness much in the same visual register as Piper does a decade later. As in the untitled painted portrait discussed above, Mendieta invokes blackness, but the performance component of the piece, which the photographs document in vignettes, also allows her to comment on the process of racialization.

Blackness, in this particular still from *Untitled* (Glass on Body Imprints) (figure 1.14), is arrived at through the violence of the spectator's gaze. The recognizable sign of blackness is created relationally, yet, by being framed as one along a spectrum, it is revealed as a construct and process, one reliant on the external gaze for recognition and actualization. While blackness is conjured through manipulated sightlines, Mendieta is also concurrently, through the presence of her body in performance, troubling the sightlines' coherence. She forces into focus the artificiality of what we understand as black, or even, given the slippage between racialized otherness and blackness, race. Mendieta conjures blackness yet relies on the sightlines that make her legible as nonblack to render the recognition she provokes as false. But she is, more importantly, calling attention to racialization processes as manipulable, unreliable, and incoherent. Mendieta addresses the gaze of the spectator directly, both in performance and through address to the camera, beyond the reach of the photograph to the indefinite spectators of the future, who are constituted as individuals through the abject spectacle. In *Untitled* (Glass on Body Imprints), she invites a relational contempla-

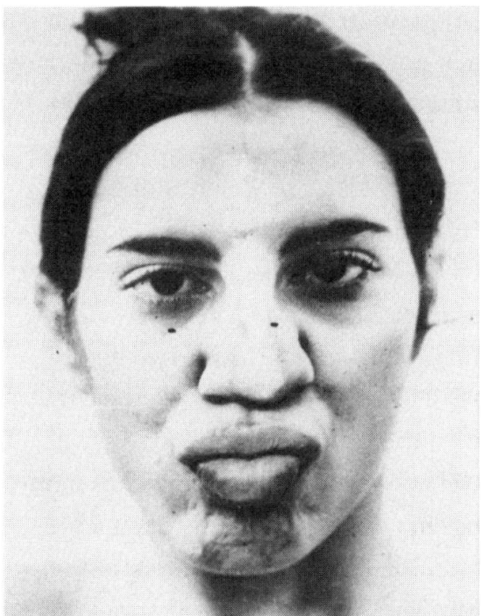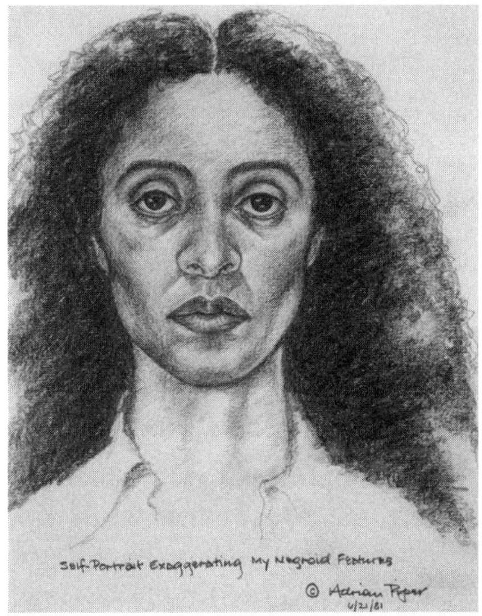

FIGURE 1.14 (LEFT) Ana Mendieta, detail, *Untitled (Glass on Body Imprints)*, 1972.
One of thirteen lifetime black-and-white photographs, 10 × 8 inches (25.4 × 20.3 cm)
each. Collection Princeton University Art Museum, Princeton, New Jersey. Copyright
The Estate of Ana Mendieta Collection, L.L.C. Courtesy Galerie Lelong, New York.
FIGURE 1.15 (RIGHT) Adrian Piper, *Self-Portrait Exaggerating My Negroid Features*, 1981.
Pencil on paper, 8 × 10 inches (20.3 × 25.4 cm). Collection of Eileen Harris Norton.
© Adrian Piper Research Archive Foundation Berlin.

tion on the process and social logics that otherize subjects and make them abject, but also cohere the viewing audience.

In a related piece from the same year, *Untitled* (Facial Cosmetic Variations), a series of eight studies similarly recorded as tight portraits of the artist's face, Mendieta alters her appearance using, simultaneously or consecutively, a brassy-blond or dark-brown wig, dark makeup, and a ripped stocking (plate 2). Mendieta is transformed with the aid of these quotidian materials, sometimes inserting cotton balls inside her mouth to further alter her appearance. In the documentation of this piece, we are presented with eight different women, wearing expressions that range from sultry to solemn. The stockinged faces of four of the images bear traces of wear. The artificial dermis is textured with scratches, torn from ab/use. Their eyes are largely shut from the pressure of the stocking, as are their mouths. The four muted portraits have countenances slightly darkened by the stocking except for the scars along the stocking runs that reveal Mendieta's lighter skin. The hair is largely matted, held in place by polyester, or covered by artificial hair. Shot from a slightly worm's-eye view that highlights the dark roots and disheveled eyebrows, these four shots evoke dis-ease and ambiguity. The runs in the stocking evoke not only a working-class femininity aspiring for sartorial dignity and failing, but also the violence of beauty standards that most women will fail to meet, especially women of color. In turn, the remaining four images, actively and powerfully, refuse beauty standards counterintuitively through acquiescence to abject excess.

Relieved of the stocking, the remaining four portraits reveal two heavily made-up blondes alongside two expressive brunettes, all meeting the gaze of the spectator. One brunette appears on the brink of tears, mouth swollen, chin tucked tightly into her neck. Her brunette twin brandishes her teeth. No longer limited by the stocking, her mouth is slightly open, chin tilted upward, with the sharp edges of her teeth bared. The expression on her face is somewhere between seductive and belligerent. In the remaining two images, Mendieta has darkened her skin offset by a dewy luminescence, topped by a harshly highlighted brassy-blonde wig. In the most haunting image of the series, Mendieta dons the blonde wig and has lightened her eyebrows and eyelashes, heavy on her lids. Her chin is tucked but, unlike the brunettes of the series, this is not paired with a swollen face and fragile expression. Instead, the subject's mouth is curved, creating a shape between smile and grimace. The photograph appears to have been created with a softer focus than the other pictures, producing an unnatural glow and overall uncanny effect. Considered together, all eight portraits present women who are familiar yet unidentifiable. Sightlines are approached but never aligned or matched. The spectator is indeed "hurled," in Kristeva's sense, no longer just taunted, to imagine "beyond the scope of the possible" knowable racialized subjects. Ambiguous in their identitarian performance, Mendieta's vignettes represent women who are only recognizable as Other. They avoid knowable combinations of visual markers of racial identity, instead mixing and combining elements and destabilizing the entire coherence of a visual racial apparatus.

In her article "Imitation and Gender Insubordination," Butler enacts a similar destabilizing of presumably knowable signifiers.[41] Identity categories, she tells us, "tend to be instruments of regulatory regimes whether as the normalizing categories of oppressive structures or as the rallying points for a liberatory contestation of that very oppression." She adds, "This is not to say that I will not appear at political occasions under the sign of lesbian, but that I would like to have it permanently unclear what precisely that sign signifies."[42] In this one statement, Butler performs an ambivalent embrace of identity categories, an ambivalence that Mendieta replicates in her work and career. The focus in Butler's piece, and indeed in Mendieta's early performances, is the trouble caused by these categories. Butler argues that claiming a particular identity category also produces a concealment of the way in which a category is naturalized and made legible by that which it excludes. Subjects are produced discursively, relationally, with identity categories in the service of reifying a norm, through performative repetition. Through this repeated performance, the identity category is established as well as destabilized and left open to subversion given that the repetitions are never identical. The result is a "semblance of continuity or coherence" where "there is no 'I' that precedes what it is said to perform"—much like the familiar yet unidentifiable figures in Mendieta's *Untitled* (Facial Cosmetic Variations).[43]

To think through the role of identity, Butler offers a strategy of what she calls "disclaiming" as a form of "affirmative resistance" for the "necessary" trouble provoked by identity categories.[44] Mendieta's *Untitled* (Glass on Body Imprints) and *Untitled* (Facial Cosmetic Variations), especially in their invocation of blackness and exploration of femininity, perform this disclaiming strategy. While Butler famously turned to drag to answer the question of the historically political necessity of identity markers and the trap of visibility they create for those who claim them through existing regulatory regimes, I offer Mendieta's ambiguous racial drag to similar effect. Through the use of abject aesthetic strategies, her work circulates identitarian signs in which what is signified might remain permanently unclear. Prefiguring Butler and Piper, Mendieta's performance here highlights the regulatory fiction of racial identity politics as well as what Andrea Smith writes of as, after Beth Richie, the shifting center of women of color feminism.[45]

Grace K. Hong writes that women of color feminism is "a political and intellectual practice around the very excesses that cannot be categorized and thus can only be named in fragments."[46] It is these fragments, which scholars have struggled to capture in language, that Mendieta captures in her untitled pieces. By combining both performance and photographic documentation, Mendieta manages to give a material body to a fractured fleeting condition, first in performance (using her own body to beckon forth unreliable identity fragments), then in photography (providing material proof of the fleeting performance of identity). Her consistent reference to blackness presents a Latinidad that calls us to explore our prietud, yes, but also pushes the metaphorical boundary of Anzaldúa's mestiza, which has had much currency within Latino studies. For Anzaldúa, the New Mestiza is hailed by either side of an artificial U.S./Mexico border and operates in a pluralistic mode that sustains contradictions, generating a new consciousness whose "energy comes from continual creative motion that keeps breaking down the unitary aspect of each new paradigm," performing "a massive uprooting of dualistic thinking in the individual and collective consciousness"—a paradigmatic project of women of color feminism that establishes the border, both material and psychic, as a valid site of analysis.[47] Undoing "dualistic thinking," Mendieta negotiates her Latinidad in relationship not to Chicanidad but to blackness, and insists that Latinidad consider not just its indigenous past but also its relationship to black bodies as well as the push and pull of the border. She challenges the redemptive mestiza consciousness to resist completion or resolution with her Butlerian trouble in favor of inhabiting sites of rupture and indeterminacy as productive openings for new collectivity.

Mendieta renders visible abjection's affective impulse to disrupt identity. As Alberto Sandoval-Sánchez stipulates in his work on the queer Latino subject living with AIDS: "Abject bodies are repulsive because they manifest and inflict a confusion of boundaries which punctures, fractures, and fragments the assumed unity, stability, and closure of the identity of the hegemonic subject and the body politic of the nation."[48] Accessible now only as fragmentary stills, Mendieta's *Untitled* (Glass on Body Imprints) and *Untitled* (Facial Cosmetic Variations) embody abjection by way of their elision of a fixed identity and disclosure of the processes of normative subject formation. Rooted in the body, Mendieta's performance (her literal embodiment of the abject) must be considered against its Iowa setting. To embrace the abject in dialogue with her largely white audience was, for Mendieta, a performance of "a boundary crisis" as well as "the disruption of order."[49] Constructing theories of racialization through a relational medium, Mendieta indicates the necessity for a reflective spectator, both of her performances and of the material record of that performance, which extends the spectator into the future and beyond Iowa.[50]

In 1973, Mendieta performed perhaps her most extreme embodiment of the abject—which turned out to be the most well-recognized work of her early career. For the event, Mendieta invited her mostly white male MFA colleagues to view a new piece in her apartment. Arriving for the performance, fellow faculty and students walked through an open door and found Mendieta perpendicularly bent over and tied to a table by her wrists. She was naked from the waist down. Her face lay in a pool of blood, smeared at the site where her hands were restrained, with the sleeve of the arm that cradled and partially hid her face soaked. Her bare legs and buttocks were smeared with blood, seemingly emanating from between her legs, down to the stained underwear caught at her ankles. The dimly lit room revealed broken dishes scattered across the floor, with cigarette butts in a nearby ashtray and blood mixed with a questionable ivory-colored fluid in the toilet. Mendieta sustained the pose, with corpselike stillness, for two hours. This performance installation, Mendieta's *Rape Scene* (figures 1.16–1.20), was conceived in response to the sexual violation and murder of a woman on her campus.

When I envision the details of the performance, it is the moments after the initial discovery that give me pause. Given the context of a recent death of a fellow student on campus, at some point it had to be decided whether Mendieta was performing or was the actual victim of a rape and/or murder. (Was her pulse checked?) I wonder if word of her performance spread, if an audience amassed to gaze at the spectacle of rape, or if the audience was limited to the invited MFA students. (Did anyone try to untie her?) What does it mean for an audience member to observe, to refrain from untying Mendieta or shielding her bloody, half-naked body? What does it mean to come across such a scene and not call for help? How does a piece like that end? While we know that a friend, Sheila Kelly, helped Mendieta to set up the scene, upsetting furniture, smearing Mendieta with blood, and tying her to that table before leaving her apartment door open, there is no record of how the piece ended.[51] Mendieta would later recall that several students sat down in her apartment and began a discussion of the piece as they would in a studio and were shocked when Mendieta didn't join them.

I imagine that this piece has no end. Though Hans Breder shares that Mendieta did not inform anyone about the subject of her performance, we know at least one student was asked to photograph the scene encountered upon arrival.[52] *Rape Scene* forced the encounter between bloodied body and the unknowing spectator, staged the discovery, but it also staged its documentation. We are meant to ruminate on the immediate reception of the performance but also on the encounter beyond the immediate scene. Mendieta's abject presentation is routed through the formally unbounded, through sublime limitlessness.

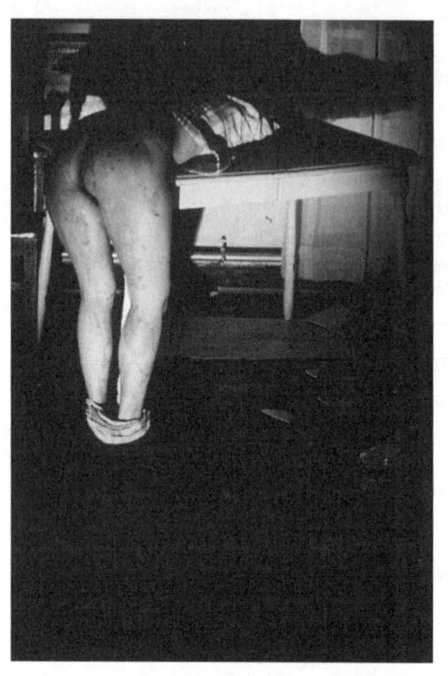
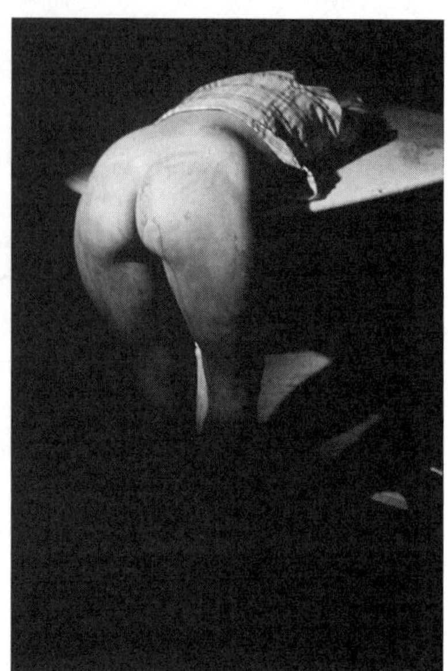
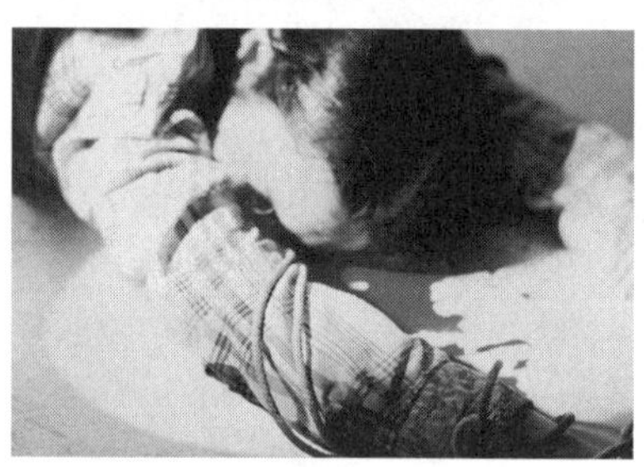
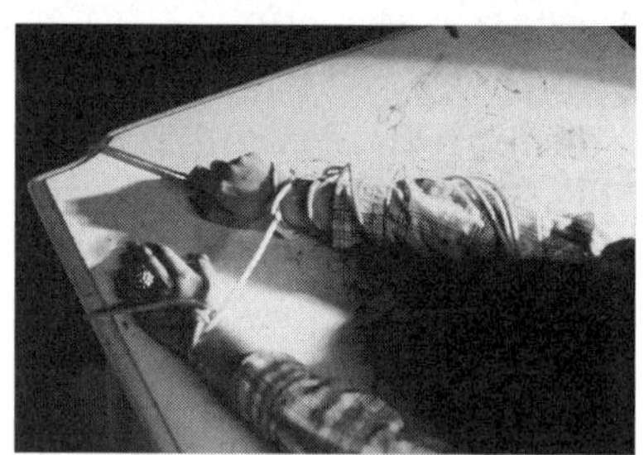
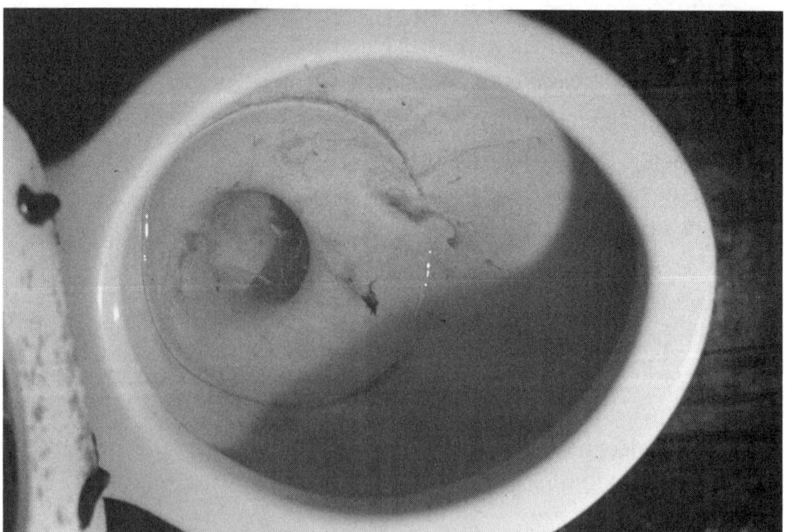

As elaborated in the introduction to this book, the Kantian dyad to the category of beauty, the sublime, designates an aesthetic judgment connected to emotion and what Kant describes as "negative pleasure." Within philosophy, the sublime has been theorized as the emotive site that frustrates reason—at once pleasurable and repulsive, an unrepresentable paradox. As Derrida tells us, the sublime is "to be found, for its part, in an 'object without form' and the 'without-limit' is 'represented' in it or on the occasion of it, and yet gives the totality of the without-limit to be *thought*."[53] While some have read the sublime as necessarily emotionally disinterested and transcendent, much like the judgment of beauty, I read in Kant's sublime a fissure of possibility from which we can mine challenges to the very political apparatus it constructs in tandem with the beautiful, activated through the use of the abject.[54] Throughout this study, the profiled cultural producers activate abjection to different though related ends. Elaborating a sublime abjection, Mendieta's performance provides the opportunity to reflect on the limitlessness of violence in and of her performance. In fact, it calls on the spectator to imagine a prior violence that created the scene they encounter. Unlike the previous pieces discussed, the primary actions that result in *Rape Scene* occur away from the gaze of the spectator, as do the actions that terminate and resolve the scene. We cannot see the violence as it occurs, nor a sequence of photographs documenting its progressing abject states. Instead, *Rape Scene* is a live installation. Its documentation extends the event endlessly into the future, suspended by photography in space.

For her audience, Mendieta re-creates not just a rape scene, but a racially coded scene cued by the bondage of her wrist with rope, echoing a lashing or lynching scene through the invitation of what Ken Gonzales-Day has elaborated as the "wonder gaze"—"the notion of the spectacle or of the scopic pleasure audiences found in looking at or reading about" lynching.[55] *Rape Scene* produces a viewing public around a presumably private violence, putting into question the scopophilic pleasure of the contemplative judging spectator, Kant's imagined ideal judge. In his essay "Race under Representation," David Lloyd argues that Kantian aesthetics rely on and produce an unmarked subject, Kant's disinterested judge, that functions as a regulative figure through whom the universality of the public

FIGURES 1.16–1.20 Ana Mendieta, *Rape Scene*, 1973. Estate print 2001, suite of five color photographs, 16 × 20 inches (40.6 × 50.8 cm). Copyright The Estate of Ana Mendieta Collection, L.L.C. Courtesy Galerie Lelong, New York.

sphere is established while providing the defining logic that structures racist discourse. The spectator of performance, be he the ideal subject without property of Kantian aesthetics or not, is part of a larger ideological framework engaged by the artist. Mendieta confronted her entirely male peers with a contemplation of their participation in systems of domination in her own home—a challenge that would be eerily echoed in the trial of Carl Andre following her death. Given the recorded response of the other MFA students—of sitting to critique the piece—and Mendieta's refusal to join them, we can read her actions as challenging the suspension of ethical reaction supplanted by disinterested contemplation. Indeed, in an undated journal entry Mendieta writes, "Ver en calma un crimen es cometerlo" (To calmly view a crime is to commit it).[56] She creates a correlation between aesthetic structures of viewing ("ver"), judging, and exhibiting, and those of racialization that enforce boundaries.

Mendieta's *Rape Scene* provokes an awareness of sexual violence against women in general and women of color in particular, but it does more than stir empathy and a reflection of audience responsibility, as has been suggested by existing interpretations of this piece.[57] *Rape Scene* collapses the private and public realms and points to the culture of silence around the mistreatment of women that the audience then itself replicates through its (our) "wonder gaze," thereby indicting fine art culture and its role in societal violence. Audiences of the live performance (as well as those of the documentation) stand and watch the rape spectacle, violently impotent. Both performer and viewer carry with them the violence of the scene met by silence. Mendieta makes visible the Kantian expectation of a disinterested spectator but also the violence and complacency inherent in the passive contemplation of the taste-bearing judging subject. This work does indeed expose purportedly private forms of violence, bringing it into the public space of art, but it does so by bringing the disinterested Kantian bearer of judgment into the private space of the home in order to show how the apparatuses that the spectator participates in already permeate private spaces.

As an installation without end, *Rape Scene* haunts me beyond the writing of this chapter, but it is in its sublime limitlessness, as in the transience and uncertainty of the earlier performances, that I uncomfortably see Mendieta's reach to provoke a transformative social response to power. Mendieta here mobilizes abjection as "socially constituted affect" in response to structures of power.[58] In my reading of Mendieta, I attempt to invoke Da-

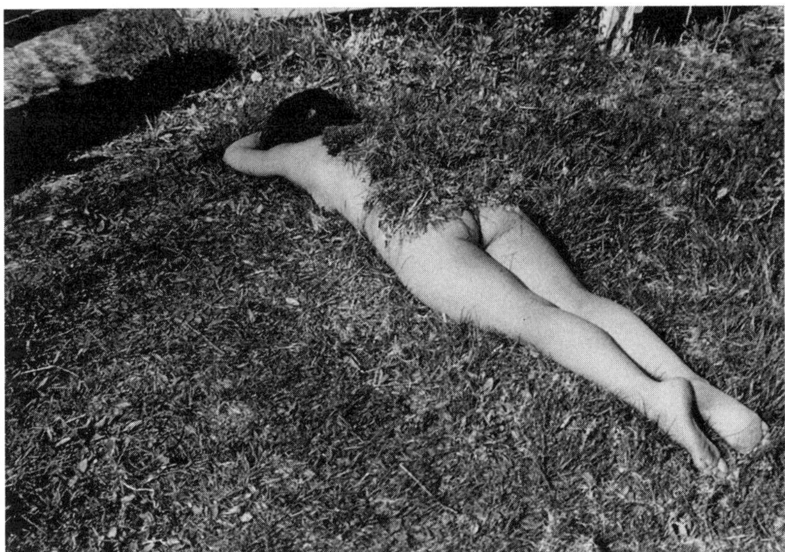

FIGURE 1.21 Ana Mendieta, *Untitled* (Grass on Woman), 1972. Copyright The Estate of Ana Mendieta Collection, L.L.C. Courtesy Galerie Lelong, New York.

vid Halperin's understanding of abjection, for her work activates abjection as "an experiment with the limits of both destruction and survival, social isolation and social solidarity, domination and transcendence."[59] Her performances, echoing Anzaldúa, "call us on a lot of shit like our own racism, our fear of women and sexuality" by taunting the disinterested spectator out of passive contemplation.

The Body Abjected

Mendieta's body, so forcefully present in these early performances, lies face down partially upholstered by the grassy blades of the green field on which she rests (figure 1.21). Just beneath the textured green atop her back from shoulder blades to hip bones, Mendieta's nude, rounded bottom gives way to exposed legs held close together. So arranged, Mendieta composed her first earth-body work, *Untitled* (Grass on Woman), the same year as her untitled facial cosmetic variations, 1972. The ratio of exposed to upholstered flesh favors flesh; in an aerial lateral view of Mendieta, the long line of flesh from raised elbow through partially encased torso to limbs dominates. It is easy to see how this work will give way to another recumbent body held taut in an open Oaxacan tomb in which her body is almost entirely ob-

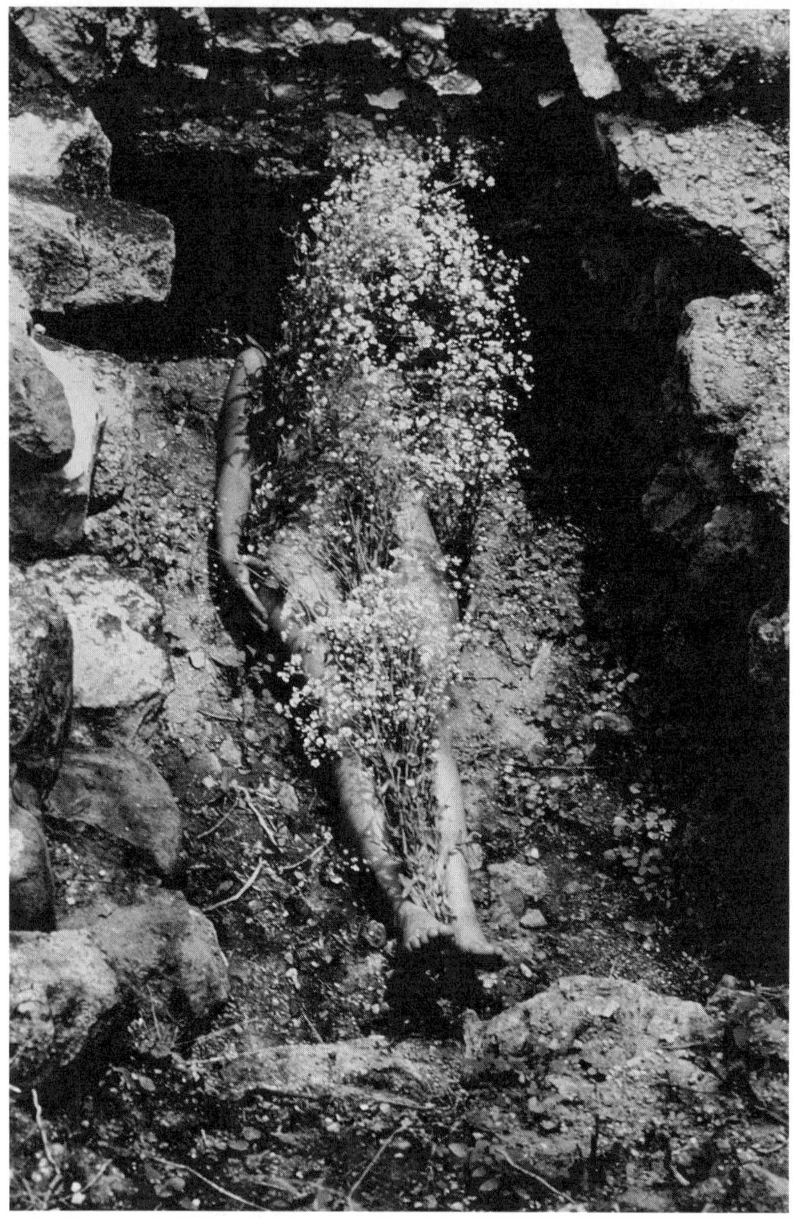

FIGURE 1.22 Ana Mendieta, *Untitled* (Silueta Series, Mexico), 1973. Copyright
The Estate of Ana Mendieta Collection, L.L.C. Courtesy Galerie Lelong, New York.

scured by green foliage offset with small white blossoms—Mendieta's first self-identified Silueta, *Untitled* (Silueta Series, Mexico) (1973, figure 1.22), created the summer just after her *Rape Scene*—and then from *Untitled* (Silueta Series, Mexico) to the Siluetas for which she is most known, and from which her body is finally absent.[60] While it is tempting to imagine a linear progression from one aesthetic mode to another, one political strategy evolving into the next, I am interested in reimagining the political work of Mendieta's Silueta Series through her abject performances, elaborated palimpsestically to her first earth-body works.

Critical race theorists, especially those with a focus in Latino studies, have sought to read the removal of Mendieta's physical body from her work as a strategy that reveals a desire for a connection to home through land, exemplary of exilic longing rather than as an essentialist gesture toward representing the "Everywoman" and more.[61] Of essentializing narratives, Kaira Cabañas writes that "inscribing Mendieta's art with the fixed language of essentialist feminism impoverishes its meaning" and that "in their appropriation of Mendieta, essentialist feminists colonize the work and consequently whiten its content."[62] Cabañas explains that instead of a biological determinism, Mendieta "[emphasizes] the different sociocultural circumstances of her body," a body she elsewhere cites as a representative of the individual-collective body—"a community of experience of exile and ethnic Other"—through the incorporation of Santería and the conflation of "land with home" in her Silueta Series.[63] I want to linger, here, on Mendieta's conflations and appropriations to tease out some of the silences around Mendieta's practice by focusing not on the "individual-collective body" but on the absent body or, rather, the abjected body whose lingering contours— a silueta—can be read as a utopian methodology for Latino studies.

Though Mendieta performed earth-body works in Iowa, her first self-identified Silueta, *Untitled* (Silueta Series, Mexico), (1973, figure 1.22), was created during a trip to Oaxaca, Mexico, with the University of Iowa's Intermedia program. The program's multiple summer trips to Oaxaca participated in the larger trend of artists and academics visiting the area, "captivated," Olga Viso tells us, "by the nostalgia and mysticism of this relatively unknown region of Mexico."[64] Though Mendieta had visited the region before for fieldwork with an archaeology class, her Intermedia visits were significantly shaped by Breder, who encouraged a disregard for material conditions that lay beyond the process of art making. For Breder, there was to be "no caution, no thought of getting jobs, of making money, of making 'it.' There was only the work and the world of creation into which it brought us."[65]

I read these prescriptions for lack of caution as deeply embedded in and enjoyed through multiple institutional privileges of which Mendieta was now the beneficiary. In addition to her association with the university program, she could also enjoy these privileges through her newly acquired U.S. citizenship, which was procured through the special privileges granted Cuban refugees in the Cold War era through the Cuban Adjustment Act.[66] We know from the archives, for example, that Mendieta and others from the program moved through Mexico with a level of access that was beyond the purview of the Mexican citizenry who served as a backdrop to their "magical" source material. Ranging from personal tours headed by the owner of the Hotel Principal where they stayed during most of their summers in Mexico, to gaining permission from the head anthropologist to work in and photograph archaeological sites, Mendieta enjoyed an enabled creative process.[67] Additionally, the owner of the Hotel Principal, who lent his rooftop and courtyards for installations and performances, took Breder and Mendieta to small local cemeteries and churches where Mendieta observed local traditions from which she would borrow for her Siluetas. Mendieta's hair was braided every morning by the housekeeper of the hotel with whom she shared her enthusiasm for the sites and her enjoyment of *"gente sencilla"* (simple people), whose ritual practices she would put into conversation with the Santería she observed in her youth in works that incorporated flower blossoms, blood, and ash. Finally, Mendieta's not-quite-spontaneous first Silueta, installed with the help of Breder and a couple of friends in a shallow Oaxacan grave, we know, was crafted and documented with the speed necessary to avoid the attention of security guards and the objection of locals, who would have surely been offended by Mendieta's nudity at this sacred site.[68]

I am attempting to highlight the distinctly different social location Mendieta enjoyed for the emergence of her first Silueta from which the series would grow. What do we make of the solidification and expansion of this significant aesthetic form at a moment of increased access to state privileges and cultural capital? And further, what do we make of the narrative, propagated by art historians and Mendieta herself, that her time in Mexico was a time of reconciliation with Cuba after the displacement of her adolescence? For example, Mendieta shared that summers spent in Mexico "working within a culture closer to [her] own . . . helped define the concept and vocabulary of [her] work."[69] Relatedly, Julia Herzberg writes that "Mexico—the closest thing to Cuba by virtue of the fact that it was Latin America—became an alternative motherland where the artist reconnected to roots from which she had been forcibly severed."[70] Similarly, Guy Brett explains that, "Mendieta did subscribe to the more general notion of 'Latin America' . . . that, despite great disparities between the individual countries, there were similarities between Latin American cultures that were collectively different to North American culture."[71]

The problematic narrative around Mendieta and Mexico, a narrative that collapses regions, has surely contributed to the charges of essentialism in Mendieta's work—charges that are nonetheless of limited use. I am more interested in thinking through the ways that the Siluetas come into focus not through the body that indents, but by the way the negative space the silueta forges then makes legible the environment against which it is carved. Mendieta's Siluetas are not interesting to me for what they tell us about Mendieta's interiority or a perceived connection to her "homeland" (through the earth in Mexico or Iowa) but rather for those ideological structures that remain even when her body does not, with a material mark as significant as the outline she creates, however ephemeral. We must contend with Mendieta's U.S., and indeed Cuban American, privilege as central to the heuristic her work offers us. If, as I have argued above, we understand her early abject performances as working through racialization with a relational and comparative model, her time in Mexico shows us the need to constantly assess our shifting geopolitical locations even while seeking out affinities.

I am not, then, interested in a hagiography of Mendieta. Rather, her work proffers useful political strategies and cautions. The space Mendieta's Siluetas give shape to emerges from complex negotiations of an unnamed Latinidad triangulated through Cuba to the U.S. Midwest and to Mexico. Given her generative engagement with comparative racialization through her earlier and concurrent abject performances, I want to believe that what can and has been called essentialist in her Siluetas is an entirely more complex staging of the dynamics that are both problematic, as described above, but also productive. This productive affinity would later lay the groundwork for recognition of the coalitional possibilities for communities beyond national borders developed in her late curatorial work at A.I.R. Gallery (specifically the decolonial impulse communicated in *Dialectics of Isolation* discussed below). Framed though her abject performances, we can understand this affinity, and the work of coalition, as requiring our critical attention and constant assessment of shifting and socially assigned privilege.

Within the space designated by the Siluetas, by its contours, we can situate the abjected body, which Mendieta has removed but repeatedly indexes. For Kristeva the abject is an intermediary position, neither subject nor object, a disruptive force of the "in-between, the ambiguous, the composite."[72] Building on Kristeva, Christine Wilkie-Stibbs has argued that the abject marks the very process through which an individual becomes subjected.[73] In her Siluetas, Mendieta gives us neither object nor subject through her physical absence. Instead, we encounter dissolving ephemeral traces and, significantly, the marked contours that reveal the abjected as shaped by social and political conditions that facilitate its emergence.

In her book *Imagine Otherwise: On Asian American Critique*, Kandice Chuh offers subjectless discourse as a model that imagines the Asian American Other primarily through the configurations of power/knowledge that render the subject legible. Chuh argues for prioritizing difference by foregrounding the constructedness of subjectivity; not the subject herself but rather the discourses that bring the subject into being. This subjectless approach, she argues, is a conceptual tool for a political project of strategic antiessentialism that would provide a discursive space for new practices of subjectivity and create a field of study that consistently questions its own boundaries. Subjectless critique has a root in queer theory, developed by Michael Warner as establishing "'a wide field of normalization' as the site of social violence." Elaborating a dynamic similar to the ambivalence of abjection, Eng, Halberstam, and Muñoz explain how Warner's concept brings "attention to those hegemonic social structures by which certain subjects are rendered 'normal' and 'natural' through the production of 'perverse' and 'pathological' others" that prioritizes "resistance to regimes of the normal."[74] This model disallows a proper subject of queer studies but simultaneously tends to prioritize white gay men. Eng, Halberstam, and Muñoz, however, insist on an epistemological approach that includes "other fields of inquiry, such as women of color feminism, queer of color critique, or queer diasporas," a theoretical genealogy of which, I am arguing, Mendieta is undoubtedly a part.[75] Reconfigured in this way, subjectless critique has the ability to perform a "continuous deconstruction of the tenets of positivism at the heart of identity politics."[76]

I am proposing that while Mendieta's abject performances offer a similar deconstruction of positivism, reframing her Siluetas pushes subjectless critique further. The Siluetas show us that there is not only not a proper subject of Latinidad but also that instead of defaulting to a privileged subject—the mestizo Chicano in Latino studies who we might understand as a cognate to the white gay male of gay studies—it is instead important to attend to the structured and shifting constitution of the subject in formation as it is performatively rendered. In the space demarcated by the Siluetas, we might think of Chuh's antiessentialism working against earlier charges of essentialism in Mendieta's Siluetas. This body of work, then, vibrates with the tension and complexity that shapes Latinidades; a sense of otherness and also shifting terrains of privilege, as well as the promise of a strategically antiessentialist heuristic that offers an approach to the field alive to tension but also possibility.

Dialectics of Isolation

In her curatorial statement for the 1980 exhibition *Dialectics of Isolation: An Exhibition of Third World Women Artists*, Mendieta writes:

> There is a certain time in history when people take consciousness of themselves and ask questions about who they are. After World War II, the label Third World came into being in reference to the people of Africa, Asia and Latin America. The movement of Unaligned Nations was founded in 1961 with a meeting which took place in Belgrade. Their aims are to end colonialism, racism and exploitation.
>
> We of the Third World in the United States have the same concerns as the people of the Unaligned Nations. The white population of the United States, diverse, but of basic European stock, exterminated the indigenous civilization and put aside the Black as well as the other non-white cultures to create a homogenous male-dominated culture above the internal divergency.
>
> Do we exist? . . . To question our culture is to question our own existence, our human reality. To confront this fact means to acquire an awareness of ourselves. This in turn becomes a search, a questioning of who we are and how we will realize ourselves.
>
> During the mid to late sixties as women in the United States politicized themselves and came together in the Feminist Movement with the purpose to end the domination and exploitation by the white male culture, they failed to remember us. American Feminism as it stands is basically a white middle class movement.

As non-white women our struggles are two-fold.

This exhibition points not necessarily to the injustice or incapacity of a society that has not been willing to include us, but more towards *a personal will to continue being "other."*[77]

The first paragraph's explanatory "they" notably offsets the shift to "we" of the second paragraph, in which Mendieta names herself and the women in her exhibit Third World people with the shared aims of ending "colonialism, racism and exploitation." Mendieta presents an ungendered community of color linked in spirit to the Unaligned Nations that rejected binary Cold War politics. She exhibits recognition of the similarities between communities of color in the United States and those abroad under shared conditions of capital. Her statement extends the unbounded sublime of her abject aesthetics into political groupings. The ontological question that follows in the opening of her third paragraph names the inhuman realm that the abject inhabit. If relegated to the role of cohering the normative subject, "Do we exist?" Will normative aspirations ever be successful? A confrontation of this reality leads Mendieta to verbalize a political project that embraces abjection. What will the project look like? Not like the "Feminist Movement" she disparages in the next paragraph for "[failing] to remember us." Instead, Mendieta acknowledges the political imperative requiring the use of certain discursive signs in her personal will to continue being Other.

In *Methodology of the Oppressed,* Chela Sandoval provides a useful cartography of U.S. feminisms to help us understand Mendieta's navigation within and beyond what Sandoval would call the hegemonic feminist movement. Hegemonic feminism is composed of a much-cited four-phase history of consciousness, including liberal, Marxist, radical/cultural, and socialist feminisms. Women of color, Sandoval argues, moved among and between these and other oppositional movements, being relegated to the periphery of each while developing what she calls a differential consciousness. Writing in the wake of postmodern pessimism and its charge for the need of a new vocabulary of resistance, Sandoval suggests that U.S. women of color feminists identified this oppositional subject and enacted and performed it differently than other politicized subject positions. One can see this oppositional consciousness at work in Mendieta's early performances, along with the challenges those performances leverage against aesthetic ideologies linked to representative politics and indeed her ambivalent participation in the mainstream feminist movement.

After joining the collaborative in 1978, Mendieta helped organize programming that challenged the boundaries of an organization struggling with charges of racism from its own members.[78] She spoke on a panel called Latin American Women Artists, convened another called Racism in the Visual and Performing Arts, and participated in the panel Theoretical Concepts in Feminist Art at the invitation of Harmony Hammond.[79] But it was perhaps *Dialectics* that most forcefully communicated her critique. As director of A.I.R., Kat Griefen tells us in her "Ana Mendieta at A.I.R. Gallery, 1977–82," *Dialectics* was perhaps Mendieta's largest contribution to the gallery. Coordinated with Kazuko and Zarina—who focused on installation and catalogue design respectively—the exhibit included the work of Judith Baca, Lydia Okumura, Zarina, Beverly Buchanan, Janet Henry, Howardena Pindell, Selina Whitefeather, and Senga Negudi. While described with racial and national descriptors in fund-raising letters for the exhibit, *Dialectics* identified the women only as Third World women in the United States.[80] Each provided a statement for their work in the catalogue paired with an image of their gallery contribution. These were, in some cases, similar in length to Mendieta's powerful curatorial statement. While the exhibit has been read as Mendieta's personal passion or declarative project, the collaborative nature seems important to underscore as it is emphasized not only in Mendieta's curatorial statement but also in the notable absence of her own artistic work on the walls of the gallery or in the catalogue.

The contributing artists displayed a range of strategies. Judith Baca shared sketches of large-form murals for which she is now famously known and wrote about the importance of community engagement and the responsibility of a socially conscious artist. Beverly Buchanan, on the other hand, provided descriptive notes on the production of her minimalist columns and the experience of spectatorship. Though seemingly visually diametrically opposed, their inclusion in the same space, physical as well as theoretical, tells us of the multitudes contained by the exhibit—a sublimely abject gesture. These multitudes included Lydia Okumura and Serena Whitefeather's treatment of earth's landscape and flora, Janet Henry's miniatures reflecting on class and the process of coming to terms with material desire and lack, Nengudi and Zarina's poetic reflections on materiality and theme, and Howardena Pindell's damning critique of white feminism—an amplification of Mendieta's. In an echo of her Siluetas, Mendieta's body (of work) was absent. She nonetheless offers an instantiation of the political project of her aesthetic practice, of the recognizable otherness invoked in early performances, her "personal will to continue being 'other.'" In *Cruising Utopia*, Muñoz tells us that the aesthetic "frequently contains blueprints and schemata of a forward-dawning futurity."[81] *Dialectics* provides a productive presentiment, a political imagining of what a subjectless approach to addressing difference, with the body abjected, might look like.

Mendieta deftly calls attention to the limits of the hegemonic feminist movement to address the concerns of communities of color. That she did this within an exhibition space birthed from the feminist movement she critiques speaks to Mendieta's careful negotiation of oppositional spaces, performing what Sandoval identifies as differential consciousness. In her curatorial statement, Mendieta captures the structure of feeling, an affective "set with specific internal relations, at once interlocking and in tension," of women of color feminism.[82] There were those who implied that while at the forefront of the avant-garde, the young Mendieta was uninterested in feminist politics, and that later as a feminist member of multiple women's collectives, she had no interest in race.[83] But here and in her early performances, we see that her aesthetic practice was deeply committed to thinking race, identity, gender, and class as intersecting projects whose constitution indicates practices and relations of power that become concretized in what we understand as identities. In her rejection of the politics and institutional logic of A.I.R., we see a theory that was first articulated as praxis in Iowa.

Mendieta offered her performative and curatorial work in response to dissidence in the movement. Her curatorial statement and earlier aesthetic praxis display a commitment to coalitional politics and to transnational struggles for social justice "allied through the apparatus of emancipation."[84] For Sandoval, U.S. women of color aligned theoretical domains into intellectual and political coalitions. Women of color feminists issued anticapitalist, anticolonial, and antiessentialist critiques, expanding liberation projects and affiliations across geographical and psychic borders to forge alliances beyond the nation-state and its juridical citizen-subject. They also challenged the reified liberated subject of dominant social movements, shifting the grounds on which demands for social justice are made from a civil rights platform to the level of structural and institutional critique. Mendieta's *Dialectics* clarifies this same strategy in her Iowa performances. An uncertain otherness is placed at the center of analysis in *Untitled* (Glass on Body Imprints), *Untitled* (Facial Cosmetic Variations), and *Rape Scene*.

It is achieved by a purposeful embodiment and deployment of abjection. Mendieta's shifting aesthetic strategies and their connections to ways of imagining collectivity and subjectivity prompt us to move beyond a politics of liberatory visibility that is often paired with an aesthetics of respectability. Abjection, as an aesthetically based political strategy, can serve as the basis for addressing political injustice, invoking broader collectivities beyond conventional identity categories even as we remain attuned to the particularities that create the abject realm. When paired with the model of subjectless critique offered by Mendieta's cultural production—performative, earth-body, and curatorial—we are invited to consider privilege as a central analytic to abjection, especially of different Latino populations as they move within communities of color in the United States but also across national borders. This frame is essential to an expanding transnational and comparative field. The project of contributing to a more capacious and critical Latino studies is augmented in chapter 2 through a reconstitution of our understanding of productive community and collective affects.

CHAPTER 2

Phantom Assholes
Asco's Affective Vortex

Dressed in a bust-hugging sleeveless top of red flowers on a field of white and crisp khaki slacks, Asco's Patssi Valdez sits above an urban drainpipe. She faces the audience with bare shoulders opening out from a side straddle, legs splayed over the cement wall that contains the pipe. The counterclockwise corkscrew of her torso's twist creates a sight line that draws the spectator's gaze down Valdez's leg to her dramatically platformed heel, kissing the edge of the cavernous, "orificial" pipe opening, and diagonally across the dark expanse from her shoe to the waste that stains the cement wall like a seeping brown tongue.[1] Her foot, barely within the frame created by the pipe's opening, serves as the punctum—that element which for Barthes punctuates the field of vision to provoke an adventure for the spectator.[2] Flanking Valdez to the viewer's left, Gronk (Glugio Nicandro), in a dark suit offset by a light panama hat and pocket square, echoes Valdez's stance: his body in profile gestures up and diagonally toward her. Like

Valdez, his body caresses the curved edge of the asshole designated by the performance's title. Diagonally down and to Valdez's right, Willie Herrón III, in a charcoal three-piece suit, directs his body and shaded gaze to the camera. Perched at the document's far right stands Harry Gamboa Jr., who has set up his camera, shutter delayed, to capture the frame within which his collaborators enact this performative composition. The leaking asshole between Valdez's legs captures the simultaneous seduction and repulsion, the pull of the punctum and push from the gag of disgust, provoked by Asco's abject production.

The photo-document described above, *Asshole Mural* (1975), emerged from a day spent surveying Los Angeles from east to west in a performance created to declare "civic landmarks, monuments, and preservation zones."[3] The document is one of many phantoms surrounding the collective known as Asco.[4] A different image circulates, considered the official record of the performance by the photographer, in which Valdez stands to Gronk's left. In this image her legs are held together, casually crossed, but directing a sight line at her legs' crease away from the seeping asshole and toward the image's left bottom corner (plate 3). One hand is in her pocket while the other supports her weight against a cement step that extends from the rectangular architecture surrounding the pipe. Her body and Gronk's are now parallel to the spectator's plane, altering the queer sensual proximity and suggestion of their bodies to the pipe opening present in the phantom image. A copy of this image as the approved official record, with the word "Ascozilla" emblazoned above the pipe and the dates "August 4–21, 1975" printed on the bottom, was used as the flyer for *Ascozilla*, an early exhibition.[5]

I first encountered *Asshole Mural* in C. Ondine Chavoya's essay "Internal Exiles: The Interventionist Public and Performance Art of Asco," which features the phantom photo-document with which I began this chapter. The spectral quality of the image—at that point a photocopy of a photocopy, blurred, it seemed, by rumor and suggestion—inspired the direction of this inquiry. I am drawn by the way this phantom document haunts the official image, which congeals a performance into a single frame, and by the ways it locates the four individuals commonly considered the core or original members of the collective that is known and studied as Asco.

By most accounts, the four began collaborating in 1972, with the group fluctuating in size after 1975 as the original members diverged to pursue individual projects and new collaborators, Ascotas—*mascotas* or mascots of *asco*—came and went until its official disbanding in 1987.[6] Here, I treat Asco less as a concrete group and more as a porous organizing energy, an abject structure of feeling, traversed by collaborative productions, beckoned by personal ties to the individual members collectively called Asco and the "asco"—meaning nausea or disgust in Spanish—that propelled this countercultural community. Following José Esteban Muñoz's belief that a "general turn to affect might be a better way to talk about the affiliations and identifications between radicalized and ethnic groups than those available in standard stories of identity politics," I turn to Asco as an affective abject vortex in order to imagine, through them, a contrapuntal political project to contribute to our understanding of abjection's political dynamics.[7] Asco conjured affective communities through an ambivalent embrace of a decidedly queer abject aesthetic. They deployed a familiar Chicano *rasquachismo* partnered with the glittery veneer of an alternative protopunk scene that rendered their daily bodily presentation and public street actions an affront to the heteronormative, patriarchal ideal upheld by the Chicano nationalist project focused on affirming representation, defended by East Los Angeles's inhabitants.[8]

While, as Ricky T. Rodríguez and others have argued, "the Chicano movement cannot be classified as a monolithic entity, requiring instead comprehension as a social force emerging from distinct regions and multiple social justice trajectories," the ethos of the Chicano movement with which Asco was critically engaged is crystalized in privileged cultural texts—*corridos* and murals—that elevated and crafted a vision of a bronze people bound to one cause: the mestizo nation of Aztlán, anchored in a mythic past, defended by revolutionary warriors, nurtured by its farmers, and its future concretized in the nuclear family.[9] What has come to be understood as the preponderance of Chicano nationalism's heternormativity has been roundly critiqued, most poignantly and immediately by Chicana feminists. This chapter builds on that criticism and situates Asco's abject choices as a unique counter to the movement's connection to representative presence as the grounds for enfranchisement.[10] Asco's mode of engagement with abjection resists the broader movement's reparative critical move toward discursive wholeness—fortified interiorities and coherent complete subjectivities within unified communities. Instead they engage with the fractured incompleteness and loss that, as Antonio Viego argues, "[generates] metaphors of possibility, even excess and not metaphors of scarcity and lack and the placid gloom of renunciation," despite, even because of, their focus on and use of negative affect.[11] This historical framing of Asco's art practice allows us to see the ways Chicano nationalism, as an ideology, upheld and participated in dominant U.S. culture, not only in its enshrinement of the normative family but also in its cultural struggle to be represented, politically and aesthetically, by a proud, bronze protagonist whose historical presence grants him rights for official representation if not national self-determination.[12] By harnessing asco, indeed willing its transmission, desiring a visceral audience response, Asco reveals an aesthetic collectivity that dwells in and amplifies a sense of displacement, discomfort, and disease, cohering around and validating feelings of disenchantment through embodied public responses to social situations throughout Los Angeles.[13]

Asco's moniker, adopted after years of collaboration, invites contemplation on the parameters of the abject and negative affect. This is an invitation that has been accepted by a cadre of more recent scholars, particularly in its quotidian circulation—revulsion, disgust, profanity—who together cement, as Robb Hernandez proposes, that Asco has become the "archetypical site for scholarship and art historiography of Chicano avant-gardism in 1970s Los Angeles" and by extension, Latino art.[14] Engaging with negative affect as a project for Latino studies is an endeavor that requires thinking through the modes of subjectivity that have been central to the field. In his *Dead Subjects: Towards a Politics of Loss in Latino Studies*, Viego argues that the predominant mode of subjectivity is one shaped by ego psychology, with an "undisturbed dream of ego mastery, wholeness, and completeness" that "inform[s] how ethnic-racialized subjects craft a politics of recognition and redistribution" as well as "the types of social and legal redress we seek."[15] The "obscenely full and complete ethnic-racialized subject, transparent to itself and to others" that Viego identifies is at the core of the project fueled by what political scientist Cristina Beltrán identifies as the politics of unity in Chicano and Puerto Rican nationalist movements, which we can link to a politics of respectability.[16]

Asco's asco seeks to disturb such respectability in a Mexican American context—applicable to a broader Latino context—through a nonnormative political vision of both their individual and collective bodies—a mode we can only call queerness, a theoretical root of abjection as articulated in this book. By queerness, I want to indicate what Muñoz describes as "a mode of 'being-with' that defies social conventions and conformism and is innately heretical yet still desirous for the world, actively attempting to enact a commons that is not a pulverizing, hierarchical one bequeathed through logics and practices of exploitation."[17] Scholarship that addresses the queerness of Asco, primarily by Amelia Jones, Rita Gonzalez, and Robb Hernandez, has served to blur the boundaries around a stable understanding of the collective principally by expanding the cultural landscape against which we read Asco actions and highlighting the explicitly queer work of collaborators.[18] It is in the wake of this work that I propose a conceptualization of Asco as an abject structure of feeling brought in focus predominantly by, but not exclusively through, those members we now understand as the Asco collective, while seeking out alternative narratives of group formation.

In the interstices of Asco's institutional archive, we can glean a queer counterarchive that troubles what has become a too-utopic presentation of a group of artists who are considered the progenitors of a politicized Chicano avant-garde. For me, the archive indexes institutions that amass, preserve, and legitimize a material record; the items beyond institutional homes inclusive of catalogues and scholarship that reproduce some of the effects of the archive alongside its contents; but also what Ann Cvetkovich has famously called archives of feelings, "repositories of feelings and emotion, which are encoded not only in the content of the texts themselves but in the practices that surround their production and reception."[19] I strain to listen to and am pulled into the vortex by rumors and whispers, the *chisme* that rises like a plume where the materiality of the archive unravels. For instance, in response to a request for an interview, the former Ascota Daniel J. Martinez responded, "The history of Asco is completely fabricated and they are comfortable with living in a lie. I will respectfully decline your offer for a conversation due to the fact that there is no real reason to alter the consensual hallucination everyone holds of an Asco that never existed."[20] Further, recent interviews with all four members reveal the tenuousness of Asco's collaboration, which was much more defined by coincidence, proximity, feelings, and personal relationships than by a teleological narrative of Chicano politics.[21]

Thus, central to my argument on Asco's abject aesthetics is a renarrativizing of existing accounts of Asco's formation and unifying ethos that rely heavily on Gamboa's expansive, personal, and artistic archive, largely compiled and made available to the public in his *Urban Exile: Collected Writings of Harry Gamboa Jr.*, edited by Chon Noriega.[22] As the self-designated archivist and primary documentarian and photographer, Gamboa cataloged and disseminated documentation of Asco actions to "as many art world luminaries as he could think of," creating an invaluable archive while enacting an aggressive delimiting curatorial practice within a collective whose boundaries seem to have always been in question.[23] In his *Archive Fever*, Derrida tells us that "the first archivist institutes the archive as it should be, that is to say, not only in exhibiting the document but in establishing it. He reads it, interprets it, classes it."[24] Indeed, in his archival practice Gamboa brought into focus specific shining stars of a larger constellation, thereby determining the recognized core members of Asco. He preserved certain actions, framing and structuring their boundaries, giving shape to what would be recognized as the Asco repertoire. Gamboa also crafted a teleological narrative arc of the collective's formation and eventual disbanding—an arc that begins with Gamboa's invitation to the other three to illustrate for the Chicano political and literary journal *Regeneración*, for which he was then editor (1970–1975), and ends in 1987 when, as Gronk reports, "We did a performance at LACE [Los Angeles Contemporary Exhibitions] and it wasn't quite up to Harry's expectations of what the piece [should be], and that's kind of the point where he just went home with the ball and said we're not going to play anymore."[25]

What I am calling Gamboa's Asco archive reveals the tensions and challenges in archive creation. In his charting of a mariconógraphic theory and archival practice, Robb Hernandez argues that "despite subversive art practices in figurative and more experimental components of Chicana/o art production, counterarchives opposing racial hostility can reinforce a blindness for non-heterosexual subjects."[26] He then pointedly challenges us to approach the archive differently: "If the prevailing heteromasculinist visual discourse of Chicana/o art production is what the archive makes visible, then it is of paramount importance to make the cultural authority of the archive transparent in the present moment by attending to those troubling images it sought to delay, subordinate, or hide: the iconography of the maricón."[27] To be clear, I am not suggesting Gamboa attempted to "delay, subordinate, or hide" Asco's queerness. Rather, I am stipulating that the "heteronormative visual discourses" that Hernandez argues "image archives" make use of provide a challenge to any project of institutionalization.[28] Gamboa's project reins in a queer abject structure of feeling, and while his curating invaluably insists on Asco's relevance for art historical archives, this carefully archived legibility gives a normative recognizable shape and narrative to a wily uncooperative structure we can only call queer in its formal promiscuity.

From the configuration of the collective to comprehensive details of their early work to questions of authorship, Asco is elusive. Their archival presence indexes absence. I am interested in those moments that render the "consensual hallucination" known as Asco a fractured entity, by tracing the abject resonance that nonetheless coalesces a queer grouping invested in a critique of the normative through the aesthetic and therein challenges standard configurations of community. In what follows, I focus on moments of disjuncture, ephemerality, and even discord, made tangible, if fleetingly, through the use of a queer methodological lens, what Hernandez might call mariconógraphy.[29] A focus on these discordant affects opens up sights and sites of community composition facilitated through abjection. Further, following scholarship that seeks to highlight Valdez's contributions to Asco and the art community in general, I center Gronk and Valdez to highlight the queer resonance that reverberates through Asco's network of affiliations and to trace the world-making possibilities of the aesthetics of abjection.[30]

Se ve, se siente, el pueblo está presente

The year 1968 was an international flashpoint for revolting youth whose antimilitarization projects were often accompanied by challenges to cultural and aesthetic norms.[31] In East Los Angeles, during what comes to be called the Chicano Blowouts, ten thousand youths across sixteen different high schools walked out of their respective educational institutions in protest of a system that produced few graduates and many hopeless dropouts under the supervision of violent and racist faculty.[32] A cascading series of protests, from December 1969 to August 1970, culminated in the largest gathering of people of color, the Chicano Moratorium, protesting the high number of Chicano bodies sacrificed in the Vietnam War as they marched down East Los Angeles's Whittier Boulevard.[33] Its violent suppression by police equipped with riot gear and the resulting deaths—most notably of *Los Angeles Times* journalist Rubén Salazar—made evident the need for continued protest through the clarification of the relationship between a disenfranchised Chicano community and enforcers of law and order. The Chicano Moratorium would serve as a key site for many accounts of Asco's formation and art actions.

Chicano political upheaval, like parallel global movements, was paired with a cultural renaissance of aesthetic experimentation that produced, as one expression, recognizable movement art. While there were a number of different regional cultural expressions, specific cultural texts have become enshrined and contemporarily understood as instantiations of key collective movement ideologies. For instance, Corky Gonzales's 1967 corrido, "I Am Joaquín: An Epic Poem," quickly became a cultural cornerstone of the movement.[34] Widely circulated and immensely popular, it was adapted into a film by Luis Valdez, of El Teatro Campesino fame, in 1969.[35] As Rodríguez argues in his *Next of Kin: The Family in Chicano/a Cultural Politics*, "I Am Joaquín," reduces *la raza*, the people, to a family of (one) man, the family that figured "prominently in various organizational practices and discursive strategies put forth by movement leaders."[36] It also works hard to establish the historical presence of la raza, a strategy which Beltrán argues presumes that "racial presence" indicates "not only racial progress but justice."[37]

Reflecting on these key cultural texts reveals the political work of the aesthetic arm of the movement and particularly how collectivity is hailed. In the corrido, the speaker Joaquín enunciates multiple points of identification—politicians, despots, revolutionaries, virgins, mothers, wives—most appropriately summed up by the utterance "I am the masses of my people and / I refuse to be absorbed. / I am Joaquín." From "Aztec prince" to "Christian Christ," the speaker reflects on the legacy of colonization in Mexico, adopting all subject positions for himself in a broad embrace of a mestizo "brotherhood which is Joaquín"—a brotherhood, or *carnalismo*, that becomes central to a nationalist ideology of Chicanismo, "regularly synonymous with la familia" and "more often than not . . . an allegiance between heterosexual men, excluding women and gay men who threatened the potency of homosocial—not homosexual—bond."[38] Formally bifurcated by a unifying "I" at the poem's center, the act of reading brings Joaquín across the border from Mexico into the United States; the "I" that cinches the poem serves as a textual performative of a border identity, an exemplary Chicano ethos. The border crossing takes Joaquín from landed and regal to dispossessed and raped. The speaking protagonist diagnoses the situation as follows:

> And still I am a campesino,
> I am the fat political coyote—
> I,
> Of the same name,
> Joaquín,

In a country that has wiped out
All my history,
Stifled all my pride,
In a country that has placed a
Different weight of indignity upon my age-old burdened back.

Joaquin is now the coyote, the name given to those who help the undocumented cross the border. As a "political" coyote, "fat" from the profits of multiple crossings, Joaquin calls out those politicians who benefit from the Latino immigrant presence, who help them cross over to a mainstream that "burden[s]" this community. Indeed he goes on to say:

I sometimes
Sell my brother out
And reclaim him
For my own when society gives me
Token leadership
In society's own name.

Joaquín condemns tokenism and the assimilationist immigrant model, while announcing a fierce refusal to "be absorbed." Yet he enshrines and aggrandizes a different past; the Mexico of revolutionaries, especially the Zapatistas, the Aztec gods, and the nuclear family that is:

Poor in money,
Arrogant with pride,
Bold with machismo,
Rich in courage.

These traits are extolled in what the speaker calls "things of value," the expressive culture of the people: the "cleansing fountain of / nature and brotherhood"; "The art of our great señores" the muralists "Diego Rivera, / Siqueiros, / Orozco" whose work is "but another act of revolution for / the salvation of mankind"; "mariachi music"; and "the corridos." The importance of these cultural forms and their creators is elaborated in the movement's twin canonical text, "El Plan Espiritual de Aztlán."

The proper movement artist's role is captured in what has come to be understood as the organizing manifesto of Chicano nationalism, "El Plan Espiritual de Aztlán," written in part by the activist Rodolfo "Corky" Gonzalez and the poet Alurista at the Chicano Youth Liberation Conference of

1969.[39] The central responsibility of the movement-sanctioned artist was to "produce literature and art that is appealing to our people and relates to our revolutionary culture," for the "cultural values of life, family, and home will serve as a powerful weapon to defeat the gringo dollar value system and encourage the process of love and brotherhood." This "organizational goal" was meant to "strengthen our identity and the moral backbone of the movement" and "[unite] and [educate] the family of La Raza towards liberation with one heart and one mind." "El Plan" demands the Chicano artist represent the Aztlán it conjures: a gilded brown nation for a "bronze people" reliant on brotherhood and carnalismo to defend against "gringo" encroachment. Movement artists were to honor its laborers, "[with their] hands in the soil," through whom, they would "declare the independence of [their] mestizo nation."[40]

"I Am Joaquín," "El Plan," and the accompanying art practices described above performed an important intervention. "El Plan's" call for that which is "appealing to our people and relates to our revolutionary culture" was interpreted as that which honors family and tradition and results in the realistic, accessible rendition of these subjects, most commonly executed in the grand mural form exalted in "I Am Joaquín." In response to the imperative to "strengthen [the] identity and the moral backbone of the movement," Chicano muralists established the parameters of revolutionary, politicized aesthetics. Their iconic motifs included pre-Columbian imaginings of the mythic Aztlán, renderings of defiant farm workers and *familias*, Day of the Dead *calaveras*, *virgencitas*, and quotidian rural and barrio scenes. The nationalism it proposes, grounded in family and brotherhood, counters the dominant pathologizing of minority families, but it does so by ascribing a heteropatriarchal and romanticized notion of the family as its structuring ideology. Its related notions of brotherhood and carnalismo create a homosocial bond that, as Eve Kosofsky Sedgwick has argued, is often triangulated and cemented through misogyny and homophobia.[41] Furthermore, the focus on a pre-Columbian heritage establishes a historical presence on U.S. soil as an antidote to national amnesia, while offering a counter to the "culture of poverty" model.[42] However, it also reproduces a dominant narrative that crystallizes in the past an indigenous present, while establishing presence as rallying grounds for political action, radical civic engagement, and ultimately national belonging. As visual manifestations of the primary cultural texts of the movement, the scenes created by movement artists sought to counter negative expressive iterations of Latinos in popular media, to fill a void with positive representation and establish presence in the visual landscape.

The four members of what would come to be called Asco were thus immersed in protest and revolutionary affect of the time and place though they did not all directly engage in conventional politicized actions. Gamboa was vice president of his school's Blowout committee, for which, among other activities, he was deemed among the "hundred most dangerous and violent subversives in the United States" by a U.S. Senate committee, while also contributing to activist periodicals *Carta editorial, La Raza,* and *Regeneración.*[43] Gronk was engaged in street performances and contributed to *Grassroots Forum* and *Con Safos,* figuring out creative ways to avoid and protest being drafted.[44] Valdez was performing and painting, often as a self-conscious political feminist act, while Herrón was developing his painting skills and planning murals, a medium the Ascotas would often riff on and come to critique.[45]

It is significant that the most repeated account of the genesis of the collective is set amid the turmoil of the 1970 Chicano Moratorium, which brought out a record number of protesters. Gamboa describes it as true activist lore, narrating in his "In the City of Angels" as follows:

> On August 29, 1970, the largest antiwar protest demonstration to occur in East L.A. brought a highly publicized Chicano community together for a massive display of unity. The Chicano Moratorium, as it came to be known, was the target of a well-orchestrated plan for disruption by the Los Angeles Police Department, the Los Angeles County Sheriff's Department, and other police agencies. The demonstration ended violently when riot-equipped police attacked members of the community. . . . As the police onslaught at the park intensified, Francisca Flores, publisher of *Regeneración,* a Chicano political and literary journal, encountered Harry Gamboa. As they ran from the clouds of tear gas and swinging clubs of the police, she handed him a copy of her journal and then disappeared into the havoc of the surging crowd.[46]

At this galvanizing site, a torch is passed between the then editor of *Regeneración* and Gamboa. She hands off a copy of the journal and shortly thereafter its editorship. Gamboa self-narrates his editorship at *Regeneración* as an extension of his on-the-ground activism and is then credited for recruiting future Asco members to illustrate its pages, thereby providing the scene for the group's formation and lending their future conceptual collaborations an inherently, and familiar, politicized root. The framing of their collective through this political publication makes their future conceptual art actions legible as political, while their drawings, which started out as individual productions and developed into collaborative *cadavre exquis*, provide a perfect analogy for a practice that draws together disparate elements to create one piece. Additionally, the claim that they were "brought together" at Gamboa's invitation—the Ascota most readily recognized as politically active given his role as an organizer for the Chicano Blowouts and the Chicano Moratorium, and as a contributor to a number of political publications—provides a plausible leader for the group's formation. I want to excavate a different root, one that delves into the archive in order to heed Gloria Anzaldúa's supplication that "Chicanos need to acknowledge the political and artistic contributions of their queer," to "listen to what [their] *jotería* is saying," and explore the unruly organism it nourishes: the 1969 Belvedere Park performance of *Caca-Roaches Have No Friends*, a collaborative production between Robert Legoretta, Mundo Meza, and Gronk (figure 2.1).[47]

Abject jotería

In 1969 Gronk distributed flyers for a performance at Belvedere Park: *Caca-Roaches Have No Friends*, a riotous protest performance featuring Robert Legoretta as Cyclona with a cameo by Valdez and costume work by Mundo Meza.[48] Together with a flock of running children whose erratic footfalls accompanied an insistent drumbeat, Valdez and her sister each played a big lip from a disembodied mouth as part of a surreal backdrop for Cyclona's climactic performance.[49] Cyclona interrupts the visual chaos of the set, entering in a black knee-length nightgown, its lace bust covered by an aluminum foil and cardboard corset, whose red cardboard boning loosely contains Cyclona's corpulent torso. His face is made up in white, lips stained blood-red and eyelids heavy with dark shadow—a glamorously eyelashed calavera (figure 2.2).[50] In this *catrina* drag, Cyclona discards his corset, slides the straps of his gown down his arms and off, and rolls the gown down to his waist, revealing a rounded hairy chest whose dark curls are offset by the blond fur stole encircling his neck.[51] In this state, Cyclona proceeds to undress the actor with whom he shares the stage.

His stage partner dons a shift made of white netting, fitted with red-and-white-striped shredded sleeves. A matching sash at the waist holds in place a decorative piece of fabric, printed with fuchsia and chartreuse di-

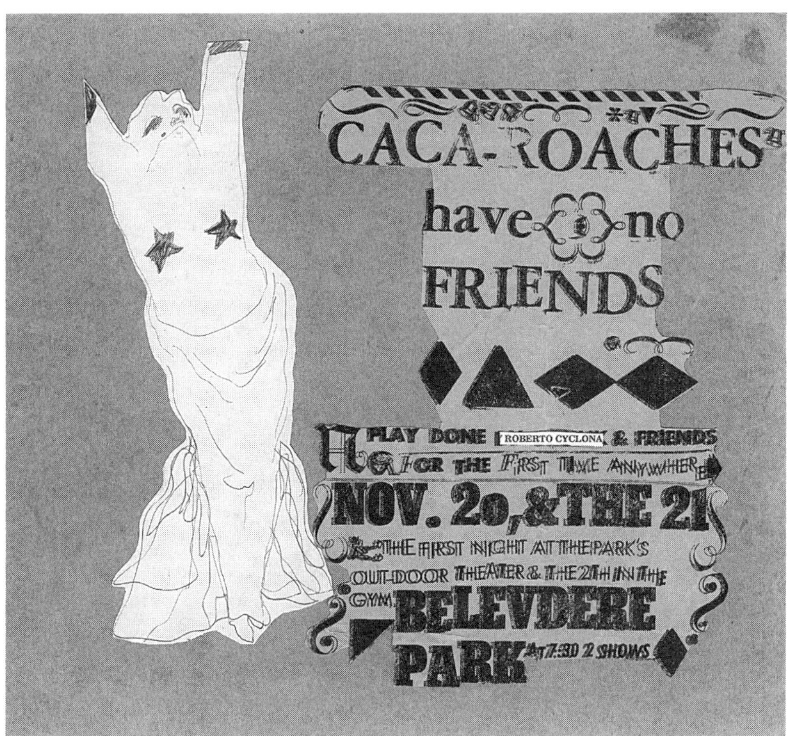

FIGURE 2.1 *Caca-Roaches Have No Friends*, flyer, 1969. The Fire of Life: The Robert Legorreta-Cyclona Collection, 1962–2002, Coll. CSRC.0500. Courtesy of the UCLA Chicano Studies Research Center.

amonds, creating an asymmetrical peplum skirt. Cyclona undresses him down to a pair of small denim cutoffs, adorned at the groin with a pair of eggs attached to a water balloon within a pair of fishnet stockings (plate 4). Cyclona then "castrates" him by cracking his *huevos* or eggs—the Spanish slang for testicles—and popping the balloon in violent simulated fellatio and manual stimulation. A bite and twist to the balloon inside the fishnets attached to the actor's body brings on the ejaculative pop.[52] The performance ends here as a hostile audience, predominantly made up of Chicano families, largely from the Estrada Courts housing community, throws eggs of their own, lights fires, and calls the police.[53] The families had been drawn to the site by a listing in the *Belvedere Citizen* that mislabeled *Caca-Roaches* "a play for the whole family."[54]

To use Anzaldúa's theoretical terminology, *Caca-Roaches Have No Friends* is some loud jotería—insistent on engagement with "the whole family,"

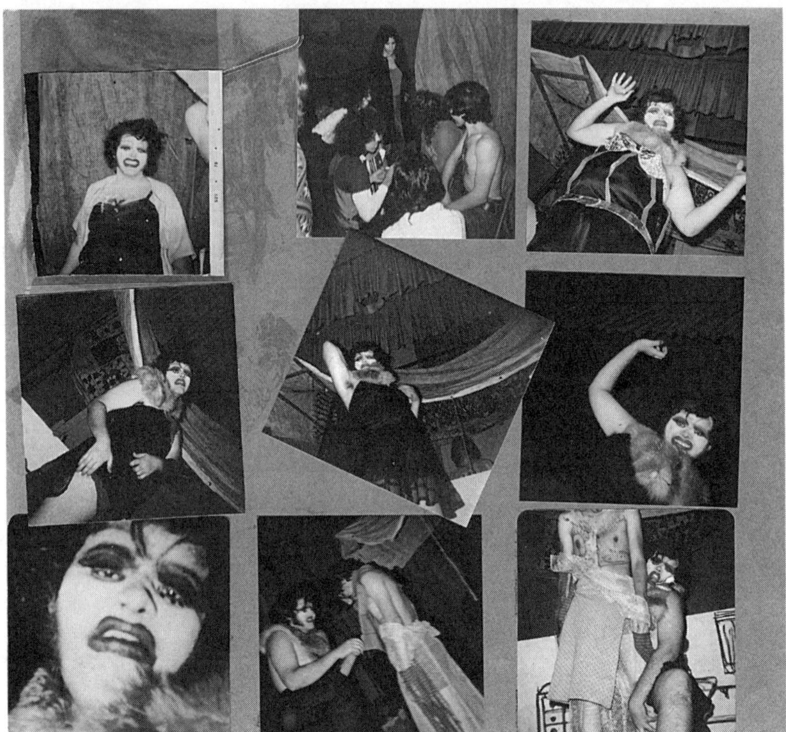

FIGURE 2.2 *Caca-Roaches Have No Friends*, scrapbook documenting performance, 1969. The Fire of Life: The Robert Legorreta-Cyclona Collection, 1962–2002, Coll. CSRC.0500. Courtesy of the UCLA Chicano Studies Research Center.

the very one so central to cultural nationalist projects. Cyclona's gender-bending persona, his incorporation of feminine dress along with his exposure of biological maleness, challenges the vision of a united protesting Chicano nation "bold with machismo" that enshrines the heteronormative family. In an interview, Gronk describes the male performer that Cyclona undresses as a "high school guy and he's wearing a poncho," also described elsewhere as a "*serape.*"[55] His liberal interpretation of the traditional Mexican garment aside, we can read the man destructively fellated by Cyclona, to a familiar Aztlán-conjuring drumbeat, as a Chicano youth activist. The serape-wearing *carnal*, who the movement arms with bronze, is exposed to the public through undress. More importantly, the performance makes evident the carnal's vulnerability to those in whose hands (and mouths) he places his virility—women and homosexuals—simultaneously revealing a not-so-subtle threat to carnalismo's phallic power. The ejaculative pop that deflates the phallus and the crack that shatters testicular fortitude symbolically eliminate the future of Aztlán through biological reproduction. Further, *Caca-Roaches* refigures the abject feminized erotic opening from a site of passive receptivity to one of violent activism that demands an alternative queer paradigm of community and family formation not modeled after the nuclear family.

Gamboa has argued that "Chicanos have been defined by exterior sources that have generally drawn lines to exclude undesirable qualities or conversely to focus attention on the negative incidents and personalities of the culture."[56] I read Gamboa as describing the ways the discursive construction of the abjected, in his case Chicanos, consolidates dominant white identity. Applied to the reception of *Caca-Roaches* described above, however, we can understand the audience's active rejection and refusal of Cyclona's gender and sexual performance as a mimetic consolidation of dominant Chicanidad, one reliant on normative gender performance and private, conjugal sexual practice. In the Belvedere Park reception of *Caca-Roaches*, we see the audience's aspiration to proper normative subjectivity, an identitarian wholeness constructed only through the casting out, or abjecting, of those who challenge borders internally, therein strengthening their demand for inclusion in the nation at large. The refusal is all the more poignantly displayed in the presence of Aztlán's bronze future—the children who witnessed the performance that day in the park.

The audience's strong response was not only a consequence of the queer abject display—the same-sex ambiguously gendered public intimacy—but was also a response to the aesthetic mode in which *Caca-Roaches* was crafted. Exhibiting the confusion of boundaries that Alberto Sandoval-Sánchez identifies as representative of the abject through formal permeability and unboundedness, narrative ambiguity, and the blending of desire and disgust, the chaotic performance was a far cry from the aspirational murals that served as the primary mode of engaging the community in urban settings or even the cathartic performances by Teatro Campesino for workers in the fields.[57] In the reception/rejection of the aesthetic mode used in *Caca-Roaches*, we see the Chicano purchase into and reproduction of a dominant cultural logic through a demand for beauty, accessibility, and truth. These demands would be defied in the abject affective vortex sometimes called, but not limited to, Asco.

It is here, at the 1969 *Caca-Roaches*, that I locate the pivotal moment of

Asco's formation as an affective vehicle; it both marks its queer theoretical genesis and serves as the scene of recruitment for future Asco actions. Gronk wrote and organized the performance, and while Legoretta and Meza were his main collaborators—individual artists with unique creative contributions—he used the performance as an opportunity to approach Valdez, drawn by her sartorial "notoriety" with her "exotic . . . sort of like Sophia Loren kind of quality . . . but in high school."[58] The intangible, indefinable affinity between Gronk and Valdez resulted in collaborations that would sometimes be called Asco but that also precede and exceed the most agreed-upon dates of Asco's existence. Valdez in turn brought a small cohort to see her perform: her then boyfriend, Herrón, and her best friend Sylvia Delgado, who came with her beau Gamboa.[59] The four understood to be the chief collaborators of Asco then, Gronk, Valdez, Herrón, and Gamboa, were gathered—all participants in the affective parameters of the performance. I want to underscore the presence of other actors who were part of the countercultural queer Chicano network through which this affective vortex swirls, which I aim to highlight here, but who are not present in the normative Asco archive. I do not mean to appropriate their contributions on behalf of that normatizing Asco project but aim, in fact, to open up the "Asco that never was" to instead approach its hallucinatory effects, jumping into its vortex in effect here at *Caca-Roaches*. Gronk, Valdez, Herrón, and Gamboa's time at *Regeneración* provided the opportunity to succumb to queer modes of kinship on display that day, fostered by an interest in the abject reality of Chicano existence and a refusal to reform to meet the standards of bronze beauty or homogenized community propagated by the *movimiento*. The strategy of formal and social disruption links a critique of a social realist aesthetic to their accompanying projects of civic recognition.[60]

But that wasn't the only affective pulse of the performance. Of *Caca-Roaches*, Gronk reports the following exchange: "I did the piece *Cockroaches Have No Friends*. Patssi was in it. Her sister was in it—Karen—as well. And she said, 'Well, my boyfriend's like really upset that I'm doing this thing, but that's why I'm going to do it because I'm getting him upset.' 'Who is your boyfriend?' 'It's that quiet one over there.' And here was this guy with long hair and wearing like a Sgt. Pepper outfit. [laughs] And I said, 'Oh, he looks like Rod Stewart' [laughter]."[61] In this account, Herrón looms as a quiet brooding macho. The sartorial nod to the gender bending of a music-affiliated counterculture, which earned Herrón the nickname *cha-*

vala from his brothers, does not disguise the controlling impulse against which Valdez is active.[62] His participation in Asco events, and Valdez's, are haunted by this controlling presence and led to her frequent exclusion. Indeed, while the collaborations that began to include Herrón and Gamboa, those that mark Asco's beginning in most accounts of the group, retain the use of agitprop, humor, fantastically fashionable costume, and strategic use of the nonsensical, morbid, and grotesque, they also contribute a different energy that is shaped by a normative desire for institutional recognition and an ascription to traditional masculinist gender roles.

For a series of early collaborations carried on through 1973, Ascotas engaged in subversive street art actions collectively referred to as Midnight Art Productions.[63] Their "nighttime activities" included "tagging or going into the streets and doing different kinds of graffiti and stuff like that with political slogans. All kinds of different things that we sort of like did in the middle of the night."[64] Titled *Instructional Destruction Projects*, their tags included "Pinchi Placa Come Caca" (fucking cops eat shit), "Gringo Laws = Dead Chicanos," "Comida Para Todos" (food for all), "Yanqui Go Home," and "Viet/barrio." These messages were transmitted in the highly surveilled and criminalized medium of debased vandalism used by their abjected community peers in gangs critiquing the police force that patrolled their communities and the racist exploitation of Chicanos in the Vietnam War. The amalgam "Viet/barrio" captured the idea of communities of color living as internal colonies by creating a link to warfare abroad while "Comida Para Todos" gestures to a shared condition of poverty beyond the barrio. Yet Gronk reports, "It was kind of sad because Patssi didn't participate initially on [*sic*] a lot of that activity. And one [reason] was because her boyfriend was Willie, and Willie was very protective: 'No, Patssi, you can't run fast enough. If we have to run, you're probably going to trip and fall and they'll catch you.' So I think she had to deal with stuff like that. She had this macho guy who was like . . . a lot of people never even realized Patssi was doing work at the time."[65] In Gronk's report, it is evident that Herrón curtailed Valdez's participation and recognition in what gets documented as Asco performances.

Valdez's exclusion is most glaringly notable in Asco's famous 1972 *Spray Paint* LACMA, also known as *Project Pie in De/Face* (figure 2.3). To rehearse the well-known account, *Spray Paint* LACMA is narrated as Asco's response to a museum curator's claim that the underrepresentation of Chicano art within LACMA was a result of Chicanos being in gangs and not making

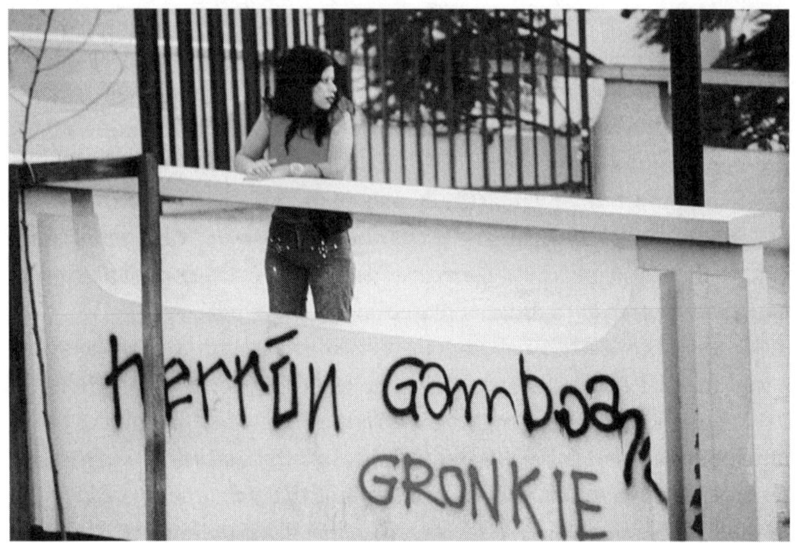

FIGURE 2.3 Asco, *Spray Paint LACMA*, 1972. Photograph by Harry Gamboa Jr. © 1972, Harry Gamboa Jr.

art.[66] The bold response to this curatorial declaration is documented by Gamboa and published in his collected writings with the following caption: "All Entrances to the Los Angeles County Museum of Art are spray-painted with the names of Herrón, Gamboa, and Gronkie, transforming the museum itself into the first work of Chicano art to be exhibited at LACMA. Pictured: Patssi Valdez."[67] In his description, Gamboa provides the four names of the actors generally considered the core and original members of what gets called Asco though with key and distinct roles.

Widely lauded as the formative work of Chicano conceptual art that marks an approach to politicized aesthetics distinct from that of Chicano movement muralists, *Spray Paint LACMA* can be thought of as a work in two parts: the late-night spray paint defacing of the white institution by Herrón, Gamboa, and Gronk; and the staging of the conceptual work that incorporated Valdez's body as signature. The photo-document by Gamboa, described above, has become the iconic, most circulated image of *Spray Paint LACMA*, despite existing photographs of just the spray-painted signatures.[68] In the iconic photo-document, Valdez leans against a balustrade, shoulders raised in a frozen shrug, facing away from the camera and the spectator. Her presence has been read as adornment or as recognition of her role as muse, not as author. Full authorship in this innovative piece of conceptual artistry is denied.[69] In his essay "Conceptual Graffiti and the Public Art Museum: *Spray Paint* LACMA," Noriega builds on Mario Ontiveros's reading of this signature image to argue that it captures a gender politics alongside a conceptual action as "one and the same."[70] The group, he tells us, "manifest[s] in name and body before the public art museum," with Valdez's body "marking the space of the male artist's ephemeral authorship vis-à-vis the museum."[71] Noriega here acknowledges Valdez's embodied performative signature, even as it is captured by the authorial photographer whose signature also appears within the compositional frame. This brief diagnosis does not elaborate on how this dynamic shapes Asco's political imaginary. The piece crystallizes a political paradigm alternative to that of a unified raza advocated by movement activists, who, Beltrán writes, "chose to rhetorically produce a more homogenous vision of the community rather than grapple with [a] more complex reality."[72]

Valdez's posture and striking profile indicate to the viewer the same "but that's why I'm going to do it because I'm getting him upset" ethos that propelled her participation in *Caca-Roaches.*[73] Valdez accompanies Gamboa to document the piece, but in her embodied signature appearance she enhances the work's critical reach to address institutions beyond those of the art world and Chicano representation as articulated by Gamboa. Like Cyclona in *Caca-Roaches*, Valdez is author of her performance, but her very presence effects the movement of Asco's vortex to highlight the offerings of asco as an abject structure of feelings. Compositionally, a sharp diagonal encouraged by the red of Valdez's ruffled-cap-sleeve top, matched by the tag "Gronkie," draws a connection between Gronk and Valdez that can be gleaned throughout the Asco archive. The warm red hue against an otherwise cool field of grays, blues, and blacks flirts to conjure sexual and erotic undertones but also recalls the red of blood. In doing so we are reminded of the sexual threat in the evocative castration scene from *Caca-Roaches* during which Cyclona and Valdez were linked symbolically through representative orality. Additionally, with his use of the diminutive suffix "-ie" in "Gronkie," Gronk displays a playful queering of the territorial act of writing, or tagging. The diminutive, in Chicano culture, is used as an endearment but can also infantilize and feminize. Additionally, Gronk's use of it, alongside color choice and clumsy capitalized lettering (as opposed to the stylized script of Gamboa and Herrón in black spray paint) insists on an abject queerness—a queerness rendered in solidarity with female exclusion when considered in tandem with Valdez's own playful dismissiveness as she poses for Gamboa. Their untenable affective link enhances the critical work of *Spray Paint LACMA* beyond institutional critique to raise questions about internal community and group dynamics. Asco's queer formation need not be one of consensus and the homogeneity of carnalismo or *la gente unida* (the united people). Instead, their abject aesthetic choices allow us to read dissent and disagreement as part of community formation, not the antithesis of it.

Where movement murals emphasized historical presence, harmonious coming together, and semipermanence on urban walls, *Spray Paint LACMA*'s completion comes with its own absence and loss. As a work of institutional critique, *Spray Paint LACMA* reveals racist discrimination and exclusion as well as medium hierarchies, as the piece was whitewashed and painted over the next day. The use of the base graffiti medium kept Asco's actions illegible as conceptual art to the art community—functioning as the abject that consolidates proper fine art forms. But we also see that the piece comes to fruition in its loss and through its failure to be recognized. The piece's institutional critique is achieved when it is destroyed—its failure to be recognized as a conceptual work of art legitimizes Asco's complaint of Chicano exclusion from the museum even while the artists chose a medium that played on the accusation of Chicano expressive capabilities, given graffiti's association with gangs. Beyond this, a queer reading of the archive, the document created by Gamboa, sees in Gronk's tag a recognition of Valdez's absence during the graffiti protest action, while Valdez's presence in the photo-document refuses the politics of equal inclusion by resisting the camera's—and Gamboa's—gaze.

And yet the four often collaborated, giving in to the pull of the affective vortex they would come to retroactively call Asco.[74] Gamboa's writing on shared meetings held to work on the production of *Regeneración* reveals something of the affective parameters of their shared concerns that would create a vortex of collaboration we might understand as "being with." This is, in the words of Muñoz, "an insistence on wanting more in the face of scarcity, which does more than simply reject negation, but instead, works through it to imagine a being-in-common within the negative."[75] Valdez, Gronk, Herrón, and Gamboa shared nights of discussion on

> drop drills, Guadalupe tattoos, smeared lipstick, no privacy, off ramps, foreignness, disagreements, blind curves, comics, pinkeye, jump starts, Dick and Jane, no heat, stray bullets, Spam, alleys, fake genuflections,

riot squads, photo booths, cucarachas, bongos, dunce caps, low riders, Molotov cocktails, the twist, lard, dead ends, grinding without music, Che, pompadours, 24-hour daydreams, Daffy Duck, hostile crowbars, bumble-bees, bubble asses, tunnel vision, Peter Lorre, bruising pinches, *Alarma*, cliques, spiked heels, racist TV, La Llorona, hit-and-run insults, flat puppies, pachuco fairy tales, English only, false eyelashes, last dimes, black spray paint, Mr. Machine, Beatle boots, ditching parties, zero chance, lizard faces, unholy water, no air conditioning, dancing curls, psycho-cholos, quicksand, outcast treatment, La Cruda, tacit extortion, doomed love affairs, mariachis, false invitations, blistering belts, hero as-sassinations, Heckle and Jeckle, white bread, laughing in public, melted crayons, official low expectations, transparent lamp shades, bitter *pan dulce*, search and seizure, cheap funerals, fire ants, suspicious stares, rude service, black widow hairdos, jalapeños, hiding in fear, brown skies, missing cuff links, lysergic acid diethylamide, Migra magots [*sic*], shat-tered glass, Dolores del Rio, barbed wire, chorizo sin huevo, hip-hugger bell-bottoms, flaming monks, drunken wild teens, stained blades, cold burritos, baby trigger fingers, El Cucui, vinyl upholstery, barrio barriers, and rip-off artists.[76]

I have quoted at length to highlight the shifts and interrelated treatment of issues ranging from popular youth culture (low riders, Daffy Duck) to traditional Chicano icons and cultural figures (Guadalupe tattoos, Che), to the local political situation (stray bullets, riot squad), and to the absurd and grotesque (pinkeye, flat puppies). This stream-of-consciousness list, remi-niscent of the counterculture Beat generation, builds a world of abject and Chicano signifiers that makes tangible, in content and style, the fleeting ex-periences of desire, revulsion, and despair. The quick run of "flat puppies, pachuco fairy tales, English only" communicates Asco's humorous inter-play with violence, racism, and Chicano culture. Politically motivated, the artists "wanted to reach inside and pull people's guts out."[77] This desire to provoke a visceral, abject response demonstrates a twist on the movement artist; fueled by similar political concerns, Asco's strategies would offer an aesthetic challenge that would rechannel the political project.

When discussing the Chicano art scene in Los Angeles with an inter-viewer, Gamboa explained, "People felt that they could single handedly define what it was to be a Chicano."[78] When asked why that might be, he responded, "Ego. Ego. Desperation." We see here the "obscenely full and complete ethnic-racialized subject, transparent to itself and to others" of ego psychology that Antonio Viego argues furnishes racist discourse with the mode of subjectivity it needs to be effective while also functioning as the predominant mode of imagining subjectivity in Chicano and Latino studies.[79] Latino studies, and Chicano studies in particular, emerged as fields of academic study as a result of the same civil rights mobilizations that Asco was immersed in and critiqued. Though Gamboa could not have anticipated the aptness of his response, Viego critiques precisely this essentialized subject defined through "ego" and "desperation," who seeks to achieve wholeness through identity recuperation and national belonging. In the same interview, Gamboa alludes to the political changes wrought by an embrace of abjection and a desire to provoke asco over identity-affirming and ego-boosting bronze pride when he reports, "And for me, it was really striking because I think up until like the early seventies, I was really bent on the idea of really following the constitution, my constitutional rights. And I felt it was a real legitimate approach and I felt that politics were really an answer up to that point."[80] Gamboa's comment is tinged with disillusion marked by the words "up to." Constitutional rights—those rights that a civil rights–focused Chicano movement sought to guarantee through an emphasis on historical presence and recuperative pride—come across as hollow, lacking in efficacy. Instead, Asco, immersed in abject affect, self-consciously challenged the movement-sanctioned role for artists. They embraced the ephemerality of performance over the permanence of murals, and the abstract and conceptual over the accessibility of journalistic representation within an affective vortex taut with tension and a form of collectivity alive to disagreement.

Asco's asco

On Christmas Eve of 1971, Gronk, Gamboa, and Herrón executed a garishly costumed, mile-long processional that began at the busy intersection of Eastern Avenue and Whittier Boulevard and ended a mile away at a U.S. Marine Corps recruiting station. For the occasion, Herrón dressed in a white robe trimmed with a wide richly colored sash from shoulder to hip and at the robe's hem. His chest was emblazoned with an iconic sacred heart while his face was transformed into a familiar calavera through makeup, framed by the waves of his long dark hair—a contemporary Christ with urban Chicano flair.[81] Over his shoulder, Herrón-Christ carries a fifteen-foot-long cardboard cross, the long post behind him while the

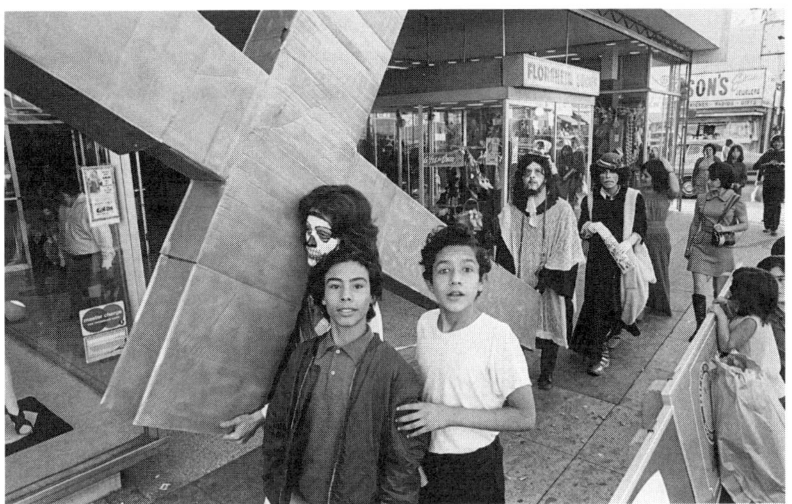
FIGURE 2.4 Asco, *Stations of the Cross*, 1971. Gelatin silver print. Photograph by Seymour Rosen. © SPACES—Saving and Preserving Arts and Cultural Environments.

shorter perpendicular burden lies down the front of his chest to be cradled in the cups of his hands. Holding the longer crucifix's post, Gamboa shares Herrón-Christ's burden, following behind him as a "zombie-altar boy" accessorizing his black wide-armed robe with a long lace bib, white face paint, and an animal skull headpiece, worn on the back of his head, nestled in unruly long curls, to "ward off unsolicited communion."[82] Gronk trailed the processional as a liberally interpreted Pontius Pilate in suit and long overcoat with a green hat perched atop a carefully rounded curly Afro.[83] Like his two fellow Ascotas, his face was painted white, but his cheeks were adorned with large pink teardrops—achieving a look between clown and calavera that lent his Pilate a playful coquettishness. Last in the processional, Gronk carried popcorn in a large furry satchel, which he sprinkled at the different stations along the way. Their attire irreverently alludes to the Catholic practice of reenacting the series of events preceding the crucifixion of Christ known as the Stations of the Cross, also the adopted title for the performance. The three walked in silence along Whittier Boulevard among a bemused public of what they describe as "shoppers, cruisers, and police," whose recorded responses include hostility and amusement.[84] Once they arrived at the recruiting station, they propped their cross against the entrance and held "vigil" for five minutes before Gronk "blessed" the site with popcorn, and the three quickly dispersed (figure 2.4).

Their procession was not without real material risk given the concentration of police surveillance in East Los Angeles as a consequence of political unrest like the Chicano Moratorium and the student Blowouts. Police agents established neighborhood checkpoints and canceled community gatherings such as Christmas Eve parades and *posadas*. *Stations of the Cross* took the place of these culturally affirming community events at the very location of the community-gathering Moratorium.[85] In place of a holiday celebration, the public action presented a scene that surely provoked questions about the relationship between Christ's sacrifice and the young men of the processional, as well as between a prostrate cross at the door of the Marine Corps recruiting station and the young Chicano men abroad in Vietnam.

After World War II, some Chicano veterans, who saw in war a patriotic duty abroad, returned to use their services as the basis to demand better treatment at home. In their performance, however, the three men of Asco shun this mode of patriotic engagement where participatory presence should equal national inclusion.[86] The calavera Christ of the performance deposits his cross at the base of an equivalent site of death for many young men in the community, refusing his burden, while Gronk's Pontius Pilate delivers a strong critique against the East Los Angeles Chicano community through analogy. In the Bible, Pilate is the government agent that sends Christ to his death, capitulating to the demands of a mob, but then washes his hands in a symbolic gesture of resignation and abdication of fault. While we can read Pilate's actions as illustrating how government decisions about minority experience can be determined by a hostile majority, Gronk transforms Pilate's refusal to accept guilt into an act of insistent spectatorship.

Gronk's Pilate follows the procession not only to witness each moment in Christ's martyrdom but leaves behind a sign of his leisurely enjoyment—popcorn, the darling snack of Hollywood, spilled on the floor of the public theater. The image of sacred maize used frequently in Mexican and Chicano iconography is here transformed by the culture industry into nutritionless junk food to be consumed during spectatorship. While the audience may not recognize Gronk as Pilate, this insistent spectatorship is certainly legible. Hand washing aside, Gronk's Pilate draws a parallel between the condemnation of Christ to his death and the scopophilic consumption of and participation in the war abroad. While the community may mourn the deaths of those they lose, they problematically seek partic-

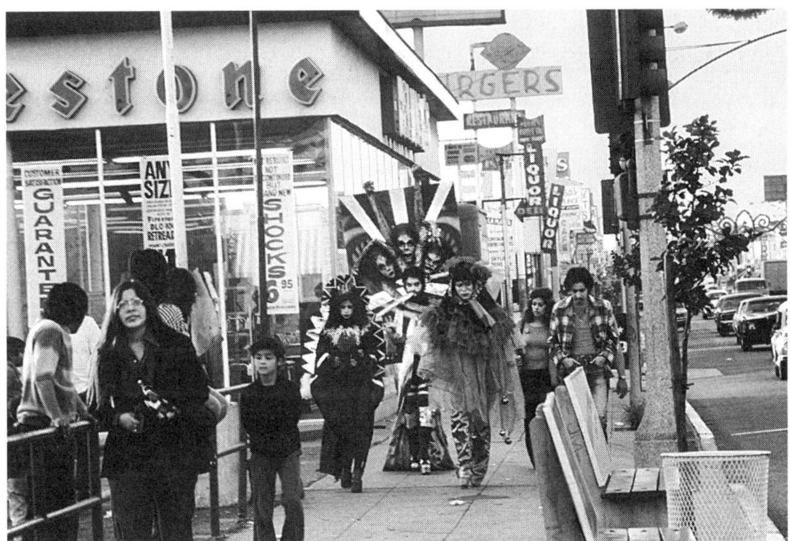

FIGURE 2.5 Asco, *Walking Mural*, 1972. Photograph by Harry Gamboa Jr.
© 1972, Harry Gamboa Jr.

ipation in the very system that requires racialized bodies to be disposable so that its imperial endeavors can succeed. *Stations of the Cross* instead insists on a consideration of loss and death by transforming a site of recruitment into one of imminent death, not national belonging. In addition to wanting to provoke "a certain kind of almost gastro-intestinal response" to "meaningless" death in East Los Angeles, a type of asco, the collective's abject display, invoking abject violence, attempts to harness loss in order to imagine new modes of political engagement or uncivic participation.[87]

One year later, Asco performed a second mile-long Christmas Eve processional departing from Whittier Boulevard, *Walking Mural* (1972)—largely considered the first Asco performance. For the event, Valdez and Gronk extended an invitation to Cyclona, who was unable to attend (figure 2.5).[88] This invitation underscores the instability of Asco membership, even within what is regarded as their first official performance, wherein participants were determined by availability and not predetermined cohesion. But Valdez and Gronk's invitation to Cyclona also highlights the queer networks to which Asco was attached as well as the queer resonance, from performances like *Caca-Roaches*, that would permeate this and other performances. By Gamboa's own account, "Gronk, Meza, and Cyclona [the three principal creative contributors of *Caca-Roaches*] would oftentimes dress in long, flowing velvet robes layered with satin, silk, and lace clothing and promenade, arms interlocked, to a quick-goose step, shoving pedestrians out of the way along a crowded section of Whittier Boulevard."[89] The available Ascotas met that day at the very same busy Whittier Boulevard for another mile-long walk among a similarly unwitting audience as for their *Stations of the Cross* and Gronk, Meza, and Cyclona's promenades: Christmas shoppers, neighborhood dwellers, and police officers. Gamboa accompanied them from a short distance to capture the piece in black and white and color slides as well as Super 8 film. Valdez, Herrón, and Gronk each dressed as iconic neighborhood symbols: La Virgen de Guadalupe—the revered virgin of the Mexican and Chicano community—a Christmas tree, and a mural. Each icon was transformed by queer abject aesthetic choices.

Valdez's Guadalupe wears a long black gown, slit to reveal a slender leg sheathed in opaque black tights, anchored by severely platformed ankle boots. She is cloaked in smooth, silver-trimmed fabric that cascades over her shoulders and down to her feet, much like the iconic blue cloak of the traditional Guadalupe. Underneath a silver crown, the texture of her hair—teased and jet black—is matched by a white, thin-feathered boa, which echoes and enhances the white makeup that covers the entirety of her face and is offset by black lipstick. A bouquet of red roses in her hands brings out the red circles that artificially blush her face. She is framed by a cardboard halo of silver and black chevrons outlined in white that bisect the front and back of her body. Her costume's back view reveals a set of silver aluminum and black labial wings, topped by an aluminum skull.

Gronk flanks Valdez in almost all documentation of the performance. His Christmas tree is achieved by layering three olive-green chiffon skirts over his shoulder, creating a voluminous petticoat poncho. His legs, which serve as the tree's moving trunk, are dressed in shimmering silken fuchsia slacks whose hem extends beyond his silver platform shoes. Gronk's skirts are hung with cobalt-blue ornaments. His tree is topped with an elaborate scarf of red feathers and a black cobalt-flecked hooded collar lined in silver sequins. A loosely structured bow of the skirt's same green chiffon kisses a white-painted chin, underneath a red star that spreads its five points from Gronk's forehead, across his brow, and diagonally over the bridge of his nose.

Herrón follows behind them both in the most cumbersome of the outfits. He wears a three-button tailed jacket upholstered in aluminum foil matching the silver of his platform shoes. His head and arms are secured, as in a pillory for public punishment, by an elaborate construction made from cardboard, aluminum foil, and paint. Broad aluminum lines radiate from Herrón's painted face. Above him are three heads, each with a pair of aluminum arms. The central figure raises aluminum fists up in the air, just beyond the top of the cardboard. Herrón is the walking mural.

The size of Herrón's costume and the title of the piece, *Walking Mural*, have led critics to focus predominantly on the work's engagement with movement murals. The piece serves as a critique of the inactivity and resulting political ineffectuality of the mural form despite the permanent presence of murals on urban walls. The processional functions as a reclamation of social space in the face of police surveillance on the streets. It brings the exalted figures of mural symbology down off the wall and into the muck of the street, but not before updating their look to speak to contemporary urban experience. Gronk explained, "A lot of Latino artists went back in history for imagery. *We* wanted to stay in the present and find our imagery as urban artists and produce a body of work out of our sense of displacement."[90] Here, Gronk addresses his displeasure with the historical trajectory so central to the political claims of canonical Chicano movement texts. Instead, he ruminates within a negative affective register, a sense of "displacement." In that embrace of what we can understand as a "without place" or "against place," Asco counters the strategy of working to establish historical roots such that historical presence is the basis on which political demands are made. Instead, by refusing to identify with a mythic past through a normative teleology imbued with a naturalized sense of inheritance, Asco favors a focus on a queer present without place, challenging us to imagine alternative grounds for disruption and inclusion through uncivic comportment.

In addition to the above, Asco had many things to say about Chicano muralists, but in Gamboa's 1974 "Cruel Profit," the opening monologue parodies what muralists said about Asco:[91]

And you wonder why I'm upset with you. It's because you don't know what you're doing and don't even care. You're too abstract. Come down to earth, hombre. Can't you understand that you're not where the people are at? You could show those pictures to anyone in the barrio, your neighbor, people in the store, the kids in school; man, no one will understand what you mean by this, only the few whose minds are all confused, and who can perceive what you mean by this madness, will be able to appreciate it, otherwise it is just a direct insult to the people. No one wants to see pictures of someone burning a baby! You should be making movies and taking pictures of people working and suffering, something they can relate to, like showing young Chicanas standing in line waiting for their food stamps or people crowding the unemployment office on Indiana Street, not some doll wrapped in barbed wire. I think that your abstraction is what is going to cause us to break apart as friends, I'm speaking to you like a brother, but I think that you better give what I'm saying heavy consideration because it seems like you might become or already are part of the problem, counterrevolutionary; things are too abstract already, the world doesn't need any more confusion, obstacles that confuse people while they try to cope with reality. People need concrete answers, not dreams! Te estoy diciendo la verdad, carnal. Don't stay the way you are because if you do you're going to find that the movement has left you behind and that you've only grown old as a burden and something to be rid of.[92]

Written by Gamboa, the above gives us a sense of his understanding of Asco's intervention regarding the role of the artist in the Chicano community. The first sin listed is abstraction. Asco's performances are "not where the people are at." The unnamed speaker berates Asco as "part of the problem, counterrevolutionary" for not adhering to a journalistic function, chronicling the quotidian local injustices in a realist mode. Abstraction appears as a threat, a "direct insult to the people" that only offers "more confusion" to a people already trying to "cope with reality." The issues raised by Asco are not seen to enhance the mission of muralists, who come across as uplifting by documenting community woes within the terms of redemptive beauty and opting not to highlight complicity and violence—those things that would only bring confusion. In their rejection of the mural form, Asco is rejecting the mode of political engagement that births the murals and is put forth by the movement. They are consequently deemed "burdens" that disrupt the teleological progress on national incorporation for Chicanos— necessarily abject such that the normative minority citizen-subject may cohere. Asco shows a clear awareness of the disdain they earn specifically because of the disruptive political implications of their "abstraction." It is indeed significant that they adopted their name, Asco, after years of collaboration or immersion in its affect, in 1974, indicating a commitment to alternative political paradigms.

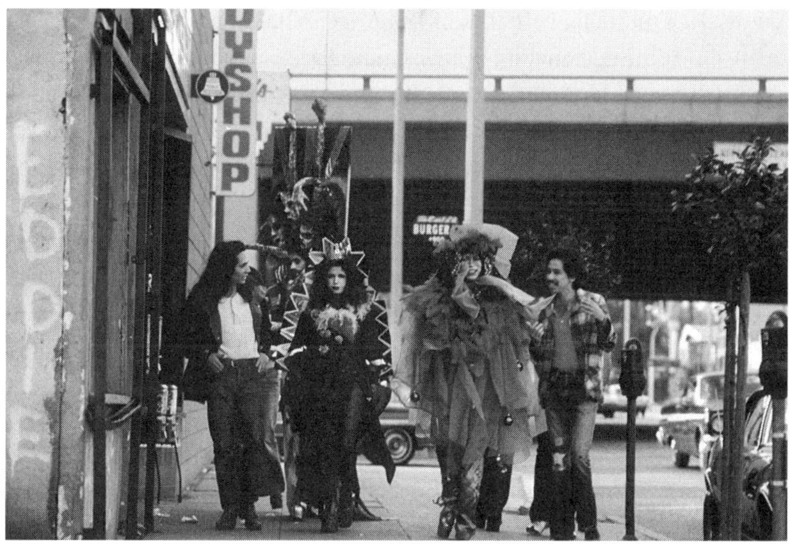

FIGURE 2.6 Asco, *Walking Mural*, 1972 (alternate view). Photograph by Harry Gamboa Jr. © 1972, Harry Gamboa Jr.

On *Walking Mural*, Gamboa reported that as Gronk, Valdez, and Herrón walked down Whittier, some people "converted in passing [and] joined their silent walk through the crowds."[93] But in his photographic documentation we see leers and the suggestion of heckling directed at Gronk and Valdez, who appear to take it in stride, in fierce unapologetically queer "goose step" (figure 2.6). Valdez's Virgen is not only a religious icon and frequent mural subject. Embracing the dark protopunk aesthetic of East Los Angeles, she has recoded the virginal mother to signal death more than birth. She is a threat to the bronze futurity promised by movement manifestos. She has left the sacred realm of religion for the abject street. By her side, Gronk's Christmas tree has left the nuclear home where he guards the hard-earned buy-in to a commercialized holiday. Queerly fashioned, he too takes to the streets. The project that emerges from Asco—the queer abject structure of feeling—moves away from highlighting historical (even art historical) presence on the wall or in the country toward the nonnormative, nomadic, and nonteleological. Where movement murals cement presence, *Walking Mural*, like *Stations of the Cross* before it, insists on ephemerality, absence, and loss.

I want to return now to the piece and image with which I began, *Asshole Mural*. For this 1975 work, Valdez, Gronk, Gamboa, and Herrón appointed themselves municipal officials of Los Angeles, taking as their primary responsibility the designation of civic landmarks and monuments. One such commemorated landmark was a storm drain, the asshole of the mural, whose negative space at the compositional center of most of the photos documenting the day serves as conduit for the city's filth and for my contemplation on queer abjection, absence, and loss.[94] Valdez's privileged compositional location in the *Asshole Mural* phantom document with which I opened, the baring of her skin in contrast to that of her male counterparts, serves as a hook, indicating the historical and gendered centrality of beauty within art history. At the apex of a pyramid constructed with brown bodies, Valdez's eyes, darkened with sunglasses, echo the vacuum of the orificial pipe in a lure that embodies the conflicting affects of the sublime—that affective counter to the classical category of beauty that Sianne Ngai has called "perhaps the first 'ugly' or explicitly nonbeautiful feeling."[95] Desire, evoked through stylized seduction, is ultimately transformed when Valdez's body turns away from the spectator and redirects the gaze to the pipe's opening. Gronk's body performs a similar invitation, the curvature of his torso and pelvis serving as a flesh outline to the orifice's lower right circumference.

The title of the piece, *Asshole Mural*, indicates a direct, if blasphemous, engagement with the sanctioned Chicano medium, memorializing the base over reverently rendered quotidian or mythic scenes. But Asco, here, also memorializes a type of uncivic engagement. Asco members stand at the end of the drainpipe, from which waste is expelled, not where it is produced. By labeling this a Chicano civic landmark, they make evident the institutionalized role Chicano communities are meant to fill, as receivers of filth, and the official infrastructure that guarantees this role—the pipe to which Valdez so brazenly calls our attention. Though the pipe's actual location is in Malibu, Ascotas deploy their bodies to frame it in such a way as to make evident the role they will always play within and beyond East Los Angeles. *Asshole Mural*'s uncivic memorialization uses the abject to make visible and chastise the city's infrastructure, the system that provides services for one community at the cost of another and the aesthetic movement that would sooner paint over all its urban blights and participate in said system. With its mural, Asco invites a reflection on space and the structures that organize participation.

As Amelia Jones has written, "The 'asshole' that Asco strategically locates at the center of their group self-portrait both illustrates and mocks the 'ego' at the center of modernist notions of artistic subjectivity and art making."[96] It also mocks the ideal subject of ego psychology that Chicano movement cultural texts work so hard to establish and which, following Viego, is necessary to the logic of racist ideology. Instead, Asco extends an invitation to be absorbed by the darkness of that negative space and consider the possibilities of negative affect, abjection, loss, and absence. Viego challenges the field of Latino studies to "stay alive to the range of losses" attributable to both the material consequences of hierarchized racialization where an investment in whiteness is structurally instituted, and to the misfire of language, where it fails to capture the fullness of the "need we try to express through its medium."[97] An engagement with this loss, he tells us, does not propose a reparative critical move toward wholeness, but rather will lead to new forms of "ethnic-racialized subjectivities that . . . are guided by the refusal of what we are currently made to be, of refusing the false amplitudes that yield from how our function in society has been reduced to our so-called difference."[98]

Asco's use of the abject highlights an understanding of a minority subjectivity that exists beyond the ethno-nationalist celebration of Chicano movement artists, who were reduced to celebrating difference. It focuses instead on the material and affective conditions resulting from the minoritized subject formed in a negative relation to power. Prominent Chicano movement artists produced a political subject that simplistically inverted the hierarchy of power relations imposed upon them by a racist hegemony. Reading Asco as an abject structure of feeling, we can view their asco as a refusal of this simplistic inversion. Instead we are invited, by dwelling on loss, absence, and failure, to imagine a form of collectivity that does not require consensus or singularity, which was often achieved at the exclusion of some of its members. It proposes a collectivity that fluctuates in size and ethos, attentive and calling attention to, their participation in subordinating ideologies and refusing respectability in the service of "being-with" and within the vortex of an abject asco.

We can follow this refusal of respectability in the performative strategies of cultural producers throughout *Abject Performances*. Here it is elaborated on the city streets, a terrain where claims for inclusion and self-determination were concurrently being made. In what follows, this refusal is performed on a simultaneously smaller and larger scale: the televisual field.

Of Betties Decorous and Abject
Ugly Betty's America la fea and
Nao Bustamante's America la bella

Bravo TV's first season of *Work of Art: The Next Great Artist* included internationally renowned Chicana performance artist Nao Bustamante among its fourteen participants.[1] Bustamante's elimination, the fourth of the televised competition, occurs after her piece, *Barely Standing* (2010), fails to elicit the measured shock called for in the episode's challenge to create a "shocking piece of art"—a calculated skill the show's judges and producers seem to think a necessary ability for the telesphere's "Next Great Artist." *Barely Standing*—an abject performance featuring a "shit flower" blossoming from Bustamante's plastic bag–upholstered pelvis—was judged as "adolescent mixed with shock-your-grandmother performance art" by the show's preeminent art critic, Jerry Saltz.[2] Her dismissal from the show served as a televisual reminder of the illegibility of performance art for a broad, popular audience and its resultant bottom-rung status on the art medium hierarchy, despite institutionalized recognition in the academy, museum, and gallery. For those familiar with Bustamante's oeuvre, it also continues her long flirtation with popular media and, indeed, her desire to invoke the genre within her practice. From her 1992 appearance on *The Joan Rivers Show* as the "sex-positive" "stunt exhibitionist" Rosa, to her performance citation of the circus and pageant in *America, the Beautiful* (1995–1998, 2002), Bustamante has often explored how "the mainstream is intervening in the art world."[3]

Work of Art: The Next Great Artist premiered just months after the final episodes of the four-season prime-time dramedy *Ugly Betty* (2006–2010), starring Honduran American actress America Ferrera as Betty Suarez. This consecutive programming placed the two in a shared telespace as Latina cultural texts at a moment marked by a surge in diverse representation on the political stage, perhaps best illustrated by the presence, within that same telespace, of the relatively contemporary hearings of Supreme Court justice Sonia Sotomayor.[4] Yet the historic appointment of this first Latina justice to the Supreme Court by another historic figure—the nation's first black president, Barack Obama—was also marked by a resurgence in xenophobic anti-immigrant legislation that supported police profiling of Latinos as always already suspect undocumented migrants. In turn, this legislation mobilized a cadre of immigrant rights demonstrations—an important backdrop against and in conversation with which the Latina texts in this chapter should be read.

Thus far in the book I have focused on performance artists whose cultural production has since been widely curated and exhibited in public-serving institutions. I focused on a time period in their careers during which they elaborated an abject aesthetic practice intersecting with a variety of publics. From performances among peers in public spaces to interventions in nature or the city, they often elaborated actions that engaged the political conversations that animated their immediate communities as part of larger political movements—feminist and Chicano. In this chapter, I take a different approach, one that juxtaposes two seemingly unrelated types of performers, in order to further broaden the scope of the reach of abjection to wider, if less concrete, publics—those of the scopic community of the telesphere. While Bustamante is a prominent contemporary Latina artist whose work, spanning what Jodi Melamed has called liberal multiculturalism to neoliberal multiculturalism, has served as a flashpoint for abject alternatives to co-optive diversity measures, America Ferrera and her Betty marked a watershed moment of Latina televisual representation that once again brought into focus a booming Latino market.[5] Together they cover a vast terrain of Latina strategies for contending with the successes of incorporation within the field of representation. With this pairing, this chapter also responds to Bustamante's flirtation with popular media and what I understand as her invitation for analysis through a comparative frame by putting into conversation two Americas: one *la fea*, the ugly, or America Ferrera's fea incarnate Betty, of the prime-time dramedy *Ugly Betty*; the other *la bella*, the beautiful, of artist Nao Bustamante's performance *America, the Beautiful* and later iterations of abject performances of femininity throughout her repertoire. These Americas are elaborated in relation to national dialogues on Latino belonging and inclusion. I want to argue for their cultural production as contributing to immigrant rights mobilizations that expose the limits of representation and a politics of respectability as well as the value of embracing queer failure as a strategy.

While there is a significant difference between the self-developed characters Bustamante embodies and Ferrera's portrayal of Betty within the limited constraints of a sitcom script based on the Colombian soap opera *Yo soy Betty, la fea*, both performers elaborate a gendered and racialized subjectivity, legible by reference to traditional standards of normative beauty.[6] Through a close reading of the series, I will argue that Ferrera's camp ugliness reifies this standard, functioning as the necessary complement to its white binary opposite and, by the show's end, coming to elaborate what we might call a mimetic minority beauty providing popular aesthetic endorsement for political strategies of racial uplift and decorum in support of the neoliberal incorporation of difference. Significantly, this mimetic minority beauty standard contains an element of quirk (difference or "color") that lends an egalitarian air to its embrace while nonetheless tracing routes of normative longing. Meanwhile, a close reading of Bustamante's contemplation of the beautiful throughout her oeuvre will be shown to deploy queer tactics that highlight the uncontainable excesses that seep through the mechanisms for beautifying the Latina body, as well as the rigid categorizations of proper normative minority identity, through an embrace of abject failure. Though seemingly disparate genres, not only does Bustamante's performative work insist we think about television as performative, she also prompts us to think of the possible reach of aesthetic interventions.

Against the backdrop of multiple surges in anti-immigrant legislation and, counterintuitively, minority political representation, the juxtaposition of these two performers provides insight on the gendered incorporation of difference as structured by cultural apparatuses. The cultural producers of this chapter contend with the institutional successes that were part of Chicano and liberal feminist movement demands alongside which Mendieta and Asco, in chapters 1 and 2, elaborated their abject interventions. Yet they also contend with nativist backlash propelled by a virulent racism. While Mendieta's and Asco's abject performances exploited the live durationality of performance, with particular attention to the long-term effects of documentation that in many ways transformed the two dimensional photo-document into a performative encounter, my focus on the television performances of Ferrera and Bustamante requires attention to narrative arc over a series of episodes. This narrative progression is distinct from, though not unrelated to, previous performances explored in this book. A close reading of Bustamante and Ferrera's performances reveals two discordant narratives of American beauty and Latina incorporation and disassociation.

Becoming America, the Beautiful

Ugly Betty capitalized on America Ferrera's rising star power as she emerged from the critically acclaimed independent film *Real Women Have Curves*. Nominated for over a hundred awards, the television show was lauded for its nuanced representation of Latinidad.[7] Indeed, Ferrera's Betty was touted as a stark contrast to the archetypes available to Latinas, identified by film scholar Charles Ramirez Berg as including the harlot, female clown, and dark lady in his study of Latinos in film.[8] Alongside critical acclaim, scholarly accounts of *Ugly Betty* enthusiastically noted the queer potentiality of the series, highlighting queer femininities on display and the queer composition of Betty's household.[9] Though critical acclaim would be tempered as the series progressed, optimism was difficult to avoid as a viewer of its first season, on which scholarship thus far has tended to focus. While developing a project on abjection, I was intrigued—between promotional material for *Shrek the Musical, Ugly Americans*, and Uglydolls—by what seemed to be ugliness's moment. I too celebrated the brace-faced, bespectacled, uncombed Ferrera through whom ugliness was established as an optic. *Ugly Betty* was indeed promising in its first season, with story lines that delved into difficult political terrain.

Though it premiered in the family-friendly 8 PM slot, *Ugly Betty* featured gay and transgender characters (problematically cast in sympathetic villain roles) as well as a protoqueer young Latino, Betty's nephew, Justin.[10] The show also explored issues of undocumented long-term residency through a story line revealing that Betty's father, Ignacio Suarez, has overstayed his visa and indeed came to the United States after committing a presumed murder. While he momentarily literalizes a racist generalization of the Mexican migrant whose status as "illegal alien" rightly renders him criminal, Ignacio is eventually revealed to be a chivalrous hero who did not actually murder anyone, but rather used appropriate amounts of violence to free his soon-to-be wife (and Betty's future mother) from an abusive relationship. This woman has passed, we learn early in the pilot episode, though her ghost will animate plot lines (especially those about culture and tradition) and fuel character development. Deborah Paredez has deftly argued that the absence of Betty's mother "serves as a representational sign of the continued legacy of the reproductive policing of Latina bodies throughout the Americas."[11] Below I show how Betty's body, and by extension America Ferrera's, and the attention it receives within and beyond the diegesis shows us an elaboration of this legacy. Here, I consider the teleological arc of Betty's transformation throughout the four-season series, deploying a close reading of key scenes to explore the ways in which Betty's purported ugliness is a necessary characteristic to narrate her coming into successful adulthood, one marked by and privileging racialized mimetic beauty that signals the incorporation of difference in a neoliberal democracy.

Though *Ugly Betty* shifts focus over its arc, it primarily follows its eponymous character as she navigates her first job after graduating from Queens College as the personal assistant to Daniel Meade, the playboy-turned-neophyte editor in chief of *Mode*, a Meade publication. From the pilot episode's opening scene, Betty's visual presentation marks her as an outsider in the *Mode* offices and the skyscrapered glitz of Manhattan as much as it marks her as at home in patinaed Latino Queens. Before the show title has aired, we encounter a tightly cropped shot of our protagonist. Betty, in close-up, is centered in the frame with the camera positioned slightly beneath her such that we gaze up at her ample nostrils, just below what will become her signature red spectacles, and above a nervously twitchy mouth struggling to contain blue-capped braces (figure 3.1). A steep stairway leading up to Meade Publications and the *Mode* offices are just behind her—the gilded gates of which are located at the center of a triptych of archways topped by the moniker "MEADE" aglow with artificial incandescence. The scene is cut by a solid yellow screen with the all-capitalized title of the show embedded in red at its center, introducing the series title but also ascribing what is presented as an obvious descriptor to our protagonist. As if

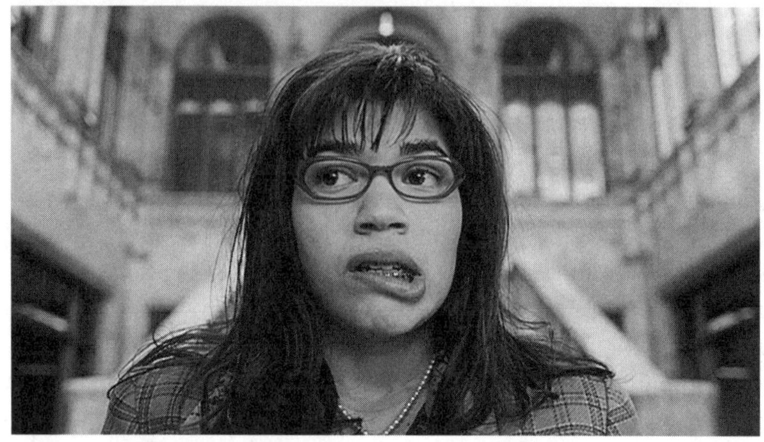

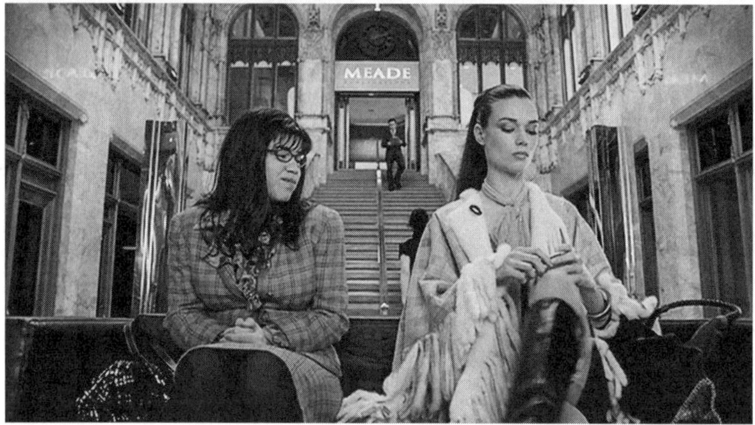

FIGURES 3.1 (TOP) AND 3.2 (BOTTOM) America Ferrera as Betty at the gates of Meade Publications. "Pilot," *Ugly Betty*, 2006.

to drive the point home, Betty, in a garish carnation pink and aqua tartan skirt-suit with a chartreuse ruffled blouse, is joined by a woman we will soon recognize as embodying the *Mode*, and indeed culturally dominant, aesthetic ideal: thin, tall, white, fashionable, wealthy (figure 3.2). The two are contrasting sides of a beauty standard. Dressed in the muted neutrals of a Dolce and Gabbana poncho, she's a chromatic fit for the environment, an embodiment of disinterest and, by Kantian standards, taste.

The consequences of Betty's ugliness soon become apparent. A gray suit–clad Meade representative descends from his office and reads out loud from his clipboard the name of the next interviewee: "Betty Suarez."

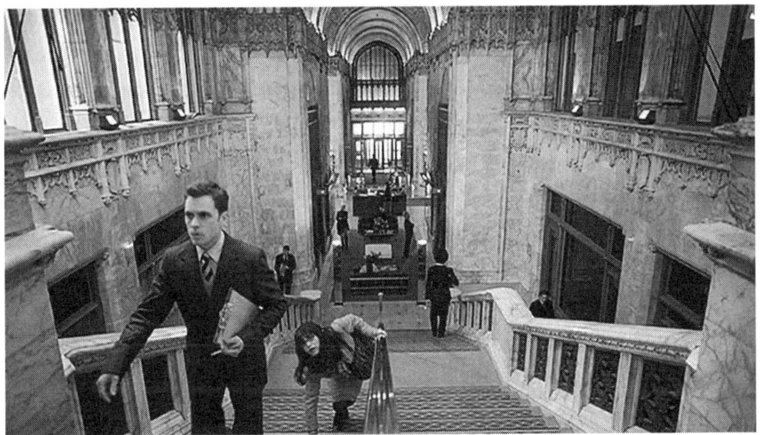

FIGURE 3.3 America Ferrera as Betty ascending toward the gates of Meade Publications. "Pilot," *Ugly Betty*, 2006.

When Betty responds to this call, his quick head-to-toe scan of our protagonist leads to an immediate announcement that the position for which she was there to interview has been filled. Betty's plucky go-getter-ness is established as she follows him in his ascent back to Meade. Her humorous groveling links Betty to the lineage of female clowns identified by Berg and thus to an established tradition of representation, donning garish color and pattern combinations complemented with comical countenance modifications to Betty-fy the striking actress, America Ferrera.[12] Her body leans toward the gray suited keeper of the gates as she articulates her attributes for successful participation and contribution to any of Meade's publications just before the closing of those gilded doors (figure 3.3). Shot from above, this scene is sutured to the gaze of Meade's white-haired patriarch and Daniel's father, Bradford, who, we learn later in the episode, will hire Betty specifically because of the ugly groveling on display. Betty's debased status is established compositionally and through supplicant gestures—appropriate for a scene littered with religious symbology—but also through Ferrera's embodiment of Betty and the racialized dynamics that can be read therein.

All too heavy-handedly, Betty is represented as an assertive, if not impeccably dressed, Latina just trying to catch a break, to climb up the corporate ladder—or marble stairs—only to be blocked, indeed dismissed, by a white man at first sight. It is significant, however, that her dismissal occurs after she has been hailed as a Latina with the declaration of her surname from a clipboard of candidates. In doing so, an egalitarian multicultural environment in which a woman of color is presumably a viable candidate is suggested, and indeed confirmed, with the introduction of Vanessa Williams's sympathetic villain, Wilhelmina Slater, who embodies the successful racial integration of the business space. But Betty's embodied base Latinidad—signaled through an excess of color, fabric, hair, and flesh—results in her dismissal, visually signaling the hierarchies that structure the myths of color blindness and full national incorporation.

This visual excess is central to designating the Suarez household as a working-class Latino space and also signals the limits or parameters of acceptable and legible multiculturalism. The interior of the Suarez home is a colorful caricature, albeit lovingly rendered, of ethnic particularity through the pan-Latino signification of a campy Chicano rasquache sensibility. It is useful to note that there is not a single Chicano among the actors that make up the Suarez family and that the demographically dominant Latino group in New York is Dominican American. A Chicano family whose household is rendered in a thoroughly Chicano aesthetic, however, allows the producers to address some of the dominant issues in Latino politics, most prominent among them immigration through the U.S./Mexico border, while also succumbing to the homogenizing tendency in popular media to represent Latinos as Chicanos.[13] Their working-class immigrant family status is depicted as inseparable from that aesthetic. In his essay/manifesto "Rasquachismo: A Chicano Sensibility," Tómas Ybarra-Frausto explains, "Very generally, *rasquachismo* is an underdog perspective—a view from los de abajo. An attitude rooted in resourcefulness and adaptability yet mindful of stance and style."[14] Additionally, "*Rasquachismo* is brash and hybrid, sending shudders through the ranks of the elite who seek solace in less exuberant, more muted and 'purer' traditions." The Suarez household is decorated in much the same shudder-inducing manner in which Betty is adorned: saturated in color, layered with texture, and accessorized to the brim—a parallel contrast to the muted spaces that stand in for Meade's Manhattan. The interior shots of Betty's Queens home revolve around the living room and kitchen, both resplendent in jewel tones and littered throughout with decorative kitsch—the most prominent of which is the serape throw that rests on the back of their couch.[15] The embrace of excess, for some, indicates not only an unapologetic Latinoness but also queerness. Indeed, Paredez identifies the series as a "queer U.S. *Latinovela*,

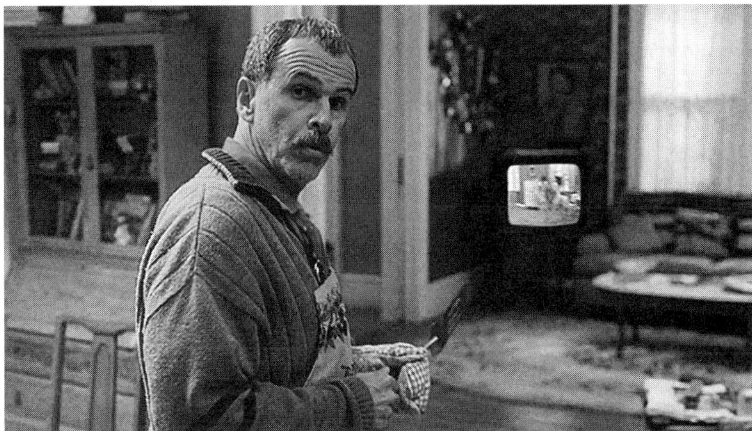

FIGURE 3.4 Ignacio with spatula in hand, telenovela and serape in the background. "Pilot," *Ugly Betty*, 2006.

an explicitly U.S. cultural product that embraces its queer and Latina/o *chusmeria*: tackiness, shamelessness, and above all, sincerity."[16]

Ugly Betty's gay inclusion can be traced to its source material, the Colombian telenovela *Yo soy Betty, la fea*, which included gay characters.[17] Its queer sensibility, however, has a lot to do with genre, both in its hybridity and in the privileging of visual excess but also its self-referential love of the melodramatic telenovela itself with its excess of affect. Swooping camera pans often reveal a *mise en abyme* of novelas on the television screen in the Suarez living room, sometimes starring *Ugly Betty* producer Selma Hayek, whose career started with roles in Mexican telenovelas. These are only interrupted by glimpses of "Fashion TV," whose TV host often dishes gossip on the Meade family. While the former is enjoyed by protoqueer youth Justin, when he manages to steal the remote control from his grandfather, the novelas entertain the patriarch of the Suarez household, Ignacio, consistently aproned and cooking—a queer revisioning of the patriarchal family (figure 3.4). But the potentiality of radical queerness offered by the Suarez home is circumscribed as, even within the first episode, the Suarez home functions as a site to alleviate mainstream anxieties about Latinos and establish grounds for liberal inclusion.

Ignacio in apron with oven mitt and spatula is symbolically contained by the apron that designates his adoption of women's tasks and his relegation to the feminized domestic realm. The emasculating, pelvis-covering apron softens the impact of the later revelation of his criminal status. Relegated to the home in this way, he also takes the place of the absent mother. He does so without evoking the threatening reproductive capabilities associated with Latina femininities—a cause of great anxiety for conservatives who dread the looming Latino minority majority. A hybrid of neutered Latino parents, he eradicates any anxiety about population growth. In the Suarez household, the Chicano/Latino home is a consumable camp of contained and managed signifiers that allow us to focus on what both Ferrera and *Ugly Betty* producer Silvio Horta have stressed is a universal immigrant story—a strategy that "[highlights] majoritarian values, fantasies and narratives."[18]

Within this space cultivated by Ignacio, still in the significant establishing shots of the pilot episode, we find Betty devouring angry forkfuls of flan on the evening after she is prematurely dismissed from the lobby of Meade Publications. A phone call prompts her to spit out her last bite, and we watch as Betty excitedly accepts a position at *Mode*, the fashion magazine that "would not have been her first choice." For her first day, Betty dons a turquoise fringe–trimmed red poncho/serape with "Guadalajara" emblazoned in acid yellow across her chest, a fashion choice inspired by the disinterested fashionista in the show's opening scene. When she enters *Mode*'s offices, scores of giggles tip us off to her failed, and comical, fashion accessory mimicry. Instead of the muted neutral tones of high fashion, Betty's ensemble literalizes her colorful otherness as linked to ethnic and therefore national outsider status—an attribute quickly associated with her ugliness as the audience learns shortly after her Guadalajara-stamped appearance that her lack of sexual appeal landed her the job. Thus her "ugliness" serves as a virtue for which she is hired with the unintended consequence of allowing us to focus on her abilities. Her arrival at *Mode* gestures toward affirmative action conversations about the incorporation of questionably qualified individuals hired for their color (designated here as "ugly"). But Betty will prove herself not only a capable assistant but, more importantly, a willing team player, and therefore an exceptional asset.

Betty establishes her stellar work ethic and staunch commitment through resilience to the hazing of her boss, Daniel, who knows he cannot fire her for how she looks. After many a hilarious humiliation, Betty reaches an understandable limit that reveals her body as a central nexus for conflict. Goaded by the photographer of a fashion shoot, Daniel asks Betty to stand in place of an absent model. When Betty complies, visibly embarrassed with hand on hip in full barely-there mod attire and patent white thigh-high boots, the pointed laughter of those on scene finally drives her to quit. Little is made of the fact that Betty is able to wear the model's outfit—with the camera's focus lingering on Ferrera's Bettyfied face, clearly legible and marked as ugly and, transitively, as of color—though it grants the audience a peek at the slender body under the frumpy Betty clothing. Betty's departure from *Mode*, however, is temporary and only leads to the infiltration of her home by the hierarchies that structure her work environment as well as the opportunity to display Betty's selflessness and willingness to forgive.

Late at night, Daniel knocks on Betty's door. He has found the "work idea" Betty had prepared for his consideration (and first ignored). This work idea, developed despite her exhaustion after a day of performing debasing menial tasks that resulted in her absence from a significant family event, is inspired by Betty's deceased mother. Daniel hopes to save an imperiled cosmetics account with Betty's pitch, which centers the relationship between a mother, her daughter, and their makeup. He begins his request for the use of her idea by first offering an apology for the way he has treated her. Betty is not impressed. After he apologizes she responds:

> **BETTY:** Well, I appreciate that, Daniel. But you're going to leave here and you're going to take your town car back to your SoHo loft and I'm still gonna be here, out of work, and dealing with problems that you'll never understand.
>
> **DANIEL:** Try me. Betty, c'mon, we've all got problems.
>
> **BETTY:** Oh and what are yours, Daniel? What restaurant you're gonna eat at? Which model you're gonna sleep with? Try spending the day on the phone with some crappy H.M.O. getting them to cover your dad's prescriptions. Or, try lining up a job, any job, 'cause you have to help pay the rent next month.[19]

Betty delivers an impassioned dismissal of his apology, making explicit his class privilege and precisely the precarious situation he has placed her in with his schoolyard bullying. The distinction between Daniel, in a pinstripe suit and carefully arranged hair, and his surroundings only serves to highlight their differences. While Betty is dressed in a muted color palate—a drab olive sweater significantly zipped over a sunflower-adorned T-shirt— her disheveled emotional excess, a racialized excess, further ennobles Daniel's sentimental elegance, a muted whiteness.

During this exchange, Betty is shot from above, with the camera posi-

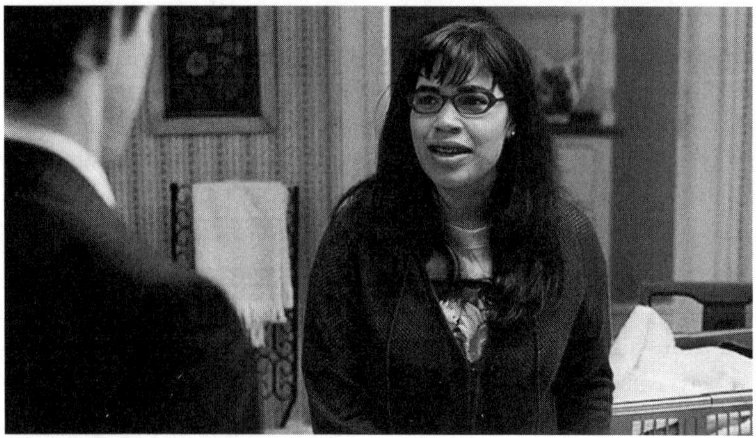

FIGURE 3.5 Daniel: "I've never quite measured up. But I am trying." "Pilot,"
Ugly Betty, 2006.

tioned just over Daniel's shoulder (figure 3.5). Indeed, it is from his point of view that we gaze down at Betty's emotional outpouring. Music from strings and piano swells as Daniel responds: "Look . . . I lost a brother a while back. He was the good one in our family and I've never quite measured up. But I am trying. Betty, I could never compare my problems to yours, but they're mine. Nothing's ever easy. I saw the layout you made. . . . I really want you to come back, be my assistant. I promise you, things will be different." After introducing him as an incompetent and shallow boss, the pilot episode's plot, here, delivers an appeal for empathy precisely when Daniel needs Betty's idea to save his own job and protect his relationship with his father. With moist downcast eyes, Daniel shares a personal account of death and sibling rivalry (figure 3.6). While he recognizes their problems are not the same, he equalizes them when he says, "Nothing's ever easy." All technical elements—camera point of view, sound score, costume, frame, composition—collaborate to render Daniel sympathetic despite the way he has manipulated Betty throughout the episode. Betty's reaction to his apology models the appropriate audience response; when she shows up for work the next morning and gives Daniel credit for her idea—accepting her job to save his and the company until another crisis of soap-operatic dimensions—the spectator is encouraged to give Daniel a second chance as well, and, indeed, to root for him throughout the series.

As the scene unfolds in the heart of the Suarez household, it manages anxieties about a working-class Latina heroine by making her climb up that

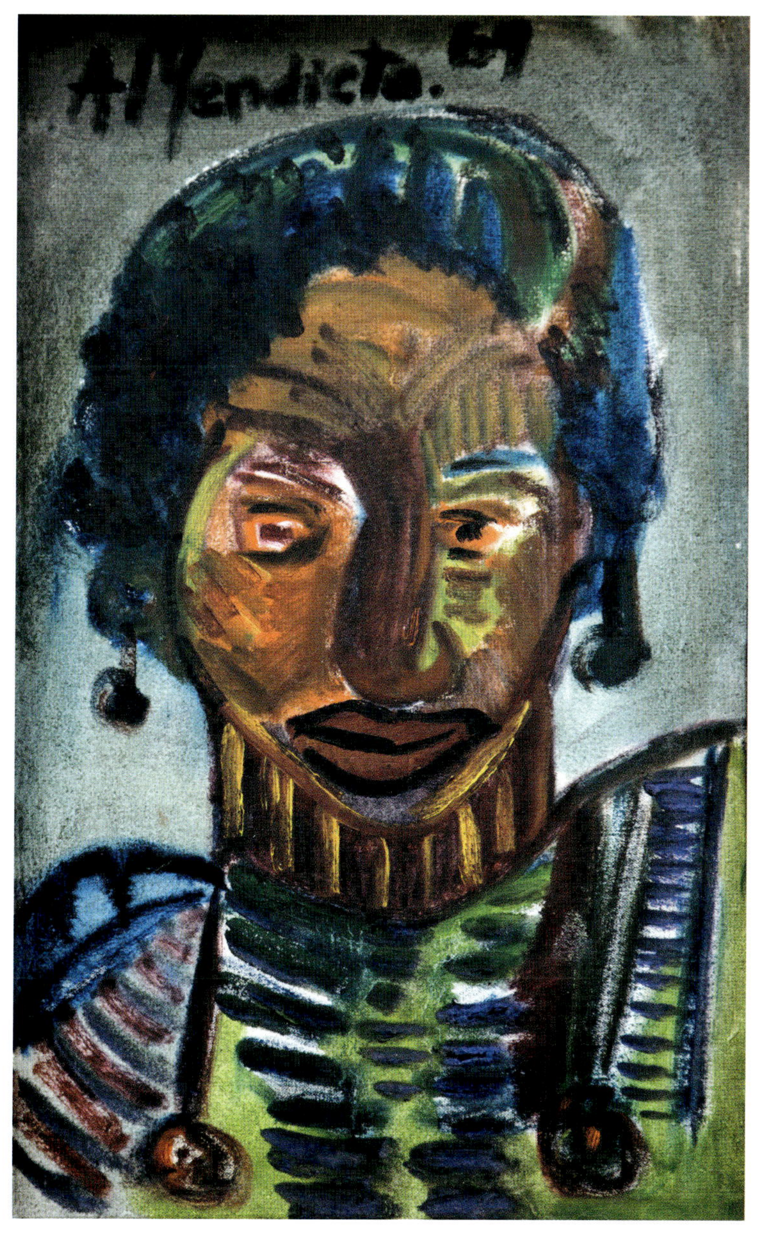

PLATE 1 Ana Mendieta, *Untitled*, 1969. Oil on masonite. Copyright The Estate of Ana Mendieta Collection, L.L.C. Courtesy Galerie Lelong, New York.

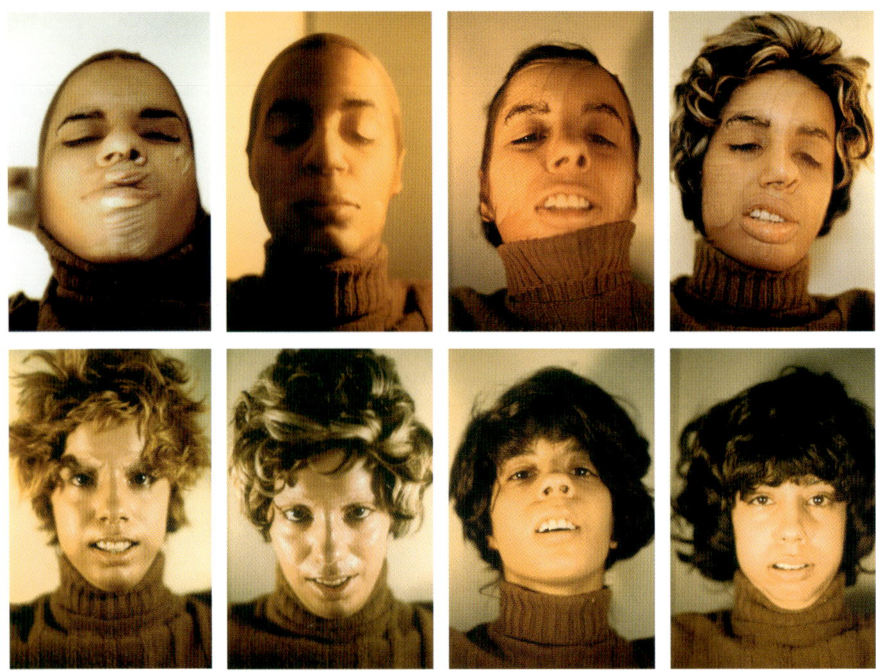

PLATE 2 Ana Mendieta, *Untitled* (Facial Cosmetic Variations), 1972. Estate print 1997. Suite of eight color photographs, 20 × 16 inches (55.8 × 40.6 cm). Copyright The Estate of Ana Mendieta Collection, L.L.C. Courtesy Galerie Lelong, New York.

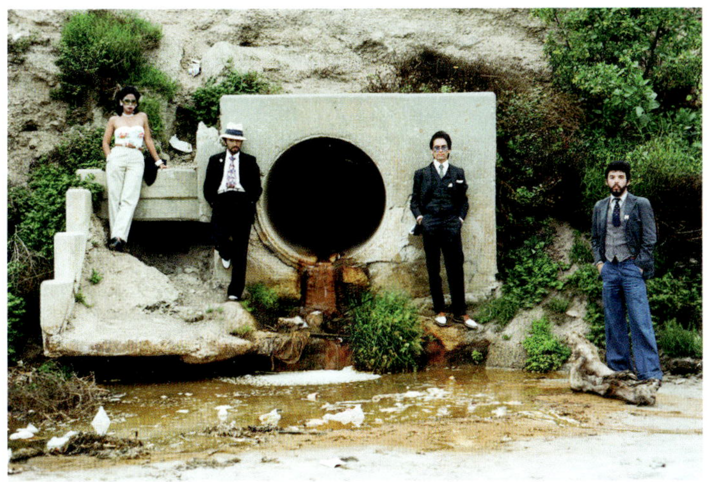

PLATE 3 Asco, *Asshole Mural*, 1974. Photograph by Harry Gamboa Jr. © 1974, Harry Gamboa Jr.

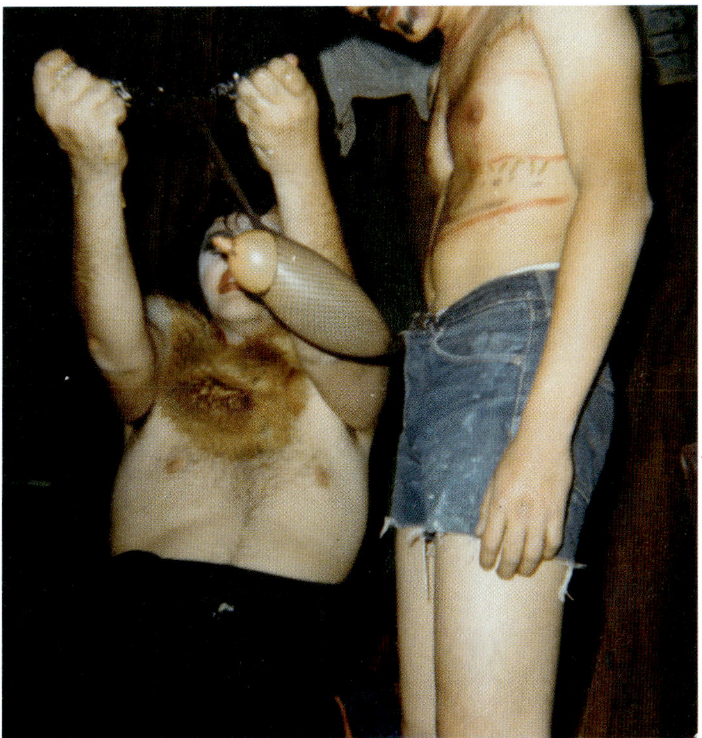

PLATE 4 *Caca-Roaches Have No Friends*, performance documentation of castration scene, 1969. The Fire of Life: The Robert Legorreta-Cyclona Collection, 1962–2002, Coll. CSRC.0500. Courtesy of the UCLA Chicano Studies Research Center.

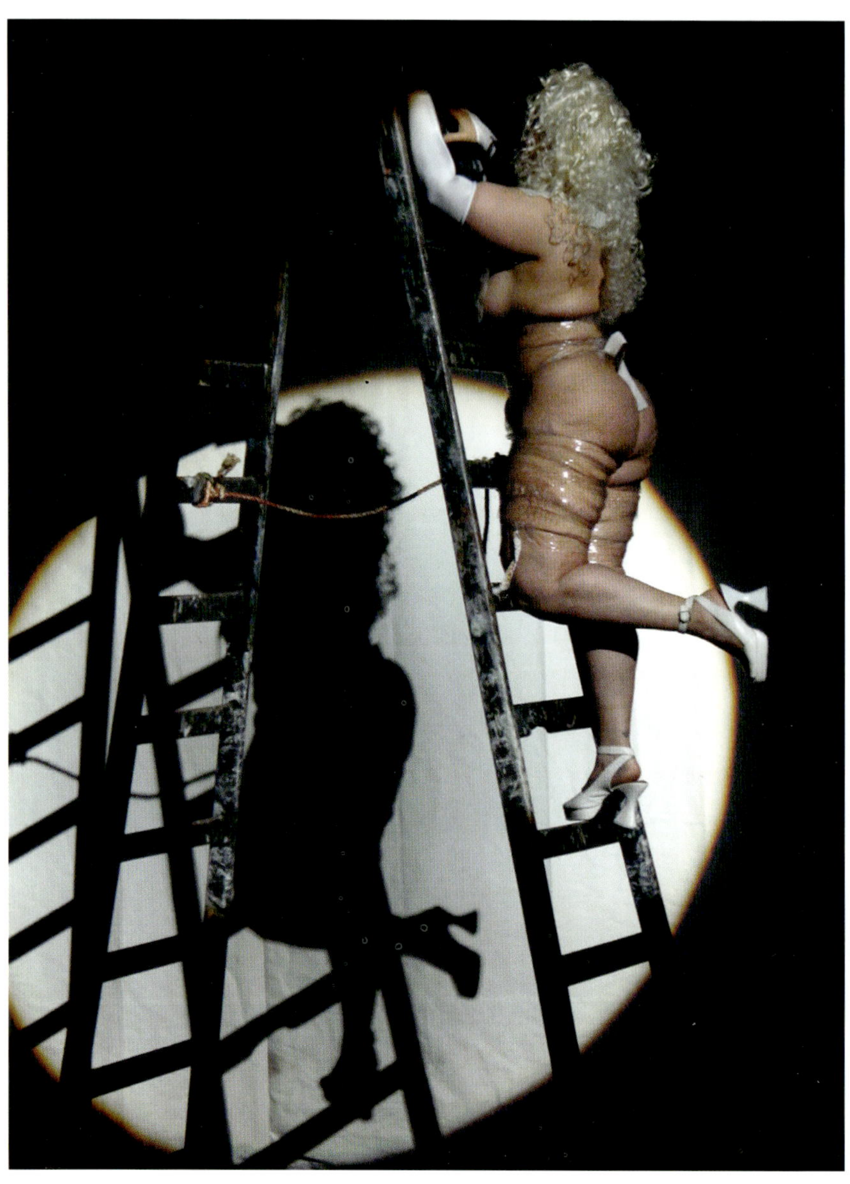

PLATE 5 Nao Bustamante, *America, the Beautiful*, 1995–1998, 2002. Photograph by Lorie Novak. Courtesy of the artist.

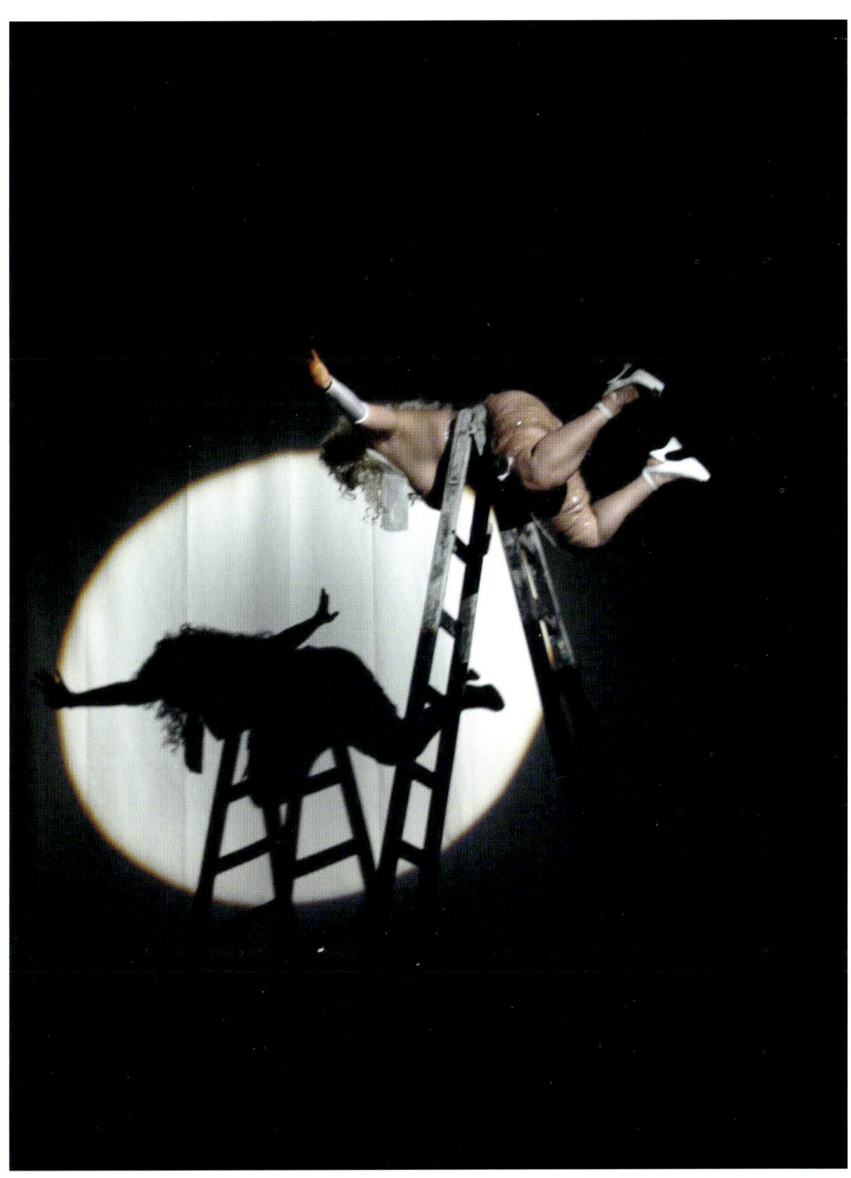

PLATE 6 Nao Bustamante, *America, the Beautiful*, 1995–1998, 2002.
Photograph by Lorie Novak. Courtesy of the artist.

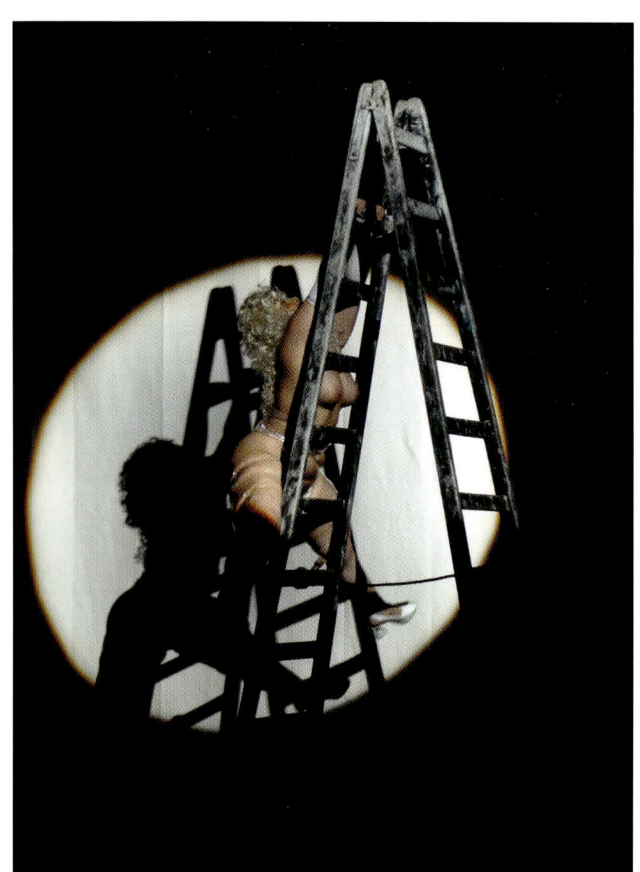

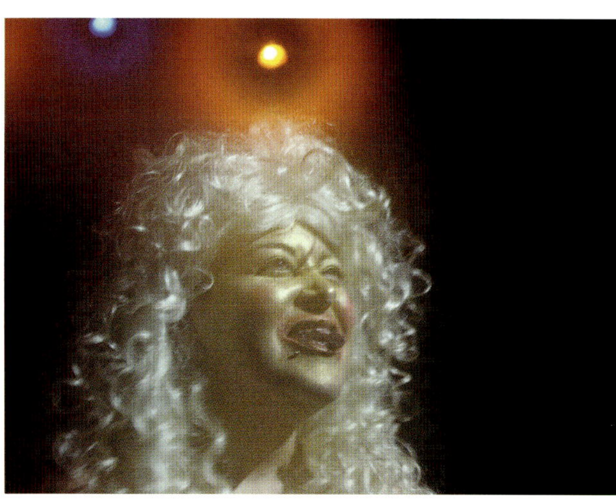

PLATES 7 (TOP) AND 8 (BOTTOM) Nao Bustamante, *America, the Beautiful*, 1995–1998, 2002. Photograph by Lorie Novak. Courtesy of the artist.

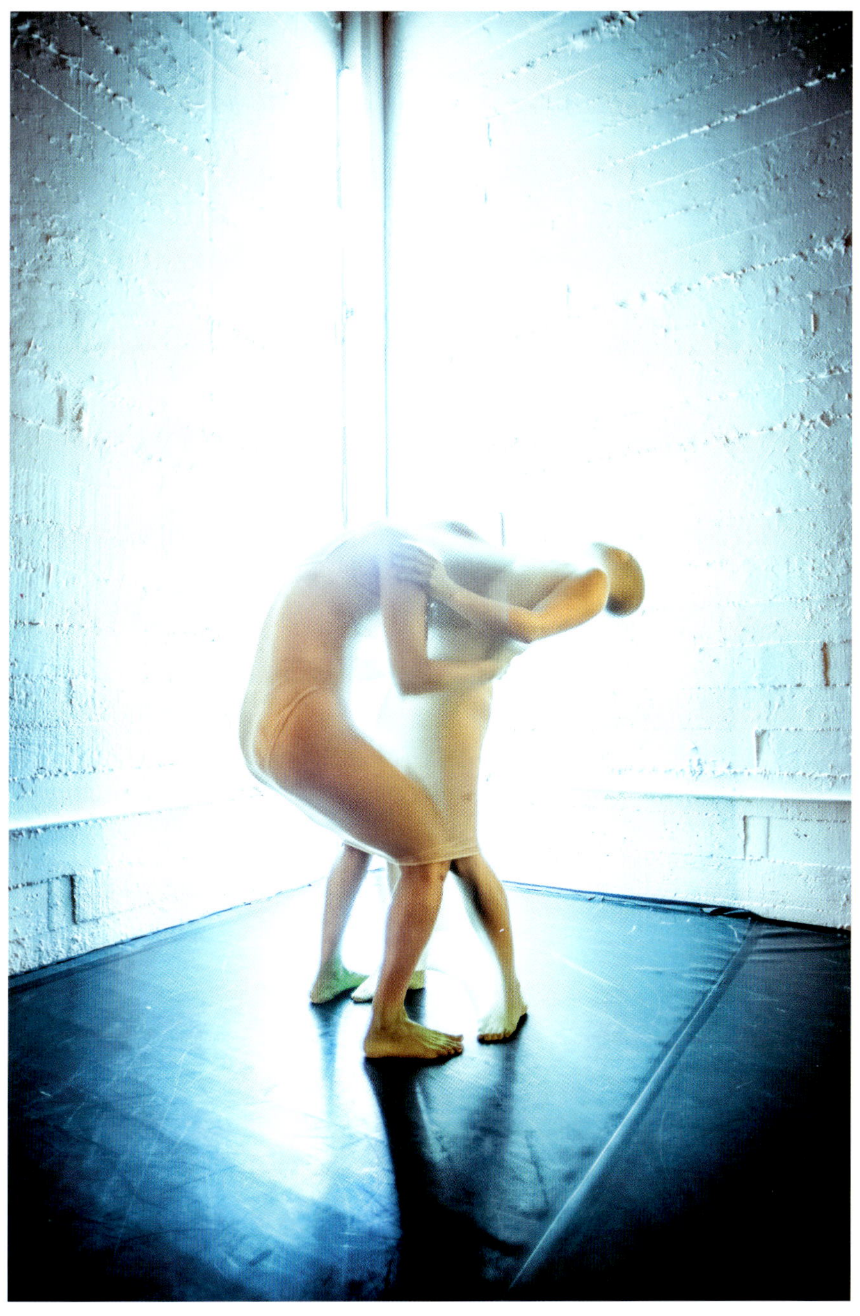

PLATE 9 Xandra Ibarra with Sophia Wang, *Untitled (skins)*, 2015–2016. Performance documentation. Photograph by Robbie Sweeny.

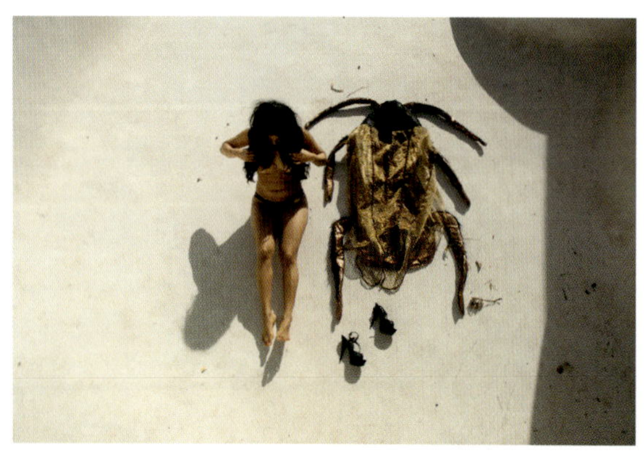

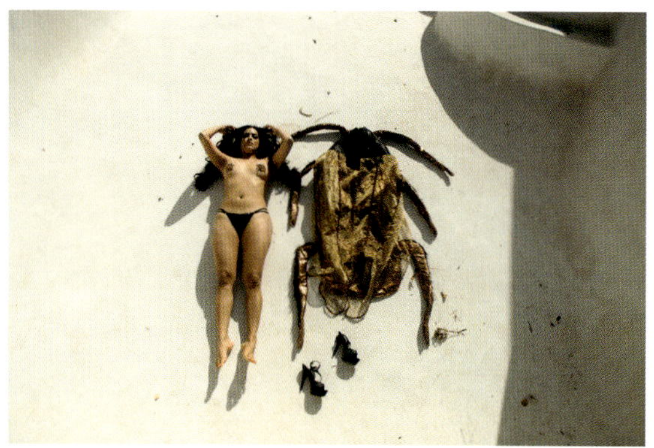

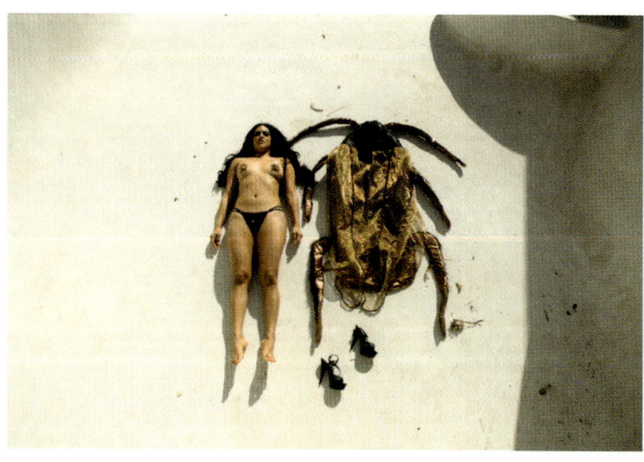

PLATE 10 Xandra Ibarra, *Triptych*, 2015, from the photographic series *Ecdysis: The Molting of A Cucarachica*.

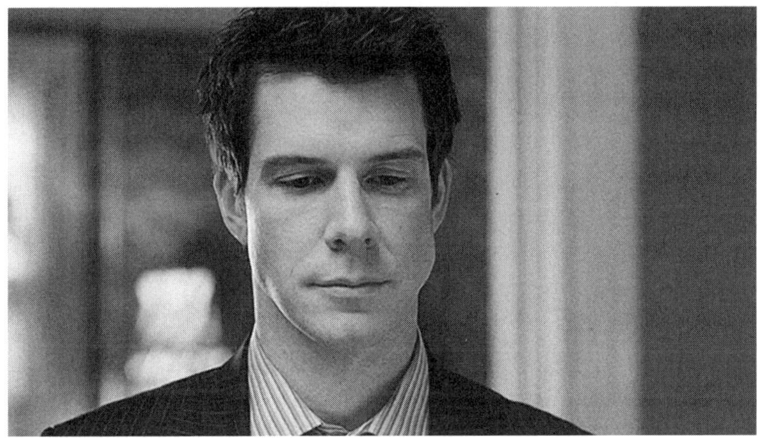

FIGURE 3.6 Daniel sees Betty's beauty. "Pilot," *Ugly Betty*, 2006.

marble Meade staircase in the service of the reigning elite. Betty's indictment of Daniel's class privilege is softened while we are assured that our representative Latina will be a productive team player—precisely the model behavior for ethnic minority participation in a liberal democracy that contributes to, but does not challenge, societal structures. Similarly, Betty's work idea, crafted in her wholesome Latino home, denotes the strong family bonds that will characterize the Suarez family throughout the series and their mode of relating to the corporate world, making multiculturalism and Latino family values work for a consumer-friendly capitalism. Her ugliness is not at all abject as it has been elaborated thus far in this book. Rather, it is a superficial and comedic distraction from Betty's true beauty.

The episode's end, after the successful retaining of their client and Betty's relinquishment of her intellectual property, reveals Betty's inner beauty, whose eventual external manifestation will be traced by the narrative arc of the series. The closing scene shows a reconciled Daniel and Betty saying goodbye. Daniel looks on as Betty crosses the street before he enters his town car, where, visible only as a disembodied manicured finger tapping, his evening's tryst awaits him. As we cut to a medium shot of Betty, who trips and then resumes a confident walk across the street, we hear the lyrics of the pop-rock song, "Suddenly I See" by KT Tunstall: "Her face is a map of the world, / is a map of the world. / You can see she's a beautiful girl, / she's a beautiful girl." We then cut to a close-up of Daniel as he watches Betty (figure 3.7). Just before Daniel steps into his car, we pan left

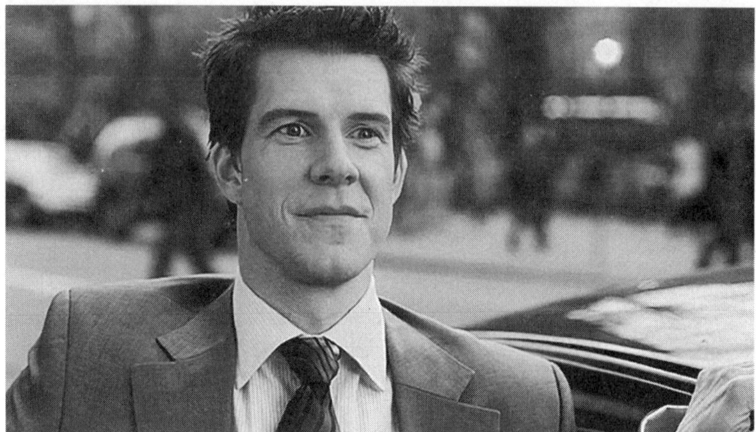

to Betty as the song continues: "Suddenly I see, / this is what I want to be. / Suddenly I see, / why the hell it means so much to me." The series title appears, again in red, superimposed over Betty as she crosses through Bryant Park while the song fades and the episode ends. At the end of the first episode, then, we see, as Daniel does, that our protagonist, ugly Betty, is in fact a "beautiful girl." That her face is a map of the world is a nod to the color, the excess, the ugliness we know she will overcome through her service to capital. The labor she will put into her job is linked to her desire to be a "beautiful girl."

Throughout this book I have been tracing the political potential invoked through abject excess, which is here hinted at by ugliness but is ultimately supplanted by an aesthetic in the service of virtuous beauty. Ugliness functions as a binary to beauty, which signals its presence and calls beauty into being through its desirous reach. The ugly in *Ugly Betty* does not explore the potential of a contestatory aesthetic but is rather a reminder of the constitution of beauty, from the inside out. While the opening shot of the pilot episode, which introduces our protagonist, highlights her ugliness, throughout the series, her ugly factor is sometimes played up or down—defrizzing Betty's mane, trimming her eyebrows, having her wear subtle makeup, shooting her from above so she looks small and demure. The focus, however, is undoubtedly Betty's inner beauty, and, as the series progresses, it is hard not to catch glimpses of America Ferrera, the actress that plays Betty. The charmed smirk on Daniel's face here at the closing of the pilot episode in recognition of Betty's inner beauty anticipates the series's end, in which Daniel follows a transformed, beautiful-on-the-outside Betty to London. Before looking at this parallel scene, I'd like to quickly note the groundwork set in seasons two and three before the dramatic transformation Betty undergoes in the fourth and final season of the series.

Just shy of midway through the first season, Betty delivers an unexpected, accessory-induced testimony to the power of fashion. During the seasonal purging of the closet, Christina, one of Betty's few friends, seamstress and keeper of the closet, has saved a coveted Gucci it-bag for Betty. To Betty, it is a facsimile of a bag her now-deceased mother gifted her as a child. After a day spent with the bag on her shoulder prompting the most compliments she has received at *Mode*, Betty trades her adored accessory for fifteen prescription refills for her father, whose HMO refuses him coverage when it becomes known that the Social Security number he is using is not his. Though willing to make the necessary material sacrifice, Betty is devastated as she confesses to her sister, Hilda, "Christina says that fashion is good for the soul, and when I was walking around with my Gucci today, it was like I was three years old again and holding Mom's purse. I actually felt pretty."[20] Betty's new appreciation of fashion, like her forgiveness of Daniel, encourages us to rethink her time at *Mode* and indeed, the role and purpose of a magazine like *Mode,* which prescribes the punishing beauty standards even its own creative director, Wilhelmina Slater (played by an actual one-time beauty queen), has trouble meeting. We root for her transformation with a little less guilt, and the transformation comes.

Betty's penchant for bright jewel tones is preserved throughout the series, but she begins to combine them in inventive analogous and secondary color arrangements that make evident the hand of costume designer Patricia Field, the well-known fashion designer and stylist responsible for the looks of the women on *Sex and the City* (1998–2004). Her hair begins to be arranged into semicoherent waves; her chunky, clumsy wedges give way to a plethora of heels (figure 3.8). Subtle lipstick graces her increasingly exfoliated lips, though their primary purpose is still to shield her blue braces. By the end of the third season, Betty's not just surviving at *Mode,* she has been promoted to Features Editor while wearing a dazzling silver skirt, ruffled blouse and pink satin sash (figure 3.9). The changes are subtle but reveal that Betty's "ugly" is an increasingly polished fabrication of the fashion industry of which she is a supposed outsider despite working within its chambers.

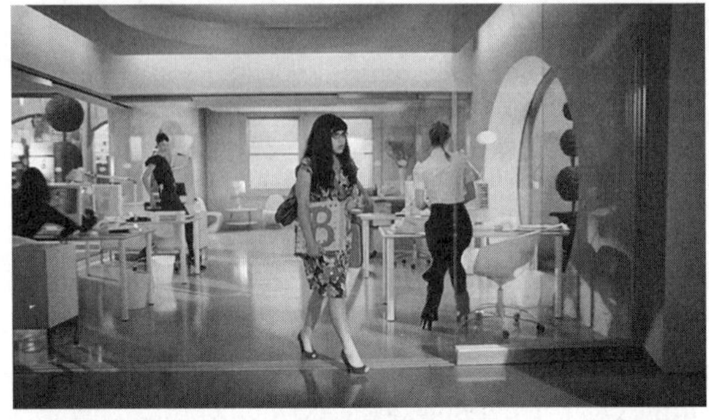

FIGURE 3.8 Betty's evolving fashion. "The Manhattan Project," *Ugly Betty*, 2008.

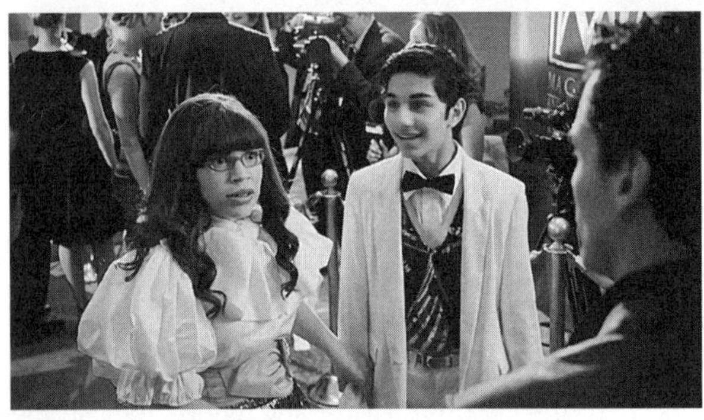

FIGURE 3.9 Betty's evolving fashion. "The Fall Issue," *Ugly Betty*, 2009.

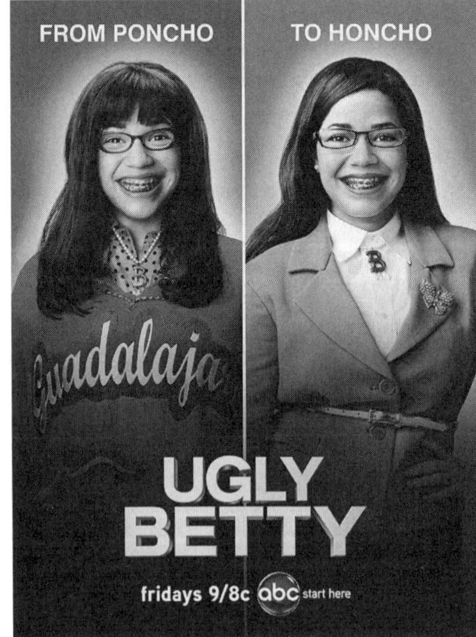

FIGURE 3.10 Season four promotional material, *Ugly Betty*, 2009.

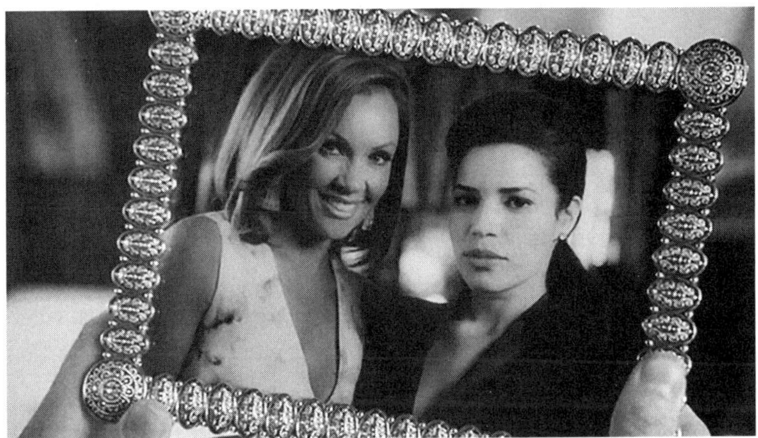

FIGURE 3.11 Parallel universe. "Million Dollar Smile," *Ugly Betty*, 2010.

The fourth and final season's promotional material hypes the fruition of a transformation we've seen coming all along. The final season's slogan, "From Poncho to Honcho," directly links the shift in her look with her rise up the career ladder—Betty is dressed for success as an editor, a honcho (figure 3.10). The opening episode of the season teases the spectator with a scene in which Betty's braces are being removed as she reclines in a dentist chair, floating in a vacuous white dreamspace. As we fade out of this scene, we hear and then see Betty sharing this dream with her sister, Hilda, in their busy home salon while helping shampoo clients. Hilda, in a performative wink to the audience, asks "When are those things coming off!"[21] But alas, the tease will not lead to oral release until nearly the end of the season. Betty's transformation does not happen in the closet, with the help of a fashionable bestie, following genre conventions.[22] Instead, the changes are small and coincidental.[23] Betty's bangs have gotten too long; Hilda is too busy to cut them; Betty sweeps them to the side. With bangs swooped, crown teased, and tresses smoothed, Betty is one braceless mouth away from looking just like the famous actress America Ferrera.

Four episodes from the end of the series, that moment finally arrives. Betty's signature comedic clumsiness at work leads to the entanglement of her braces with a valuable photo shoot prop and a bump-to-the-head-induced peek at an alternate reality in which Betty is the stunning protégé of fashion villainess Wilhelmina, with a perfect smile that covers cruel cutthroat ugliness (figure 3.11).[24] When she wakes from this alternate world, Betty's braces are cut off in the midst of the fashion community of which Betty has become a member, revealing a surprising Betty to Daniel. Throughout the ensuing photo shoot with the now-recovered prop, both Betty and Daniel keep stealing glances at Betty's new smile. While a romance narrative between these two characters is central to the Colombian-origin telenovela, the relationship between Betty and Daniel here has been kept entirely friendly, if codependent. With the show's cancellation now looming, the two characters are rushed toward each other, with each ensuing episode dripping with romantic suggestion that comes to a head when Betty takes a hard journalism job in London despite Daniel's proclamation that he "can't live without [her]."

Thus we arrive at the closing scene of the series, whose parallel to the closing scene of the pilot episode completes the arc of our protagonist. A series of shots of Betty walking in heels across the Millennium Bridge, St. Paul's Cathedral, Leicester Square, Westminster Bridge, and Piccadilly Circus establish Betty as thriving in London as she launches her own magazine (figures 3.12, 3.13). On a busy walk across Trafalgar Square, she happens to bump into Daniel, who has followed her to London on the pretext that he wants a fresh start away from a world where he is handed everything (figure 3.14). After Betty accepts his eventual invitation to dinner, Daniel watches her walk away with a smile on his face, slightly brighter than the one at the end of the pilot episode that inaugurated the series (figure 3.15). We pan out as we hear Macy Gray singing, "because there is beauty in the world."

The narrative arc of the season is not about ugliness as much as it is about coming into beauty. Indeed, it is one of moving from the character ugly Betty to the recognizable actress, America, the beautiful, we've always known was there, and who, thanks to the show's success, we've come to enjoy on the red carpet. When we see Betty, we do so in two registers: first as the character ugly Betty, and second as the actress America Ferrera, whose approximation to normative standards of beauty is the look toward which the character will progress. The promise of an America-like beauty, a true Betty in the colloquial sense, is necessary for the character to function as a visual joke.[25] Though her ascendency to star status was not characterized by a focus on her spitfire beauty, Ferrera's "real" curves establish a seemingly egalitarian beauty ideal that lends the show authenticity, not just for incorporating diversity but also the "real"istic body of America, the actress who now becomes a cipher for women of color across the nation. Structured through a familiar telos, the audience anticipates Betty's

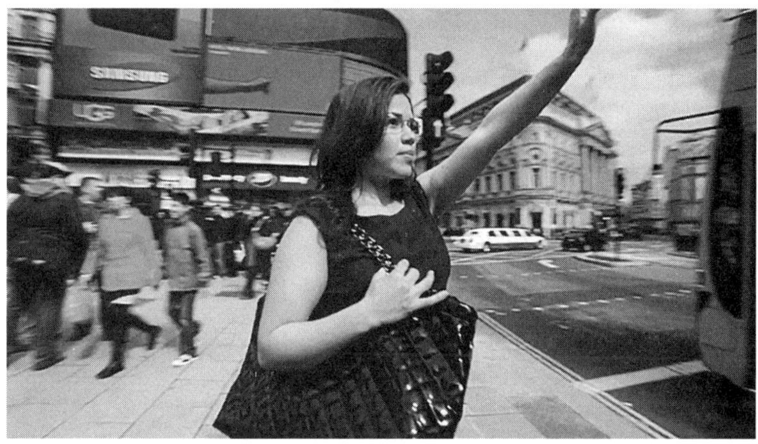

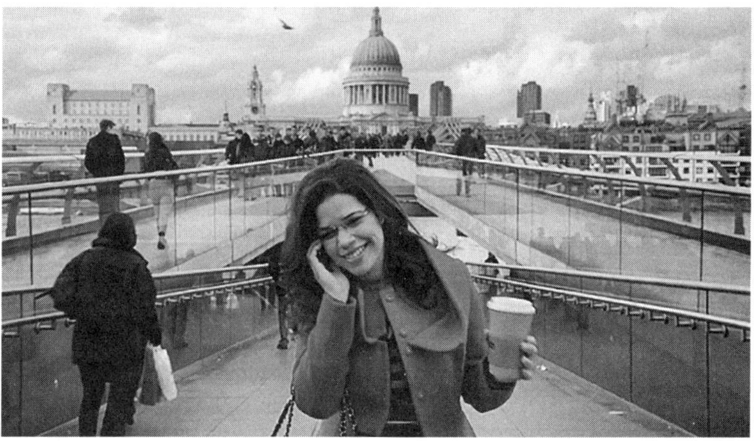

FIGURES 3.12 (TOP) AND 3.13 (BOTTOM) Betty in London. "Hello Goodbye," *Ugly Betty*, 2010.

makeover from the beginning. While the series leverages a soft critique on the beauty standards propagated by fashion magazines that require the severe disciplining of the female body, facilitated by Ferrera's real curves, the series has its most prominent opponent, Betty, convert and testify to its healing powers. Furthermore, outer beauty must be matched by inner beauty—taken largely to mean self-sacrifice to family, yes, but also predominantly to work and capital, the major publishing conglomerate that Betty comes to serve in her devotion to Daniel and the Meade family, skills she significantly applies to a global venture. While Betty leaves *Mode* for the type of journalism she always hoped to do (into which we get little insight),

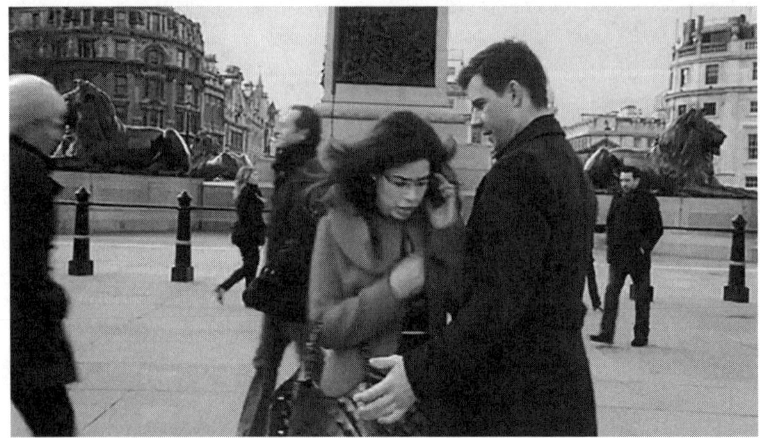

FIGURE 3.14 Betty bumps into Daniel. "Hello Goodbye," *Ugly Betty*, 2010.

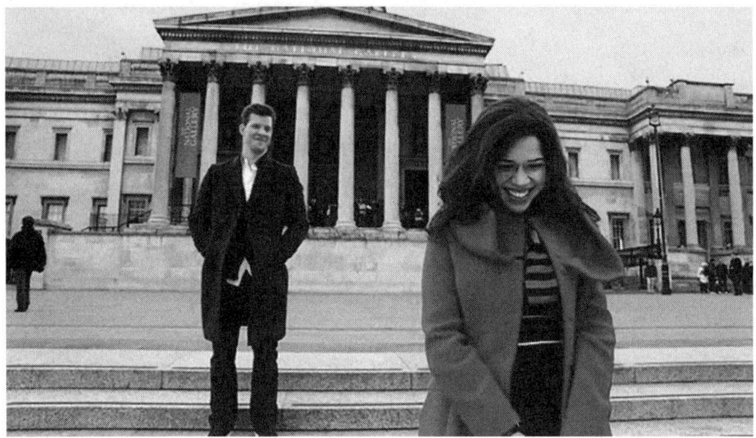

FIGURE 3.15 Betty walking away as Daniel looks on. "Hello Goodbye,"
Ugly Betty, 2010.

this career success comes as a result of her staunch work ethic in the service of capital and her indoctrination into normative standards of beauty,
for which she is additionally rewarded with the promise of a relationship
with her white superior. Indeed, this conclusion serves to illustrate the dynamic Melamed argues characterizes the neoliberal multiculturalism of
the 2000s, in which "official antiracism has attached to neoliberal sover-
eignty" such that "antiracist discourse has leapt from coding social policy
in order to endorse certain economic arrangements to being an attribute
of global capitalism itself."[26]

If, as Paredez claims, "the Latina body [is] often and variously celebrated both as the means through which hegemonic forces sought to occlude and thereby to ignore the political economic plights of Latina/os and as the site upon which Latina/o communities attempted to stage their presence within the nation," what does it now mean that this series, replete with Latina actresses, in the end promotes a moralistic brown Hollywood beauty?[27] Additionally, what does it mean that this occurs during a historic rise in minority representation in the political arena?[28] Following Rey Chow, we can read *Ugly Betty* as prescribing proper ethnic participation and acceptable mimetic minority beauty.

In *The Protestant Ethnic and the Spirit of Capitalism*, Chow argues that capitalism hails, disciplines, and rewards ethnic identities constituted by certain forms of labor. Racialized subjects, Chow argues, are hailed as "protestant ethnics" in the same dynamic that perpetuates their subordination since "resistance and protest, when understood historically, are part and parcel of the structure of capitalism; they are the reasons capitalism flourishes."[29] Betty's character is crafted in protest of the absence of rich positive roles for Latina actresses, and indeed the series leverages soft critiques of the fashion industry, superficiality, and narcissism, all of which are part of a larger culture industry that sustains racial hierarchies and material inequalities along racial lines. As her Guadalajara poncho so colorfully illustrates, Betty's "ugly" identity is linked to her ethnicity. Ethnic laborers, Chow argues, are theoretically produced "in terms of opposition and resistance" hailed by various apparatuses through what she calls "coercive mimeticism," which calls on racialized subjects to replicate internalized cultural stereotypes and in this way perform "proper" ethnicity.[30] This is precisely the role filled by *Ugly Betty*'s arc toward the beautiful America. In replicating a teleological makeover narrative, while also responding to the hail of coercive mimeticism in their ethnic Betty, *Ugly Betty* produces a mimetic standard for ethnic beauty.

Consider by contrast a failed makeover from the beginning of the series. In the episode "Queens for a Day," Betty is asked to dress up for a meeting with a photographer she has helped land. Betty turns to her sister, Hilda, whose working-class femininity serves as a contrast to the elite idealized professional femininities on display at *Mode*. Hilda takes Betty to a local salon to see Choli, who all but ignores the magazine cutout of the look Betty wants to emulate—neat French twist, understated makeup. Betty's finished look, her stylist declares, is "better." Betty's hair is heaped in dark

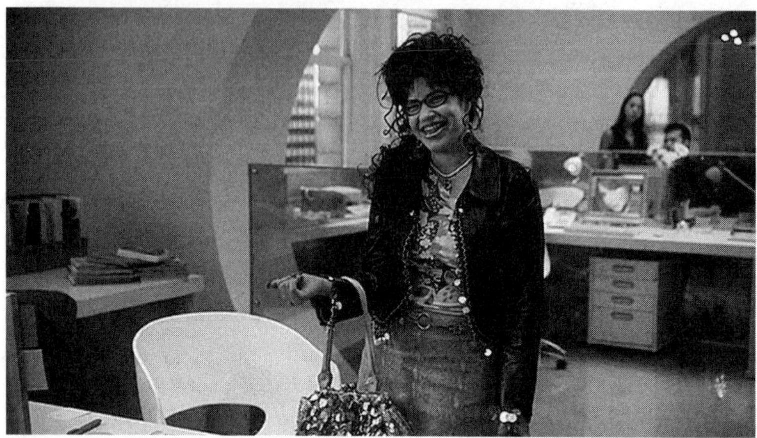

FIGURE 3.16 Failed makeover. "Queens for a Day," *Ugly Betty*, 2006.

curls on top of her head. Her newly waxed eyebrows are defined with brow liner, and her eyes dazzle behind her red frames lined with sparkling silver eyeliner, a sparkle that is echoed in the rhinestones on her long fuchsia nails. Her lipsticked smile ends in iridescent blush blossoms on the apples of her cheeks (figure 3.16). The finished look crafted by Choli earns Betty a round of applause from other patrons in the salon as well as trailing catcalls from construction workers on her way to the subway station to leave Queens for Manhattan. When she struts into the *Mode* offices on cherry peep-toes, however, she is met with laughter and mockery that reduce her to tears. Her look is an abject failure full of untapped femme potentiality.

Betty's Queens makeover, characterized by an indulgence in excess, replicates the pain and discomfort of the disciplinary demands on the body of beauty standards—Betty shrieks in pain when her eyebrows are waxed; giggles when her feet are buffed during a pedicure; contorts from a cough and gags as her hair is set with copious amounts of hairspray. The scene suggests that working-class racialized feminine beauty standards are just as painful as white normative ones, albeit withstood by Betty with little discipline. The results, however, are quite different, allowing us to see classbound conflicting and contradictory beauty standards. Unfortunately, the failed makeover is performed for comic effect, a counterpose to the proper mimesis that Betty accomplishes at the series's end that in fact resembles the magazine cutout that Choli disregarded with a flourish. Despite being surrounded by high-femme figures who perform an alternate working-class and distinctly women of color self-fashioning, the series does not, at least through Betty, explore the political possibilities this mode opens up. For those possibilities I turn instead to Nao Bustamante, whose failed performance of beauty, in *America, the Beautiful*, is called forth by Betty's abject failure.

Abject Betty

Bustamante's *America, the Beautiful* is a self-described "body narrative," a "tragic comedy that takes the viewer on a bizarre circus-like adventure of ladder climbing and breath-holding tension."[31] Performed between 1995 and 1998 (and again in 2002 for the Hemispheric Institute) in front of live audiences across a variety of venues, from the proscenium stage to festival floors, the critical gestures of the performance are best understood in relation to the political environment against which it was created.[32] As backdrop for Bustamante's *America, the Beautiful*, I'd like to note a few salient signposts that together deliver contradictory messaging about Latino national inclusion within Bustamante's home state, California, in the 1990s. The year 1992 commemorated the quincentennial anniversary of Columbus's incursion into the Americas. In an interview with José Esteban Muñoz, Bustamante reports, "It seemed like all these grants were being given to artists of color" specifically "to make work about [the quincentennial] and it seemed like there was this intense pressure to make this work."[33] Bustamante's initial response to this institutional incitement, as she shares with Muñoz, was telling a friend that she would "just wear [her] strap on burrito," recognizing that she was being invited to perform her minoritized identity in a particularly protesting way in order to establish multicultural critique as a necessary part of national narratives. In response to the hail, Bustamante wanted to poke fun at "la raza," "hardcore feminist theory," and "ritual performance art," developing the sentiment into the performance *Indigurrito*.[34] Multicultural celebration and an invitation to be a part of national narratives was paired with legislative xenophobia, most famously in the triptych of California Propositions 187 (1994), 209 (1996), and 227 (1998), which restricted access to public services by undocumented immigrants including public schools for undocumented children; ended affirmative action in California; and ended bilingual education in California, respectively.[35] *America, the Beautiful* reflects on this seemingly contradictory dynamic, a dynamic useful for us to consider in the contemporary moment in answer to what abjection might lend as strategy for critique and imagining alternatives to neoliberal incorporation and nativist attacks. I turn to this performance, visually propelled by the paths not taken in *Ugly Betty* but also as a conduit to set up and return us to the vignette with which I opened this chapter.

In one iteration of the almost hour-long performance, Bustamante first walks across the stage in black pedestrian clothing, indistinguishable from the stagehands. She adjusts the needle on an old record player, which sings out a distorted version of the patriotic "America, the Beautiful," after which her piece is named. A stagehand brings out a small step stool, placing it next to the standing record player while Bustamante carries out an old cosmetic suitcase. She places it on the floor and changes the record to a spoken motivational on the relationship between the spiritual and physical body. She nods her head in agreement as she walks a small circle on the stage, crossing herself at the mention of Jesus Christ, before walking upstage right, where she begins to undress—shoes, pants, and underwear in one tug, followed by socks and sweatshirt. She holds the sweatshirt over her pubis as fleshy legs carry her toward the audience, and nods her head in agreement as her mouth labors to form the words we are hearing from the record player—"Your body is a temple." Back upstage right, she removes her shirt and bra. Holding hands over voluptuous breasts, she walks down center stage, sits on her step stool, opens her suitcase, and pulls out a toilet seat cover through which she pushes her head, still repeating and nodding in assent with the male speaker on the record player. With this last prop, Bustamante cues us in on the complex interplay of disciplining body rituals and morality, some of which—in her upcoming hyperbolic performance inclusive of the act of vomiting—activate base bodily functions that might require a toilet.

As in most of her performances, Bustamante's bodily presence is inescapable. Her hair is cropped, chin length, dyed blonde with grown-out dark roots. She is a woman of abundant flesh—arms, breasts, thighs, legs—her stomach and buttocks dimpled. The two moments of demureness during her disrobing—when she conceals her pubic area and then her breasts—draw attention to their matter-of-fact exposure throughout the performance. The body-altering ritual that constitutes the next section of Bustamante's performance is accompanied by music steeped in ideologies of feminine sacrifice, discipline, and the promise of reward. When a warm tenor croons, "Love is a many-splendored thing," Bustamante begins to curl her lashes—holding each set trapped within a metal curler with eyes wide open—an image that recalls Salvador Dalí's iconic bulging gaze. She

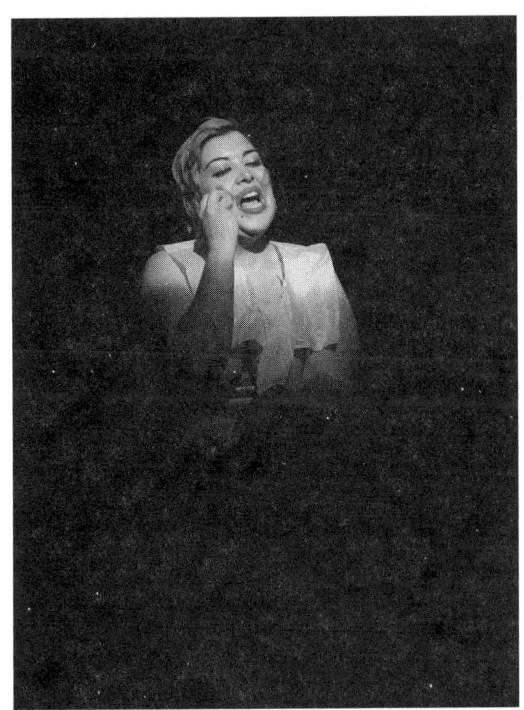

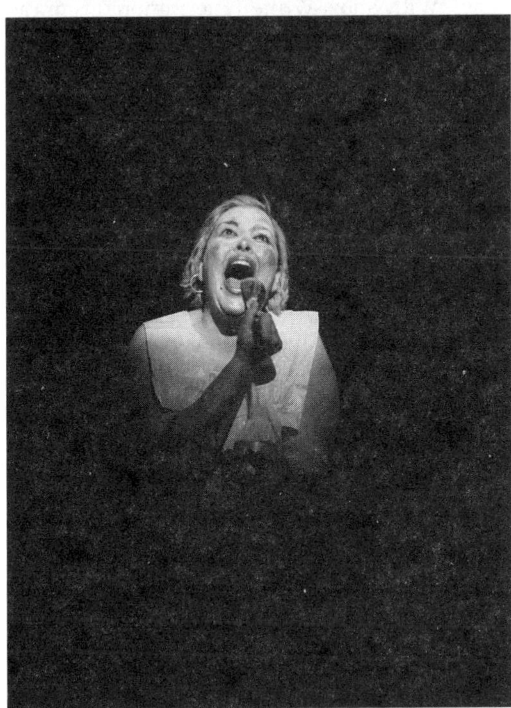

FIGURES 3.17 (TOP) AND 3.18 (BOTTOM) Nao Bustamante, *America, the Beautiful*, 1995–1998, 2002. Photograph by Lorle Novak. Courtesy of the artist.

next applies lipstick in fluid ovals, well beyond the border of her lips, past the corner of her mouth and, as the music crescendos, up to create crimson cheeks—a clown's smile and rouge (figure 3.17). She finishes her face with golden powder applied generously with a large brush, creating a glistening visage as she turns a pained, seductive gaze up to the spotlight (figure 3.18).

At the next crescendo in the score, Bustamante covers her short straight hair with a long blonde curly wig, tossing the artificial curls as she flips her head and adjusts the wig, once, twice. She sprays her curls with what appears to be the entire contents of a can of hairspray. Bustamante laughs, sobs, and gags—saliva falling from her mouth—and yet she continues spraying. Once the can is depleted, she adjusts the wig until her hair is big, blonde, "beautiful." Satisfied with her facial reconfiguration, Bustamante's character places a cigarette in the corner of her mouth but fails to light it, instead licking the lighter. The presence of the lighter and the attempts to ignite it within such proximity of the flammable cloud that still surrounds her now-drenched wig is the first of many moments during the performance when audience members might fear for the performer's safety. With her face set, the performer moves on to her body, cued by the sounds of a new recording: "He was so romantic, I could not resist. . . . Some day my prince will come." With Snow White's motivational soprano tremolo for accompaniment, Bustamante turns her attention to sculpting her body with the assistance of clear shipping tape. She begins by molding a tapered waist, wrapping the roll of tape around herself as she spins slowly like the porcelain figure of a music box. As she wraps, her breasts are pushed up and out. They achieve the torpedo shape of a miniature plastic feminine icon, Mattel's Barbie.[36] She sends the roll from around her waist down the triangle of her pubis to wrap and therein slim her thighs. A brief struggle with the roll of tape as she transitions between each leg gives way to two tapered stems. At this point in the performance, she is lit only by a red stage light positioned below and in front of her, creating a dramatic silhouette on the curtained wall behind her—a silhouette whose slimming the spectator gets to experience as Bustamante entraps her body in adhesive shapewear. So attired, Bustamante performs a series of tricks. We are alerted to the specialized effort of her deeds in part by the music (first the staccato signature song of Carmen Miranda's "Mamãe eu quero" on piano, and then Johann Strauss's "The Blue Danube Waltz") and Bustamante's own choreographed gestures, which invite applause from the audience after each feat of feminine discipline: walking in her modified body (!), putting on white platform heels (while standing on the step stool!), and finally performing terrifying feats of balance and grace on a tall ladder positioned right behind the artist.

With the addition of long white gloves, Bustamante is ready for an elegant display of her talent. She climbs up the ladder, coordinating her ascent of each rung to the cadence of Strauss's waltz. She smiles coyly at the audience as she kicks her heel back with bent knee, mimicking the pizzicato that closes each musical stanza. She struggles to balance herself between rungs, striking poses that hybridize the movement vocabulary of gymnasts and pole dancers, occasionally pausing to take breaths, assure the audience she's fine, appreciate the music, smoke a cigarette, or put on a shadow puppet show (plates 5–7). Each pose reveals the precarity of her body, the risk involved in movement always constrained by the demands of hegemonic beauty, which Bustamante has embodied to the point of clownish excess. But unlike America Ferrera's Betty, Bustamante's abject Betty does not move away from excess and the way it signals failure. Rather, she moves toward it. Bustamante's is not a genuine makeover but a pointed parody achieved through the extreme embodiment of literalized beauty guidelines. As her flesh spills from its constraints, Bustamante reveals a self that, pretransformation, is so abject it cannot be properly modified to the norm.

When she descends the ladder, Bustamante's character trembles from the strain of her performance and bows with a slight nod and outstretched arms (figure 3.19). Amid the applause, with a wide smile plastered on her face, Bustamante performs moments of false humility, shaking her head and dismissing the applause with a flick of the wrist, a gesture that indeed spurs that which it is rejecting (figure 3.20). She is tossed a bouquet of roses from stage right that she briefly holds to her chest before distributing all but one among a still-cheering audience. She invites continued applause even as she signals her performance is complete. When the applause eventually stops, the smile on Bustamante's face turns menacing, and she bites the head off the remaining rose. The temporary adulation of the applause seems not to have been enough. She paces, lashing herself with the remaining stems, her teeth stained with the juice of the rose petals she continues to chew as bits of masticated petals fall from her mouth (plate 8). She spits out the mass back onto the stems and smiles at the audience before ducking her torso behind a stage curtain to throw up. She has taken a symbol of the audience's appreciation and processed it through her body

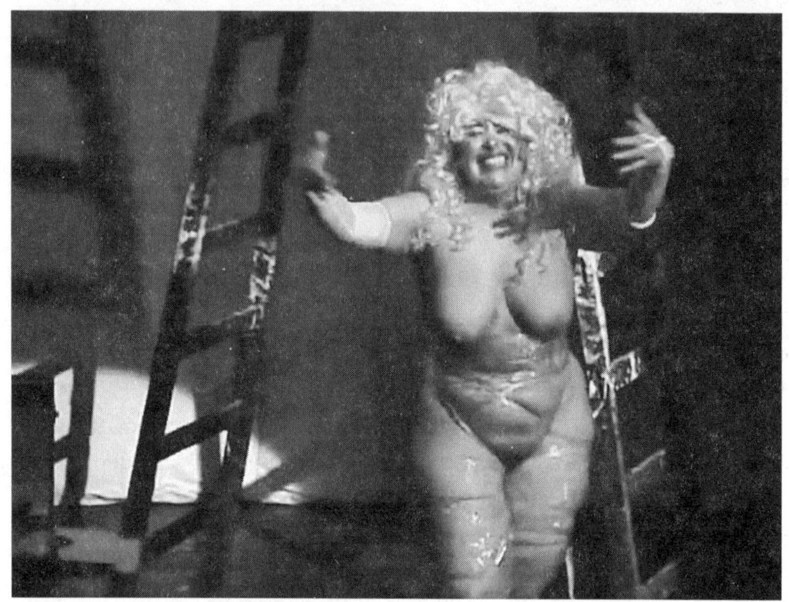

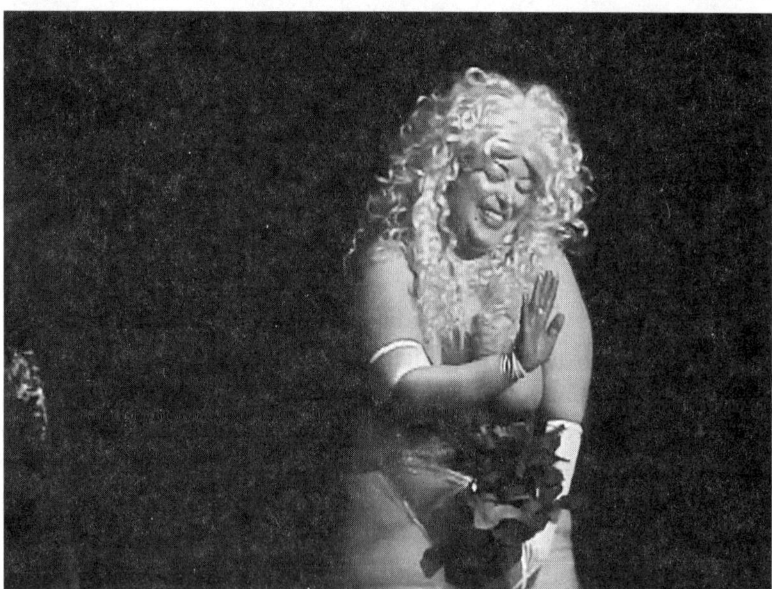

FIGURES 3.19 (TOP) AND 3.20 (BOTTOM) Nao Bustamante, *America, the Beautiful*, 1995–1998, 2002. Photograph by Lorie Novak. Courtesy of the artist.

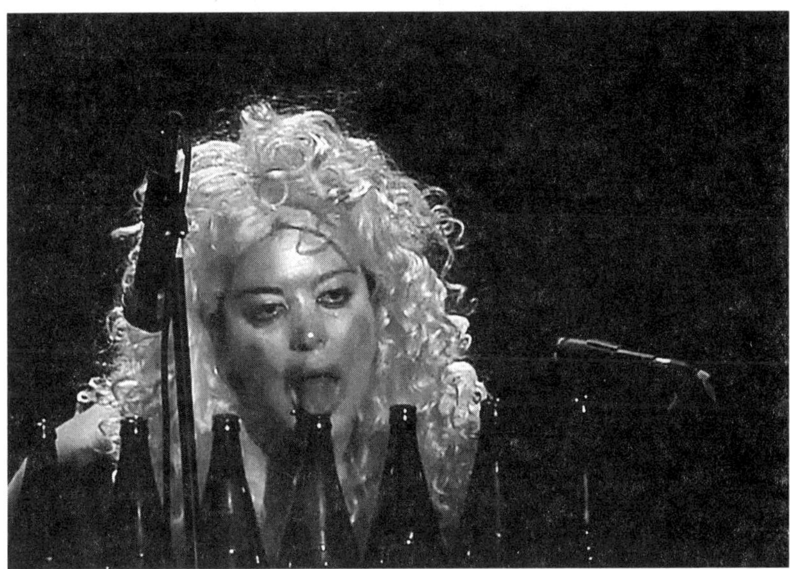

FIGURE 3.21 Nao Bustamante, *America, the Beautiful*, 1995–1998, 2002.
Photograph by Lorie Novak. Courtesy of the artist.

to produce vomit. As self-inflicted malady, Bustamante's regurgitated applause literally rejects the praise her character had found insufficient.

She returns to stage to change the record (Chuck Berry sings, "Maybelline, why can't you be true") as the lights dim to almost black. Bustamante teeters as a long, narrow table is brought out, on which she places a row of glass bottles. Having failed to elicit the desired effect—or perhaps affect—from the audience, for the final section of her performance, Bustamante exhibits another of her character's talents: she performs an off-key rendition of "America, the Beautiful" by blowing on bottles filled with varying amounts of water. She punctuates stanzas with finger cymbals and a rhythmic stomp of her heel, sometimes stopping in between hollow notes to lick or deep-throat the bottle she is blowing (figure 3.21). She then places her hand over her heart, gazes up to and beyond the spotlight, and mouths "I love you" as the lights fade with the blow of her kiss. Only a halo of curls is illuminated before the stage goes black.

As a whole, the piece makes a mockery of the disciplinary techniques for beautifying the body and the decorum of femininity. It renders these necessary performatives to incite the approval of spectators that will never satisfy the abject subject against and through whom a standard is formed. The very desire for approval pushes Bustamante's character toward a purposeful abjection. When read through the specificity of Bustamante's body, a body that Muñoz has described as "an affective beacon" that "illuminates a particular predicament around agency within the social: a feeling queer, a feeling brown, that is both about belonging and the failure to belong," the performance is an abject reflection on minority inclusion.[37] The techniques for disciplining the body that Bustamante's character follows will presumably grant her acceptance, inclusion as part of a society that favors blonde women with tapered waists. And while the audience claps, Bustamante's character is displeased with their acceptance of her. Bustamante's transformation, then, is one that critiques the terms of acceptance and inclusion. The applause is never enough given the labor spent in a makeover that hasn't quite made her over, but shows her attempts to do so. By the end, her character seems to find peace only after an embrace of her abject status—she dances suggestively, drinks from the glass bottle in her hand (possibly holding just water, but her slurred performance implies it might contain alcohol), and desecrates a patriotic enunciation with queer nonhuman fellatio. In doing so she makes evident the hypocrisy of a beautiful America that requires a certain performance for inclusion—a performance that in part encapsulates the exhibition and not elimination of her difference and the ways it attempts to approximate but never is the norm. (We are always aware of the wig and the tape, for example.) Though the piece began with the patriotic anthem after which it is named, the last section's irreverent rendition of the song transposes the disciplining of the female body to the national body, teasing out the ways beauty, morality, and nation building are conjoined but also the ways minority inclusion is part of the mythos of America's beauty.

In Myra Mendible's edited volume *From Bananas to Buttocks*, she suggests that "[in] today's global economy, the Latina body figures as a kind of negotiable currency [that] can help sell America's new multicultural image while reaffirming its most enduring myths [. . .] affirming the nation's self-image as a meritocracy with opportunity and products for all."[38] Bustamante and the character she crafts in *America, the Beautiful* refuse to be that body at a moment of incredible hostility toward the growing Latino demographic. Through "moments of failure, theatrical failure, that are built in," Bustamante reveals that the constitution of a beautiful America exists through the exclusion of certain subjects but also critiques the pathetic desire for inclusion in this system.[39]

I cite this early performance in order to frame Bustamante's appearance on Bravo's *Work of Art: The Next Great Artist,* an appearance we might read as a performance of a purposefully abject refusal of coercive mimeticism and an embrace of failure and disassociation. Again, the series premiered just months after the final *Ugly Betty* episodes. The political arena was characterized by seemingly contradictory messaging on the incorporation of people of color: halfway through President Barack Obama's first presidential term, just a little over a year after Supreme Court justice Sotomayor's confirmation but also amid an unparalleled surge in anti-immigrant legislation that recalled the California tryptich against which Bustamante created *America, the Beautiful.* Legislative efforts were galvanized by Arizona's SB 1070, largely regarded as one of the toughest anti-immigrant laws. Among its provisions, SB 1070 required that individuals carry immigration documents at all times, at risk of being charged with a misdemeanor, and gave the police broad power to detain anyone they suspected of being undocumented.[40] Arizona's SB 1070 served as model for Alabama's HB 56 and similar laws in Indiana, Georgia, South Carolina, and Utah.[41] As in *America, the Beautiful,* Bustamante's performance here is one that deploys abjection to critique but also to illuminate potential alternate approaches to minoritized belonging. In that earlier performance, popular genres (circus/pageant) were invoked with mimicking gestures. Here she infiltrates the telesphere as what Jennifer Doyle has called an "[agent] of interference," in a site where proper Latina mimetic comportment had only recently been spectacularly performed, as described above, by the beautiful America Ferrera.[42]

Work of Art episodes are divided into five distinct sections interspersed with confessional vignettes in which the artist participants directly address the camera and scenes of them beginning or ending their day at their shared living spaces. During the first structured scene, the host, China Chow, art scene regular from a family of collectors, introduces the participants to the week's challenge with the help of a guest artist/expert who will then serve as that episode's guest judge. The participants are then given a predetermined amount of money to purchase supplies at Utrecht Art Supplies, a sponsor of the show. After the artists have purchased the material they need, they begin the process of creating a work of art in a shared work space where their appointed mentor, auctioneer Simon de Pury, probes gently with questions on the direction of the participants' work and provides suggestions when he fears for the shapes their pieces are taking. The artists then exhibit their answer to that episode's challenge in an open gallery, where we see an invited public and the show's judges—Bill Powers (gallery owner), Jeanne Greenberg Rohatyn (curator, gallery owner), and Jerry Saltz (art critic for *New York Magazine*)—reacting to the participants' work. The final section consists of a critique session with those artists the judges consider the top three and bottom three for the challenge, who are dramatically selected and dismissed before a winner is chosen, and the artist who created the weakest piece is sent home. That week's loser gives a closing monologue in the final scene.

For the episode under consideration, the guest artist and judge is Andres Serrano, most known for his *Piss Christ* (1987) and the role it played in the culture wars of the late 1980s and early 1990s, characterized by political campaigns to defund controversial art.[43] After a closed-gallery tour of Serrano's exhibit at Phillips de Pury, Simon de Pury's gallery, Serrano shares that he likes to "make pieces that make people feel something. Any reaction is better than indifference." That "something" gets transposed into the episode's challenge as presented by China Chow: to "create a shocking piece of art." Given Bustamante's performance history, the challenge seems crafted for her success. The majority of her fellow participants resorted to making sexually explicit work. Bustamante, on the other hand, shared, "In relationship to art, there's not that much that shocks me. . . . I'm going to do some type of performance but I have no idea what I'm going to make." Throughout, Bustamante gives voice to a procedural state of unknowing. She both knows and doesn't what the end result will be, a measured uncertainty that, for Bustamante, is part of performance as structured around audience participation.

In the shared studio, we see shots of Bustamante busy at work. Despite ample activity, the other participants can't seem to figure out what she's up to, an ambiguity Bustamante doesn't aim to clarify. "I've pretty much been freaking out all day," she tells us, "because I'm not sure where the work is going to settle but I know that I want to create a housing for my character. . . . I'm thinking about the structure as a kind of primitive space, something that was designed almost by an insect or an animal." Bustamante is at work creating an environment for the performance that will be her piece, though she says very little about the character. During de Pury's studio visit, the following exchange occurs:

DE PURY: Tell me what you're, um, up to.

BUSTAMANTE: [laughs] Well, I'm not even sure myself. I'm in the
process of sort of going into outer space and coming back with some
information. It's gonna be pretty wacky.

She then walks him over to the structure she has been working on.

BUSTAMANTE: So my two positions will be either sitting inside or
mingling with the crowd. So it's not going to be a very theatrical
performance.

DE PURY: It's very difficult to give you any advice because whatever you
are doing now is so diametrically opposed from what will come out
tomorrow.

BUSTAMANTE: Yes, I know. Hopefully I'll be able to catch up with my process in studio so it'll make more sense, eventually.

DE PURY: Again, but since you are a performance artist, I trust that you
will be able to surprise us and provoke us with your performance.

Bustamante is illegible to both fellow participants and their assigned mentor, a man whose claim to art world knowledge comes from his role selling discrete works of art, and for whom performance art can present a
challenge. When de Pury says, "It's very difficult to give you any advice
because whatever you are doing now is so diametrically opposed from
what will come out tomorrow," he also acknowledges the challenge that a
performance presents for the very structure of the show. Indeed, we see
the ways the format relies on certain presumptions about the way art is
crafted and presented, and consequently dictates the ways it ought to be,
awarding those that play the game well. Bustamante's chosen genre—
performance—places her outside expected parameters such that, unlike
the works of her fellow participants, we know very little about hers and see
even less.

The camera struggles to capture Bustamante's contribution in a single
frame. Though perhaps technically capable, the camera fails to capture
the scope of a performance meant to occur over a period of time and principally through an engagement with a crafted environment and live audience. Additionally, Bustamante refuses to provide a legible and accessible
narrative on what she is constructing and why, providing only otherworldly
referents—the "insect or animal" world and "Mars." Our understanding of
the piece through *Work of Art*, then, is poor. What we see is a figure whose

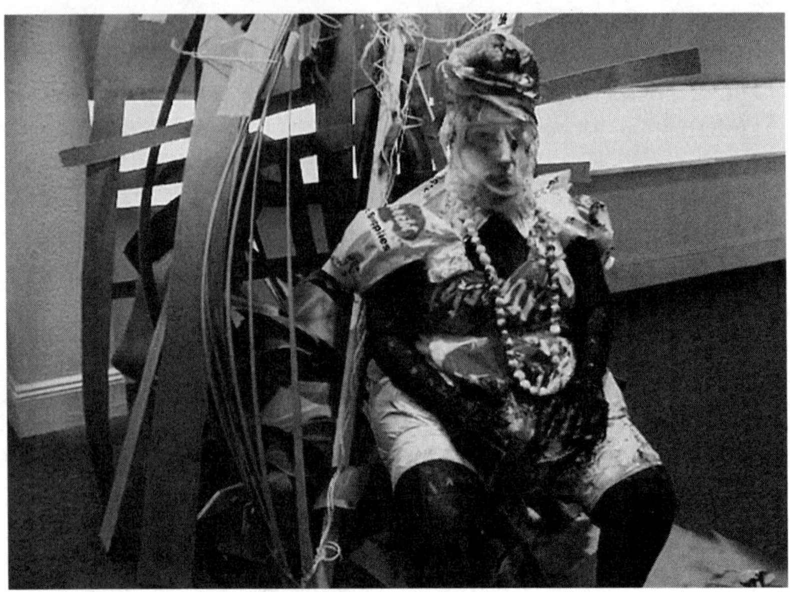

FIGURE 3.22 Nao Bustamante, *Barely Standing*, 2010. "A Shock to the System," *Work of Art*, 2010.

limbs are garbed in skin-tight black sheen, from her neck down her body across limbs and digits. On top of this she wears a garment seemingly constructed entirely from plastic Utrecht bags. They wrap her thighs, creating plastic bloomers, come over her torso and out to create puffed cap sleeves, then around her neck and up over her face and head. An ample hole over her face permits her to breathe, while the black bodysuit glistens through an opening on her chest. Around her neck Bustamante wears a necklace of yellow felt beads, matched by a yellow thread around her waist that holds in place a plastic flower out of whose center seeps a brown substance.[44] On the tops of her feet she has taped citrus fruit and on the opposite extremity her plastic bag headpiece is adorned with a piece of kelly-green latex nested within a large sponge. We see Bustamante sit in her "hut"—a pyramidal shredded cardboard construction inside of which strips of black and green paper are piled high. The edifice takes up the back half of a green paper rectangle whose front corner is painted with a brown and yellow nest. The apex of the structure is decorated with bright blue tassels (figure 3.22).

The camera captures Bustamante only as she sits on a small stool in front of her structure, one hand under her chin and the other resting on

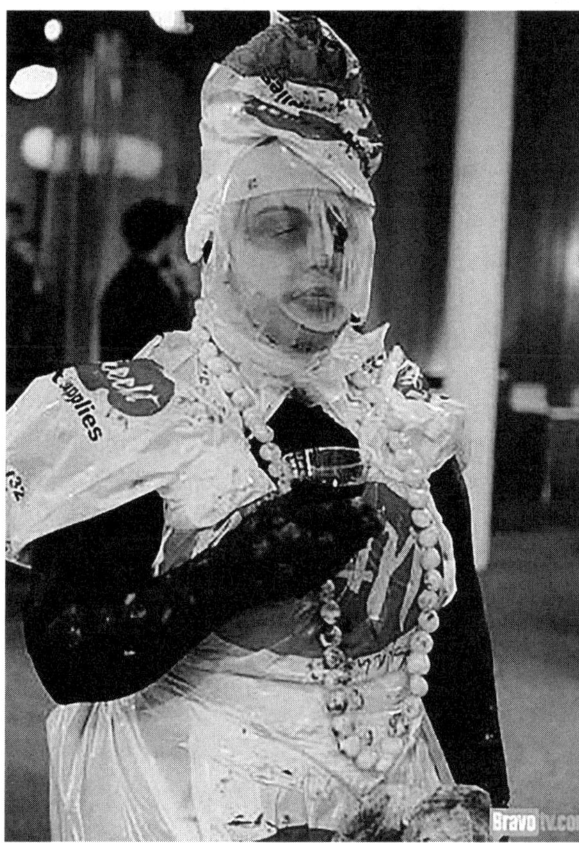

FIGURE 3.23
Nao Bustamante,
Barely Standing,
2010, outtake.
"A Shock to the
System," *Work
of Art*, 2010.

her cheek. We see her massage the brown substance oozing out of the plastic flower at her groin. In voice-over, we hear Bustamante say, "I hadn't really thought about my piece through to the point where I was going to become kind of this scatological mess. I think I was working towards shocking myself." Interestingly, we see as much of the judges' response to the performance as we see of the performance itself. China Chow leans in and says to Andres Serrano, "I think that's a bag of shit." Serrano's unfazed response: "I don't smell anything." What we don't see during the episode, which a few event photographs capture, is Bustamante walking around the gallery, wine in hand, mingling with art viewers (figure 3.23).

For the critique section of the series, the judges select Bustamante as one of the most disappointing participants of the challenge. When the group discusses Bustamante's piece, they are visibly distraught, shaking their heads, gesticulating aggressively. If not shocked, they are at least disturbed. Chow, in an almost mocking tone, invites Bustamante to *"please explain what we're looking at."* At this point, Bustamante is still in costume, though the plastic that was over her face has been torn off, spreading the brown residue from her anus flower in a fingerprint pattern around her face and shoulders.

> **BUSTAMANTE:** I was trying to get to this place of building almost like an animal would build.
>
> **BILL POWERS (JUDGE):** But why were you rubbing yourself?
>
> **BUSTAMANTE:** I wasn't rubbing myself, I was rubbing this [gestures to and strokes her flower].
>
> **JEANNE GREENBERG ROHATYN (JUDGE):** Is that supposed to be excrement?
>
> **BUSTAMANTE:** It wasn't supposed to be excrement but I think in the end it did read as excrement.
>
> **JERRY SALTZ (JUDGE):** So you don't really know what this piece is—we don't know what the piece is—and it comes off therefore, as incredibly familiar kind of adolescent mixed with shock-your-grandmother performance art.

The judges seem most distraught about the unknowable, and Bustamante refuses to narrate a palatable, consumable practice that is legible to the judgment of taste based on standards of knowable beauty, even where the judge is looking to be shocked.[45] That she herself seems to be coming to understand the performance as she discusses it with her judges runs counter to the idea of the artist as genius with a methodical reason for producing work. Bustamamte's practice is an abject one that immediately renders the judges uneasy, and they respond by vitriolically shaking their heads at her as if she were a teenager who should know better.[46] The guest judge, artist Andres Serrano, has a very different take on the piece. "For me," he says, "this is one of the more interesting pieces because it's disturbing. It made me think of homeless people, the people we don't want to look at, and especially when we were talking about your work in front of you like you didn't exist, that also is uncomfortable." Serrano pays keen attention to both Bustamante's presence (in costume) and the terms on which the piece was constructed and received. He is quick to note the ways the work calls forth the abject realm of homelessness and undesirable bodies, unpleasantries this version of the art world would sooner eliminate from their competition. I imagine the performance as bringing that level of discomfort Serrano names to the entire gallery as Bustamante, in costume, mingled with gallery attendants.

When considered alongside the challenge winner, we can see that part of the judges' frustration stems from Bustamante's lack of aesthetic accessibility in addition to the lack of legible identitarian referent in both the crafting of her work and her character on the show. Put another way, Bustamante's refusal to succumb to the pressures of coercive mimeticism results in an abject aesthetic strategy that serves as an affront to the premise of the show, structured through the Kantian tradition of judgment, taste, and beauty, while also showing how these require subjects that respond to institutional identitarian hails. The two finalists whose work most approximated a "true work of art" crafted projects that illustrate the effects of racism and explore female sexuality and the male gaze, respectively (figures 3.24 and 3.25). Abdi Farah's *I.E.D.* (Improvised Explosive Device), which would go on to win the challenge, was presented to the judges with a well-rehearsed explanation of what they were looking at:

"My piece is titled *I.E.D.* So many of our cities are so disenfranchised, stricken by poverty, family structures are destroyed and thusly kids grow up as these improvised explosive devices. So I have these three black male portraits and I'm depicting them as bombs." The work is accessible on multiple registers; aesthetically, it is representational and illustrative of the narrative he provided. Additionally, he announces the piece's immediate import as evidenced by its political content—race, class, family values, specifically through the pathological black family. He has crafted a piece that reflects on social injustice and builds a visual metaphor for contemplation that facilitates a disinterested engagement for the judges in the Kantian tradition.

It is unclear to me precisely where the shock in Farah's piece lies. His facile narrative through portraits of black men as ticking time bombs, however, seems to strike the judges as just the right kind of shock for mass-media consumption. During their critique of Farah's piece, the judges comment:

SALTZ: They have a kind of, if not shock, at least magnetic power.

POWERS: There's a quieter shock to this. It wasn't one after it's already exploded. It's the threat of imminent violence that's connected to the piece.

CHOW: It just has lots of different layers and the more that I hear about it the more I . . . *I'm enjoying it.* [emphasis added]

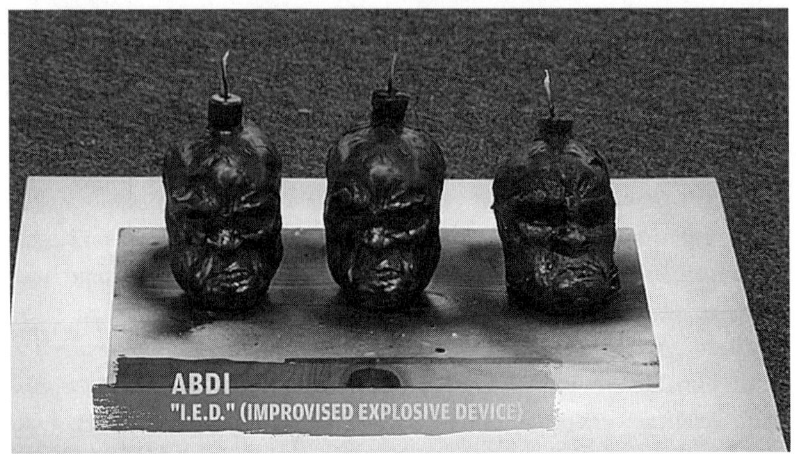

FIGURE 3.24 Abdi Farah, *I.E.D. (Improvised Explosive Device)*. "A Shock to the System," *Work of Art*, 2010.

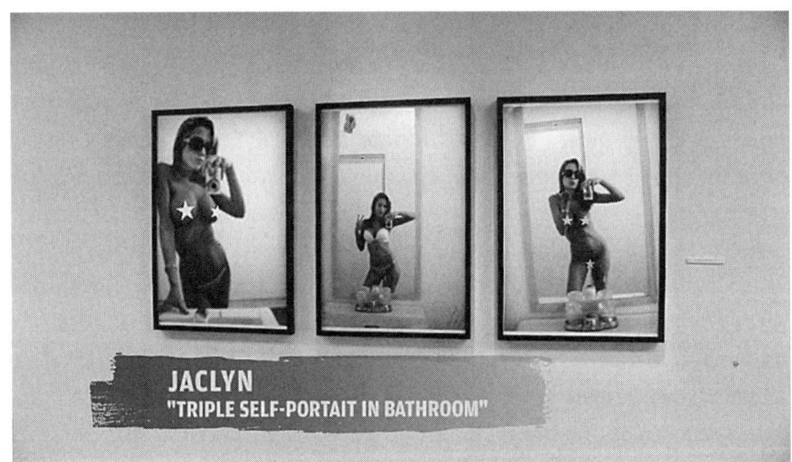

FIGURE 3.25 Jaclyn Santos, *Triple Self Portrait in Bathroom*. "A Shock to the System," *Work of Art*, 2010.

The judges are explicitly intrigued by the promise of threat to the point of gleeful enjoyment—a response Chow shares with Farah as she compliments him through a broad grin. The work is squarely within the terms of disinterested Kantian enjoyment of art, here linked to the anticipation of black men performing within racialized codes of comportment, that is, explosive physical violence. The reasons why ("disenfranchised, stricken by poverty, family structures are destroyed") seem almost irrelevant given the tantalizing threat (is this shock?) that they will explode. Farah's piece provides a safe way for the spectator to engage in ghetto gazing, allowing proximity to a theoretical racialized risk.

After the critique with the artists, the judges withdraw to decide the best and worst among them and select a winner of the challenge. Their conversation on Farah and Bustamante follows:

> **SALTZ:** Abdi's was one of the more successful pieces I thought, because it pulled you in in a kind of a weird mysterious way.
>
> **ROHATYN:** The formal qualities of his heads, it's kind of ritualistic candle art, really pushed it through. . . .
>
> **CHOW:** What did we think about Nao's performance art?
>
> **SERRANO:** It was the weirdest thing I saw here tonight.
>
> **ROHATYN:** [shaking her head] She's a performance artist! This is her trade and she couldn't come up with an explanation for this work?

Farah's "weird mysterious" piece is alluring with its racialized "ritualistic" elements, in addition to its promise of black violence—a promise that haunts the presence of the young black artist and against which his success is measured. Bustamante is explicitly called out for not being able to provide a narrative of her work, for truly shocking the judges and disturbing their disinterested contemplation with an excess of negative affect. Awarding Farah is to award the proper incorporation of special interests (e.g., race, class, gender) into aesthetic practice without disrupting contemplative spectatorship. Indeed, Farah models proper "protesting ethnic" comportment, even as his presence speaks to the viability of the bootstrap model for success and art as a pathway for escape. He presents a recognizable critique of capitalism that not only postulates a possible, plausible resolution—repair inner-city conditions and racism—but also is performing the remediation even as it performs the critique because the artist is living proof of the success of incorporative multiculturalism. This moment in *Work of Art* reveals the ways in which minoritized subjects are expected to perform in order to be judged as successful, even exemplary, participants of a multicultural society. It is no surprise, then, that Farah goes on to win the entire competition.

Of her own piece, Bustamante has said, "The piece was called *Barely Standing*. I think there was a deep sadness expressed in the work and I think that did come through for the viewers in the gallery. I also thought the work looked beautiful on TV. When I saw it, it looked so beautiful I thought I would scream."[47] Bustamante describes her work on an affective register as generated through an engagement with the gallery audience, an interaction we see little of during the show. When she says the piece looked beautiful, I, of course, think of the standard of beauty set by *America, the Beautiful*, where the beautiful serves the abject in critique of dominant standards of beauty and racialized comportment, here repurposed for a refusal of minority inclusion on neoliberal terms. When Bustamante is eliminated with the catchphrase, "Your work of art didn't work for us," I am struck by the use of the word "work," conveying not only that the piece didn't accomplish the desired aesthetic results for the challenge, but also that it failed to do the labor as a cultural product for a larger ideological apparatus, principally through Bustamante's refusal to be legible or accessible formally and along identitarian lines.

In her exit confessional monologue, Bustamante shares, "Failure is completely okay in the process of making art. We have to really push beyond our own boundaries and be able to fail. I often make work that is very fragile and very difficult." Bustamante's work failed to maintain the link between object and spectator and further to support the larger cultural apparatus where Kantian aesthetics meets neoliberal multiculturalism.[48] She is invested in the practice of pushing boundaries beyond the knowable, a queer abject aesthetic of which failure is an integral part.[49] In their recent *The Queer Art of Failure*, J. Halberstam offers that failure serves as "a way of refusing to acquiesce to dominant logics of power and discipline and as a form of critique. As a practice, failure recognizes that alternatives are embedded already in the dominant and that power is never total or consistent; indeed failure can exploit the unpredictability of ideology and its indeterminate qualities."[50] Bustamante's work engaged dominant forms and formats of representation and reproduction, and here interjects her critique into a major cultural apparatus: cable programming. As evidenced by Serrano's response, her work shows us how we might invoke projects of social justice affectively, provoking discomfort through abject nonidentitarian performance. Her use of abject aesthetic strategies to stir discomfort and expulsion challenges cultural institutions reliant on Kantian traditions, crystalized in Bravo's *Work of Art* and its judges, and refuses the identitarian labels of class and gender so carefully performed by her colleagues on the show. Instead she situates herself in the distinctly anti-identitarian abject realm of the animal, the insect, the faceless homeless, and the alien (Martian) with all its political dehumanizing implications.

While Ferrera's Betty lays out a popular culture transcript for proper Latina incorporation, easily transposed as an America-n rubric for the incorporation of gendered difference, Bustamante's abject Betties (both in *America, the Beautiful,* and on *Work of Art*) perform a refusal of this model. Bustamante instead offers us a mode of dissociation from neoliberal multiculturalism that allows, through the centering of affect, affiliation within the abject realm. This mode of critique and alternate group organization emerges from a refusal of legibility to the Kantian judge and therein a refusal of subjectivity as organized by this ideology. The figure of the genius-bearing artist at the core of Kantian aesthetics is refused as template, and with it a dynamic that prioritizes beauty, even the inner beauty of a palatably contestatory subject who ultimately does not change cultural structures but contributes labor to shoring up its expanding boundaries. Bustamante refuses that identity and subjectivity Chow argues capital has come to rely on, the consumable, protesting, mildly oppositional minority standard of America Ferrera's ugly Betty. She does not "work" for them.

CHAPTER 4

Arriving at Apostasy
Performative Testimonies
of Ambivalent Belonging

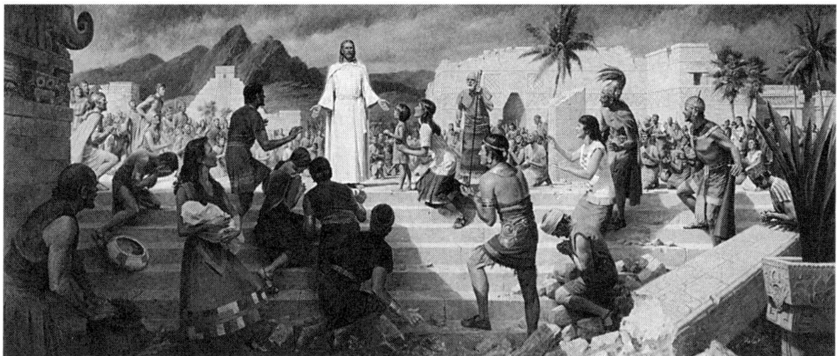

FIGURE 4.1. John Scott, *Jesus Christ Visits the Americas*, 1969. LDS Media Library.

A Divine Hailing

Eight illustrations lie within the covers of the two latest print publications of the Book of Mormon, the most sanctified text of the Church of Jesus Christ of Latter-Day Saints (LDS), whose followers are known as Mormons.[1] Depicting key figures and moments in the church's history, the images appear one after another within the first pages of the book, deeply saturated with color, in distinct contrast to the thin, black-and-white-text-filled pages. One of the most captivating images, *Jesus Christ Visits the Americas* (1969), by painter John Scott, presents a blond Christ atop a set of stairs (figure 4.1). Christ is attired in a white belted robe and cape, rendered in an incandescent glow popular in religious iconography. He stands at the

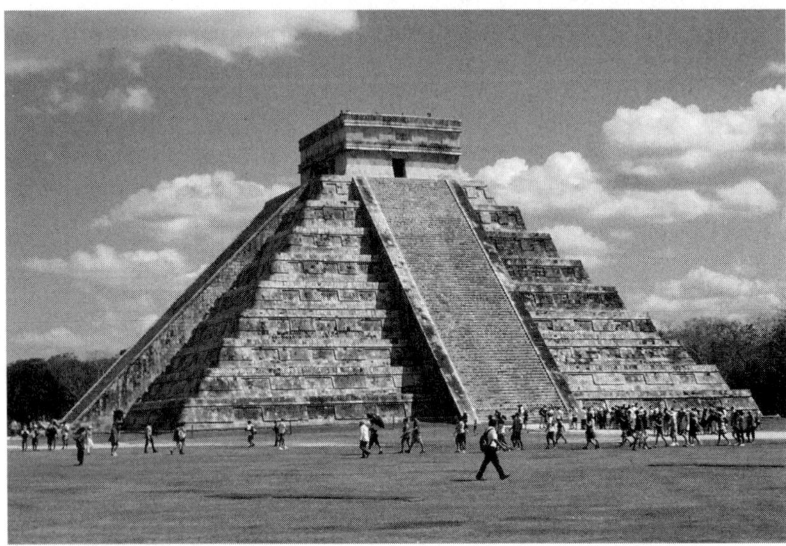

FIGURE 4.2 Temple of Kukulkán at Chichén Itzá.

apex of a pyramidal composition with arms outstretched gesturing down, triangularly, to congregants suspended in action toward kneeling. Christ's arms demarcate the active foreground of the painting. The background, in contrast, is relatively static, composed largely of supplicants propped on one knee, green sloping mountains, and—significantly—a square-top pyramid furrowed by a deep set of central stairs resembling the Mayan temple of Kukulkán at Chichén Itzá (figure 4.2).

This particular image enacts a powerful hailing, calling forth supplicants from among viewers of the painting who are made to linger on the page. The inclusion of images in the book signals the power of the visual and the importance of the role of aesthetics in religious experience, which indeed can propel an active engagement that we might think of as performative. The image illustrates the initial visit of Jesus Christ to the Americas captured in the Book of Mormon, marking a moment of revelation of both doctrine and Christ's role as savior. In *Jesus Christ Visits the Americas*, the enlightenment of the Americas' indigenous populations, performed through Christ's apparition, is captured representationally by the diagonally cast light that bisects the composition as well as the exhibition of Christ's stigmata. The painting also situates the event in a specific geographic location that equates the people of the Book of Mormon with the Maya of pre-Columbian Mexico. David Morgan and Sally Promey have argued that within religious practice, "images identify individuals as members of kinship networks, communities, or nations as well as religious denominations, traditions, or institutions. [. . . They help to] establish a *communitas*, incorporating a set of horizontal relations among individuals as well as a vertical communion with a reality greater than the self."[2] The focus of this chapter is arrived at through this image. It provides an opening out to the performative testimonial communities it hails, around which I expand an exploration of abjection.

A notable departure from the rest of this book thus far, these quotidian though ritualized performances are significant cultural products that exploit the relationship between the aesthetic, ascetic, and abjection of religious submission. I am interested here in the racialized communities we might recognize under the sign of Latino as hailed through an aesthetic engagement with the Book of Mormon and choice LDS teachings; their ambivalent belonging and contingent embrace of abjection, specifically through identification with the Book of Mormon's native Lamanites—those supplicants rendered in Scott's *Jesus Christ Visits the Americas*. As the painting's landscape evokes, the church's doctrinal and institutional foundation in the Americas directly hails those who trace their ancestry to the continent. Of special interest to my study are those Latinos for whom the ideology of mestizaje has instilled a claim to indigeneity.[3] In order to understand the parameters of Latino incorporation metonymically gestured at by the painting and its relationship to abjection, it is necessary to first briefly review the nature of the church's unique claim on the American continent.

The narrative of the Book of Mormon begins with a prophet, Lehi, and his journey out of Jerusalem with his family, including sons Nephi and Laman, and offers an account of their descendants. The Nephites were white, industrious, and God fearing, and built cities of great architectural splendor supported by an agricultural economy. The Lamanites, cursed with dark skin for their infidelities to God, were nomadic, war-making hunters. The Nephites, the Book of Mormon tells us, were overcome by their material success and turned away from God, making themselves susceptible to an attack from the Lamanites that resulted in their elimination.[4] At the Book of Mormon's end we are left with crumbling stately buildings on a continent populated by the victorious, iniquitous, dark Lamanites. Mormon, the last Nephite prophet and general of the Nephite army, recorded this history on gold plates and gave them to his son, Moroni, to hide from the Lamanites so that their future discovery would allow for the restoration of the gospel in the Americas. It is these plates that Joseph Smith claimed to find in 1827, buried in a hill near Rochester, New York, after personal revelation from the angel Moroni on how these plates should be excavated, translated, and shared with the world.[5]

Adoption of the Mormon faith asks Latino Latter-Day Saints to identify with the racialized abject figure of the Lamanite, marked by iniquity. They are taught that "whitening" follows righteousness made evident through testaments of faith—through conversion or performative proclamations of conviction—and foreshadows the second coming of Christ. As such, Latino LDS members play an integral role in the church and in heavenly plans for Christ's return. I am interested in what happens at the moment of identification with the abject figure before the turn toward promised whiteness. What does this identification facilitate? How do individual members mobilize this subject position within and beyond the organized church in the national political arena? What communitas is established textually, visually, and performatively?

I come to this material as a repentant member of this community. I am intimately aware of the way LDS church doctrine speaks to immigrant families and serves as a site for syncretic cultural affirmation not unlike the affirmation offered by Chicano nationalism through its mythology of Aztlán.[6] I attended a Southern California Spanish-speaking congregation a minimum of twice a week in my childhood, eventually building up to daily visits in my teenage years—attending seminary Monday through Friday, with service or social events on Saturday and Sunday services. The LDS church figured prominently in my personal understanding of Latinidad. I have no recollection of my first encounter with *Jesus Christ Visits the Americas* but rather remember it as having always been a part of my Chicano Mormon home, part of its ethnic architecture. Born into a newly converted household, my childhood memories are literally hung with portraits of Christ and Joseph Smith, or rather "José es-Smith," the LDS church's founding prophet. These were accompanied by Aztec calendars from the *panaderia* and popular reproductions of the Aztec princess Iztaccíhuatl and her warrior lover, Popocatépetl, as volcanoes (figure 4.3).

Representations of Aztec warriors blended seamlessly with those of Nephites and Lamanites, the warring tribes in the Book of Mormon, encountered in scripture text and illustrations but also in church animations, films, stickers, and coloring books. These were part of the visual culture of my youth that functioned as decorative performative presentation, what

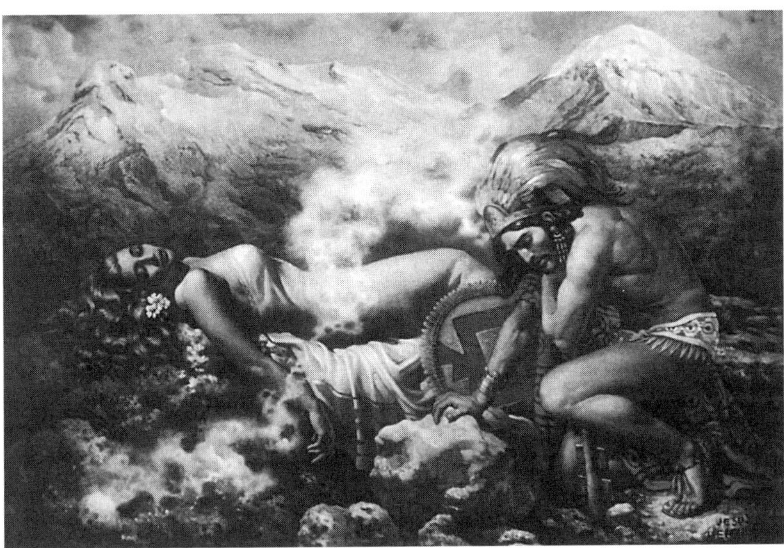

FIGURE 4.3 Postcard of *La Leyenda de los Volcanes*, by Jesus Helguera, 1940. Ken Brown Collection, 1993.

Jill Stevenson might call the dramaturgical set.[7] My father, a bishop during my teen years, taught our family and his congregation that we were direct descendants of the people in the Book of Mormon.[8] My uncle, also a bishop of his congregation, or ward, in Tijuana, Mexico, named two of his children Itzél (after an Aztec princess) and Abinadi (after a prophet in the Book of Mormon) in parallel gestures. Visual cues in the Book of Mormon, such as the inclusion of the stepped pyramid in *Jesus Christ Visits the Americas*, encouraged the association. I share this memory from my personal archive to note the contiguity of church doctrine with something akin to Chicano nationalism, as both share a transnational even pan–Latin American, appeal on the basis of indigenous belonging. As is developed below, it also affected political vision and demands within and beyond the church.

I must note the obvious: mine is not a disinterested engagement but a deeply personal exploration of the rich dynamics and contradictions of a pious Chicano Mormon upbringing, especially with regard to its deployment of an aesthetics of abjection as the basis for religious and ambivalent belonging. My own performative testimony, then, shadows my analysis, a testimony of eventual departure and apostasy, a willfully abject position that seeks to grow the kernel of abjection in the Lamanite identity—an elaboration of which closes this chapter and book. My decision to leave the church followed close scrutiny of its history and the ideologically embedded white heteropatriarchy I found difficult to countenance as an adult. Thus I struggle with the unlikeliness of faith and doctrine as a site of political possibility that challenges the dominant interpretations of the LDS church and its relation to racialized subjects. The work of feminist and Foucauldian scholars such as Marie Griffith, and her study of conservative evangelical women and their embrace and use of submission, models a way to complicate the dichotomy of "subjugation versus liberation with subtler formulations of individual and collective dissent."[9] Following this scholarship, instead of a simplistic dichotomy, I am interested in the ways Latino Mormons mobilize the abject Lamanite identity to negotiate the many vectors of power at work on and through them in the church and beyond. Below I weave together the critical inquiry at the heart of Latino studies—with its attention to power as structured by discourses of race and ethnicity—with the illumination provided by the performative, to give us an account of the politicized strategies of a growing and dynamic religious community as well as lived applications of abjection as an aesthetic strategy.

The LDS church has a history of strident criticism from outsiders who have resisted its specific family practices and violent colonial actions. Yet even as the LDS church displaced Native American communities and excluded black membership from certain ordinances, it still attracts a large number of its converts from nonwhite and disenfranchised populations, especially among immigrant communities.[10] As documented in the most recent available census, performed in 2010 but released in 2012, the LDS church is one of the fastest-growing denominations in the United States, with Latinos as the fastest-growing group within the community of converts.[11] The domestic congregation accounts for a little over a third of its 14 million members worldwide, numbering approximately 5.5 million (including communities of color). There are a noteworthy 2 million members in Latin America, half of these from Mexico, whose movement across national borders reveals the challenges of truths arrived at through statistics.[12] Though, as I argue, whiteness is part of what constitutes the doctrinal logic of the church, through strategic assimilative moves often declared as divine directives and the resultant tenets of strong patriarchal nuclear families, matrimonial sanctity, and staunch individualism, the modern LDS church serves as an archetype of American middle-class values. These changes have led W. Paul Reeve to describe Mormons as moving along a trajectory from "not securely white in the nineteenth century to too white by the twenty-first."[13]

In what follows I focus on the performative testimonies of Latino LDS, their citation of Lamanite heritage, and the affective oscillation between an embrace of abjection and cultural nationalist celebration as they navigate their seemingly contradictory status within the church: they are of unique spiritual import as well as abject subjects within its hierarchy. A focus on testimony allows me to center the aesthetic sensuousness of religious experience as testimonies often narrate the individual's sublime encounter with the divine. I do so to expand, beyond the realm of the cultural sector, what has thus far been a consideration of the politics of an aesthetic of abjection. My three previous chapters read the performative production of artists and actors in fine art and popular media spaces to demonstrate the ways abject aesthetics serve to imagine collectivity and coalition, in difference, against the ideological violence of a politics of presence and in critique of coercive mimeticism. Here I am interested in the politics of an aesthetic practice that emerges from a different engagement with the sublime, that classical aesthetic category within which I situate abjection throughout this book.

In her book *Sensational Devotion: Evangelical Performance in Twenty-First-Century America*, Jill Stevenson challenges performance studies scholars to take religious pop culture seriously. Doing so, she argues, will not only show us that what she calls "performative genres" function as "vivid, sensual, affectively oriented, and individualized" embodied practice that "reinforce and clarify the believer's faith" and their "personal relationship with Christ," but also that they affect popular culture more broadly.[14] Thinking of religious embodied expression as a performative genre offers a valuable model that I pair with a meditation on the visual culture of religion in my approach to Latino LDS testimonies that deploy the abject Lamanite. I am thus building on attention to the performative and visual in religious studies through the critical lens of Latino studies as elaborated through women of color theorizing and queer of color critique, alongside rigorous engagement with the aesthetic in its various abject incarnations as they have been elaborated in this book. I focus largely on performative narrative, the content of testimonies, and the site in which they are performed, drawing from María Josefina Saldaña-Portillo's *The Revolutionary Imagination in the Americas and the Age of Development* in which, through her reading of Rigoberta Menchú's *testimonio*, she theorizes the "theater of Realpolitik," in which "the act of testifying is itself an interpellative performance" that "issues an interpellative call to form a community of action."[15] I am interested in the multiple hailings of Latinos by the physical text of the Book of Mormon, its visuality and material performative manifestation, but more importantly the hailing within the testimonies under analysis that confirm their embrace of the doctrine yet manage, for a moment, to disrupt its structure and gesture beyond it.

For Mormon parishioners, testimony is a performative product of the affective pull of the Holy Spirit. While sporadic testimony sharing is encouraged, the church also provides structured opportunities for the performance of faith and commitment. Of these structured opportunities, the most popularly recognized are the same-sex pairs of young, suit-clad, clean-shaven, self-funded missionaries whose lives are dedicated to proselytizing for two years, in part by sharing their testimony with potential converts.[16] Additionally, Sunday services and periodic conferences largely feature members of the lay congregation as speakers, providing an opportunity for members to incorporate testimony into a meditation on an assigned theme. Most do, peppering their closing remarks with proclamations of faith. Finally, first Sundays of the month replace regular talks and sermons with an open testimony session during which volunteers from the congregation rise to the podium—a regularized stage for the performance of personal testimony. The formalization of this opportunity allows members to sporadically decide to share, as moved by the spirit, but also to prepare, to set personal goals if they so chose.[17] The church has also organized large performance events and media campaigns, the most recent of which is the "I am Mormon" media ads, whose accompanying website provides a place for members to share their testimony.

In her book *Straight to Jesus*, Tanya Erzen has argued that "the testimony, with a sin and redemption narrative, has long been a hallmark of evangelical Christianity" and is central to the process of affirming one's conversion.[18] Though Mormonism is not considered an evangelical Christian faith, I have observed this narrative structure as part of many Mormon testimonies. But something else is at work in those who identify as Latino Lamanites. Unlike convert narratives, in which what Ghassem-Fachandi calls social abjection is necessary for an overcoming such that "power chosenness, and the power of the wrath of God" is arrived at once abjection is transformed and reworked, this narrative structure of overcoming abjection reveals something different in the LDS church. Overcoming an identi-fication with the abject, for me, reveals the shortfalls and limitations of the LDS church and ultimately the Lamanite identity.[19] Using abject aesthetics as a lens to approach these performances of religious conviction reveals not only the racial dimensions implied in the sinner/saved categories within LDS doctrine, but also the ways Latino *Mormones* assert their participation in both the religious organization and the nation-state through an embrace of the personal, spiritual, and political possibilities of abjection but perhaps also the difficulty of its sustained engagement.

(Too White) Presidential Promise

In May 2012, then-presidential candidate Mitt Romney invoked his Mexican-born father during a private fund-raiser. Romney shared, "My dad, you probably know, was the governor of Michigan and was the head of a car company. But he was born in Mexico." The conjunction "but" linking his father's career history and the revelation of his birthplace designates the latter as a counterintuitive identifier that sharply contrasts his position as governor and car executive. "Had he [Romney's father] been born of Mexi-can parents," Romney continues, "I'd have a better shot of winning this." His audience responds with laughter, prompting Romney to extend his bit with, "I say that jokingly but it would be helpful to be Latino." Booming laughter fills the room with a consensual recognition of the absurdity of the desire to inhabit Latinoness, especially by someone so imbued with white male privilege.

In that speech Romney employed and relied on the understanding of a simplistic calculus wherein a presumed Latino voting block would be swayed by identitarian loyalty if only his parents had been Mexican and not U.S. citizens on Mexican soil. According to this logic, Romney implies that in the absence of a Latino candidate, Latinos will vote for another person of color, his opponent incumbent President Barack Obama. When consid-ered alongside the now infamous "47 percent" remarks made during the same speech—in which he states that it is not his job to "worry about those people" who "are dependent upon government, who believe that they are victims, who believe the government has a responsibility to care for them, who believe that they are entitled to health care, to food, to housing, to you-name-it"—Romney creates an equivalency between those Latino votes out of his reach and a horde of government-dependent, entitled "victims."

Wanting to be one of "those people," his audience agrees, is an uproarious joke laden with both dismissal and recognition of a growing Latino voting demographic.[20]

This series of statements reveals much about Romney's political beliefs and those that came to be associated with his much-publicized faith as a member of the LDS church. For my purposes in this chapter, asking how his father came to be born in Mexico proffers the consolidation of a long history between Mexico, its diaspora, and the U.S.-founded LDS church. Members of the Romney family have belonged to the church since the mid-1800s when founder Joseph Smith was alive. In 1843, following Smith's death and attacks on church members for their practice of plural marriage, the Romneys benefited from the porousness of national boundaries, fleeing to the unincorporated West. Then in 1885, with that region under the jurisdiction of the United States since the 1848 Treaty of Guadalupe Hidalgo, they fled south, away from polygamy and perjury prosecution, deep into Mexico, where they established Mormon settlements with the consent of Mexican president Porfirio Díaz, only to return to the Southwest when the Mexican Revolution threatened the Porfiriato and their lands. While quite a few of the Romneys returned to the Mexico they had come to consider their home after the revolution, Mitt Romney's father did not.[21]

Romney's family history reveals our neighboring country as a site of refuge for Mormons fleeing religious persecution and highlights the link between expansionist projects and religion.[22] The pilgrimage of bodies across national borders was accompanied by a spiritual narrative that cast Mormons as following a divinely ordained proselytizing mission to convert the Lamanites, ancestors of the native peoples of the Americas around whom the narrative of the Book of Mormon is built. Covering a vast geographic region, the term "Lamanite" has been and continues to be applied to various populations, including North American and Latin American native and indigenous communities, as well as a Latino diaspora in the United States.[23] Hokulani K. Aikau's study of Mormon Polynesian members in Hawaii reveals a community believed to descend from a related honored genealogy who thus claim Lamanite identity.[24] This chapter builds on work on the intersection of race and Mormonism, both internationally and domestically.[25] These works explore the historical paradox of what Armand Mauss identifies as a universalistic missionary program and the simultaneous avoidance of specifically racialized communities as well as the eventual dominance of a universalism that Aikau identifies as functioning similarly to a conservative color-blind approach to race that only solidifies racial hier-archies.[26] Mitt Romney, an (almost too white) embodiment of privilege and his invocation of proximity to Latinidad by virtue of his Mexican-born fa-ther, allows me to signal a poignant promise for American belonging that the LDS church offers its Latino members, an ambivalent promise that, like Romney's remarks above, acknowledges the importance of Latinos through a gesture that underscores their abject status.[27] Below I explore the relation-ship between the willful steady construction of whiteness in and through Mormonism—despite, as Paul Reeve has argued, their earlier racialized status—and its relationship to Latino communities racialized as Lamanite.

Restoration of an American Church: The Lamanite and His Keeper

The lush hill on which the LDS church believes Smith unearthed the pages that he would translate into the Book of Mormon welcomes thousands ev-ery summer for the Hill Cumorah Pageant. The pageant is an all-volunteer reenactment of the stories that make up the Book of Mormon, weaving together foundations in Jerusalem across the big ocean with the Ameri-cas and into the latter days (figure 4.4). Though the performance opens with a prayer that makes clear its testimonial function, to both strengthen member conviction and recruit nonmembers, I was most struck by the in-teractions before the actual performance. Costumed volunteer actors were available for hours before the performance to greet approaching audience members and share their personal testimonies along with a favorite scrip-ture (figure 4.5). As soon as I settled into my seat, a group of four teenagers costumed as Nephites approached a large Latino family that sat behind me, taking up almost an entire row of seats. The young men shared their testi-mony, a favorite scripture, and a brief summary of the show in which they would soon perform with the family's patriarch, whose nodding head and occasional accented response communicated his patience with speakers whose language he didn't speak well but to whom he was happy to listen. I would later learn this Latino family had made a thirty-hour road trip to attend the performance. The patriarch who had listened to the young men surely knew what he was there for as well as the role he played when the young men were sharing their testimony with him. He was familiar with the script; he performed acceptance and served as witness to their testi-mony with his presence, but also physically confirmed a good deed, a re-quired spiritual benchmark for these young proselytizers. The young men who addressed him, however, addressed him as a nonmember—a failure

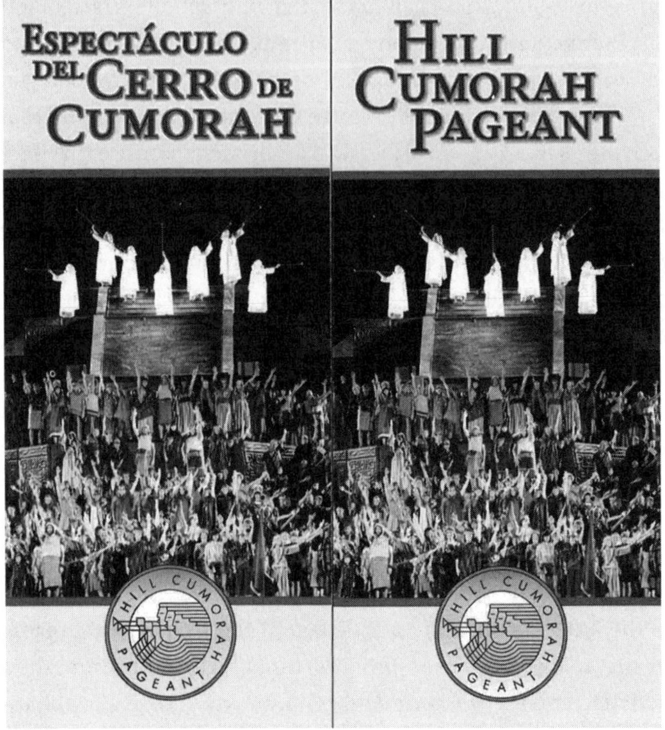

FIGURE 4.4 Promotional material for the Hill Cumorah Pageant, 2014.

of recognition of a fellow believer and his pilgrimage to the sacred site to partake in this testimonial event.[28]

Not long after, a young female duo—one dressed as a Lamanite, the other a Nephite—approached me. In addition to hearing their favorite scripture and about their experience in a singles ward, we discussed the differences in their costumes (figure 4.6).[29] The young woman dressed as a Lamanite explained that her outfit was darker and more revealing than that of her partner, whom she described as "more modest." Dominated by the bright red and fuchsia of her frayed skirt and the emerald of her almost sleeveless top, her costume was accessorized with tufts of fur, feathers, scraps of hide, and dark brown fringe leather arm and leg bands. Though she wore no face makeup or paint, she donned a sharply angled dark wig. Her partner, on the other hand, wore an outfit overwhelmed by the golden poncho that modestly covered upper arms, with blue accents that were echoed through Nephite costumes on the stage. She wore a headpiece that, while keeping

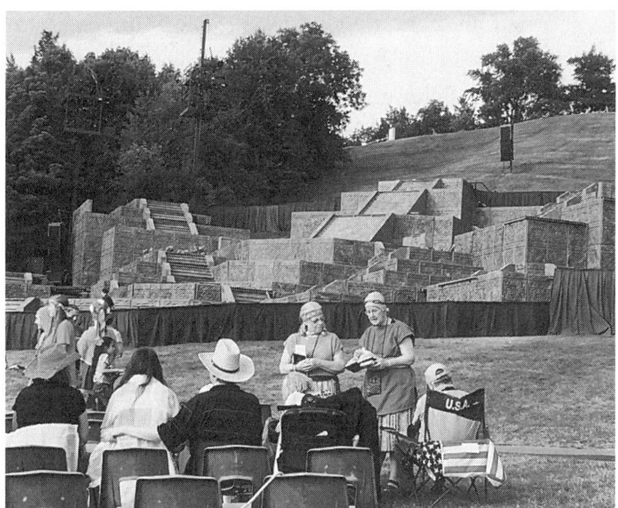

FIGURE 4.5 LDS members in costume sharing testimony before the show, 2014. Photograph by the author.

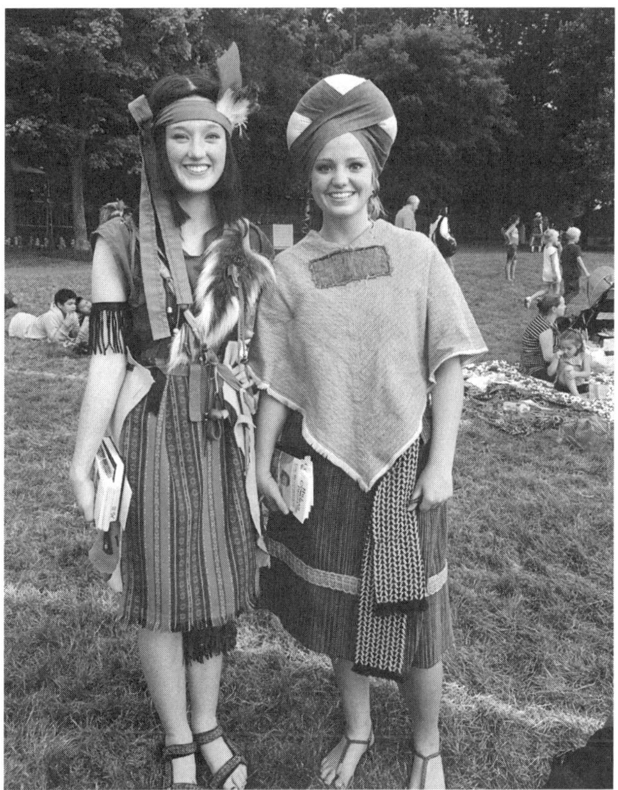

FIGURE 4.6 Two young women dressed as a Lamanite (left) and a Nephite (right), 2014. Photograph by the author.

hair from her face, revealed her natural blond tresses cascading out from a ponytail in the back. She wore no animal-derived materials except for the "anachronistic" sandals she chose to match her attire. Both carried a copy of the Book of Mormon and pamphlets about the show. When I asked about their roles in the performance we'd be watching later that evening, the young Lamanite made an effort to explain some of the choreography. Nephites, she told me, were more disciplined and orderly than their opponents, who were more "all over the place." Where Nephites would use metal swords for the fight scene of which they were a part, Lamanites would use wooden staffs. Racial signifiers abounded in the costuming, choreographed dances, and fight sequences even if overt references were carefully kept at bay.[30]

When the performance began, I recognized those eight colorful illustrations from the Book of Mormon punctuating scenes in the seventy-five-minute spectacular, complete with a running-waterfall-backed baptismal font, tower-shattering earthquakes, volcano eruptions, crucifixes and prophets aglow in fire, and an ethereal Christ descending from the darkest heavens. The Hill Cumorah Pageant literalized the performative function of testimony and its interpellative function as an embodied manifestation of *Jesus Christ Visits the Americas*, the painting whose hail opened the previous section of this chapter. It also confirmed the complexity of affective oscillation I am trying to understand. As an audience member faced with the peoples and ruins of the Americas, it is difficult to miss the importance of the descendants of these peoples, as difficult to miss as the racialized hierarchies performed onstage.

The church is unwavering in its claims that founding prophet and president Joseph Smith discovered and translated an ancient historical text buried in New York by one of the last members of an indigenous tribe of white Indians, the Nephites. While some argue that the 1827 Book of Mormon contended with the major theological questions of the 1820s–1830s, it also grappled with racial scripts.[31] The Book of Mormon proposed a complex genealogical link between the indigenous peoples of the Americas and Anglo-Saxon settlers, contributing to the many theories on the lost tribes of Israel. But the Book of Mormon's narration of its warring tribes also reflects the ideology of British settler colonialism that vindicated Anglo-Saxon encroachment on land, as I discuss below, and is further justified by the genealogical claims that undergird the church's organizational logic, with white church leaders as the administrative heads of a structured patriarchy, and their engagement with those they consider to be present-day Lamanite descendants.

In her *American Pentimento: The Invention of Indians and the Pursuit of Riches*, Patricia Seed argues that British settler colonialism was structured in part by "the nonverbal English theory of landownership: whoever farmed the land owned it."[32] As a product of its time, the Book of Mormon's casting of the remaining indigenous inhabitants of the continent, as wandering, hunting Lamanites, was in keeping with the ideological maneuvers of settlers who sought to push frontier boundaries and make land claims. Smith's narrative of the Lamanites as nomadic hunters who were a "loathsome, and filthy people, full of idleness and all manner of abominations" similarly justified Mormon expansion into unsettled territory.[33] The moral obligation to cleanse or purge implied by the adjective "loathsome" makes evident the sacred mandate that renders LDS church growth a manifestation of the era's Manifest Destiny–driven expansion of settlers into the Western frontier. But the nascent religion's claim on the American continent was not restricted to land use.

The Book of Mormon not only provides an account for the American continent unmentioned in the Bible—save for, some believe, its reference to the lost tribes of Israel—it also stipulates the roles for the tribes' descendants, and therein the relationship between Lamanites and their descendants to Joseph Smith and his white congregation. Together they share a common Hebrew ancestry with discrete God-ordained tasks.[34] Following Phil Deloria in his examination of the concurrent creation of a white American subject and an imagined American Indian based on stereotype, we can understand Smith's Lamanite people as a foil against whom he and his early white converts crafted their sense of being and belonging.[35] The Book of Mormon established a unique genealogical relationship between the indigenous Lamanite descendants and the white settlers of North America: in addition to a godly mandate to restore the knowledge of their "true heritage" to the Lamanite descendants, white members of the church were to serve as custodians of the Lamanites themselves.

In *Playing Indian*, Deloria stipulates, "Savage Indians served Americans as oppositional figures against whom one might imagine a civilized national self."[36] The same dynamic is readily visible in the early LDS church. The westward and southern movements of early Latter-Day Saints, like those of the Romneys mentioned earlier, and their accompanying settlements find reason and justification in the church's teachings. Early Mormon pioneers were not simply settling, they were preparing the continent for Christ's return by working to convert their brethren, the Lamanites, for whom the Mormon gospel offered not only a religion but also a set of values that promised them the eventual reclamation of their land upon Christ's return, inclusivity, and the whitening of their skin.[37] This promise reflects a hierarchy of culture and race that places white Mormon custodians at the fore, while promotion to whiteness, if not the role of custodian, is promised to faithful converts of color. The administration of the continent in preparation for Christ's second coming, as described above, has fueled an aggressive missionary agenda into the present, as well as the accumulation of resources ranging from livestock to radio airwaves.[38] Meanwhile, the genealogical connection between Lamanites and white LDS pioneers that accompanies the custodian, administrative, and proselytizing duties creates an affective link invoking normative family structures to naturalize a hierarchy established by the material practices of the church.

The early infrastructural demands of the church, after Smith's murder, delayed attention to the missionary work Smith had enthusiastically called for. Once firmly established in Utah, however, the LDS church prioritized a Mexican Lamanite mission. Very early on, Mormons proselytized among North American Native communities, signaling the importance of Lamanite conversion from the beginning.[39] But the Lamanite label is very easily transposed on nineteenth-century Mexican communities on both sides of the newly established border, among whom the Mexican mission had successfully converted hundreds. Again, as the Romneys show us, given that the Southwest and indeed the shifting border region of Mexico functioned as a safe haven for fleeing Latter-Day Saints, it is no surprise that this region would receive priority. Consequently, the first translation of the Book of Mormon was into Spanish.[40] Despite its liberal application to all descendants of indigenous North and Latin Americans, "Lamanite" came to be used by the church to refer specifically to Spanish speakers from Latin America and Mexico, both within and beyond the United States, who tended to be perceived as mestizos.[41] Thus the Lamanite identity as constructed and deployed by the LDS church can be viewed as managing Latinos and Latin American subjects as a population brought into the church and made subject to its management in fulfillment of its evangelical mission.[42]

As recent as 1978, church officials underscored the importance of Lamanite conversion. In his "Joseph Smith and the Clash of Sacred Cultures," Keith Parry composes the following compilation of church statements:

We possess a unique understanding of the Indians. They are Lamanites, descendants of the Book of Mormon peoples, sprung from the House of Israel. The Book of Mormon was written for them in particular, so that they might be redeemed from the curse which fell upon their ancestors. As custodians of this record of their past, a sacred record of their heritage and destiny, we have a duty to ensure that the Indians regain their true identity. We accepted that responsibility from the first—our missionaries went among the Lamanites soon after the Church was restored. Since then, our prophets have seen to it that we have done our duty by the Indians. Now, more than ever, we must meet our obligations, for President Kimball has said that "the day of the Lamanite is surely here and we are God's instrument in helping to bring to pass the prophecies" of the Book of Mormon (TSGD 1978, 74).[43]

Present-day Saints are still enlisted as "custodians" whose "duty" and "responsibility" it is to reveal the "sacred record" of their "true" Lamanite identity to "Indians" and all those marked under that sign. A reminder of a shared genealogy is issued to the converts, but so too is the abject status of the cursed Lamanites in need of redemption. With the proclamation from then-president and prophet of the church, Spencer W. Kimball, that "the day of the Lamanite is surely here," church officials communicate a pressing need to "redeem" what can be understood as a growing Latino presence in the United States. The racial hierarchy established at the church's founding remains intact in this compilation of official statements and shapes present-day proselytizing efforts.[44]

"Hey, You": Ambivalent Interpellations

During the same year Kimball prophesied the arrival of the day of the Lamanite, the first LDS Latino bishop, Orlando A. Rivera, published "Mormonism and the Chicano" in *Mormonism: A Faith for All Cultures*, the book project linked to a series of symposia on the same subject at Brigham Young University in 1978.[45] These symposia were a site to "listen to [participants] speak of the bonds that unite us in the spirit of the gospel, to note their affirmation of the spiritual substance of those bonds, [and] to enjoy their humor and the warmth of their personalities"—a stage, in other words, for the performance of testimony.[46] The book was produced for a general church audience as a hybrid of "insight, passion, and testimony."[47] In Rivera's "Mormonism and the Chicano," Rivera shows the influence of the Chicano nationalist movement in his conceptualization and deployment of the Lamanite. Largely unaddressed by scholars of Chicano nationalism, Rivera performs a sublime Chicanidad in which the identities of the Chicano and the Lamanite are conflated, and recommends that the church and its members mobilize this identity to increase the success of proselytizing among Latinos in the United States. His sublime Chicanidad transforms the affirming testimony, challenging its parameters and the church's. Reading this as an interpellative performance, following Saldaña-Portillo, we can understand Rivera as hailing communities of action through testimony, but also engaging in poignant critique. His testimony and desire for inclusion in the faith, however, reveals a complex oscillation between abject critique and the desire to belong.

Rivera begins his testimonial essay by stating, "We call ourselves Chicanos, and all Chicanos think of themselves as having an Indo-hispanic background, of having ancestral roots native to America as well as to Europe. Thus, your considering us Lamanites is in no way offensive, but rather acceptable to our people. We are proud of our native American progenitors."[48] Rivera builds on the interpellative work of the Chicano nationalist movement, which hailed a community of Mexican Americans as Chicanos. "We call ourselves Chicanos," he says, delineating an entire group of people called into consciousness by cultural texts like "El Plan Espiritual de Aztlán" and "I Am Joaquin," protests, rallies, and other consciousness-raising gatherings of the era. In his opening lines, Rivera has actively conflated the two identities, Chicano and Lamanite, based on the Chicano movement's understanding of racial mestizaje and indigenous pride. He simultaneously reveals Lamanite to be an identity structured in abjection—as he explains that it is not offensive, he reveals an understanding of it as offensive among his audience. Rivera's Foucauldian reverse discourse indicates a shift in the signifying power of the discursive sign. Rivera will not go on to say that the Book of Mormon misrepresents the abject Lamanite, but instead that he is moved by an initial abject identification.

The self-identification is contrasted by an external label: "your considering us Lamanites." Rivera's pronoun usage throughout indicates an address to a white audience of LDS members and church leaders. In the above opening lines, the "your" and "us" indicate a dominant presence that labels a Chicano minority "Lamanite" with what appears to be guilt over the shameful association with the Book of Mormon's wicked tribe. It is for them that Rivera performs an embrace of abjection and recommends the deployment of the Lamanite identity to increase the success of missionary efforts among Latinos. Early in his testimony, he both responds to the hail from the organized church and is successfully interpellated as a Lamanite but counters with his own Althrusserian "hey you"—an interpellative call that anticipates a discursive shift in power as Rivera prepares to issue a critique. Rivera's "you" capitalizes on sanctioned church roles calling on his audience as custodians to organize a better mission and therein recruit more Lamanites. But he also testifies to the interpellative power of the La-manite identity as presented in LDS gospel through terms that nevertheless reveal a cautious, poignant protest.

Rivera takes another cue from the Chicano movement and underscores collective "ancestral roots native to America" and pride at their "American progenitors." He reminds the administrators he is hailing that, as a Lama-nite, he is historically situated in the continent. Later Rivera states, "To the Indian, America came to him, not he to America. The same holds true for us. America came to us, not only because of our Spanish heritage but also because of our Indian heritage." Here, Rivera distinguishes the Chicano mestizo Lamanite, with Indian and Spanish heritage, from the "Indian" or Native American Lamanites, though they share "America's" encroachment. The "coming to us" that Rivera refers to carries two valences: the religious one, of having the restored church seek out and convert Lamanites, but also one of colonial encounters. Those familiar with the popular Chicano protest chant, "We didn't cross the border—the border crossed us," surely hear an echo in Rivera's claim, such that America coming to the Indians with Spanish heritage recalls both Spanish conquistadores that literally imposed the concept of an American continent, but also the nineteenth-century border disputes that culminated in America—the United States—coming to Mexico or rather, Mexico becoming America through the 1848 Treaty of Guadalupe Hidalgo that ended the Mexican-American War. In doing so Rivera links the Mormon mission to the growth of the United States as a colonial empire while underscoring the long-term existence of "Lamanites," "Indians," and "Chicanos" in the region.

Because of shared lineage between the Chicano Lamanite and his Mexican "brethren," Rivera argues that they are more alike than they are different. Given the similarities, Rivera's main concern is the compara-tively more successful mission work in Mexico. Why the higher conver-sion rates? Rivera responds with a rhetorical question of his own: "Is it the environment, one generally dominated economically, politically, and socially by other than our people, that holds the answer?"[49] In contradistinction to Mexican LDS converts in Mexico, Rivera identifies Chicanos as a colonized people who cannot thrive spiritually or materially. Through his performative testimony, rooted in the abject figure of the Lamanite, Rivera asks the LDS administrators to contemplate their participation in an oppressive political system and how this might be affecting their sacred duty. He achieves this precisely when he focuses on the abject status of the latter-day Lamanite. Cautiously, Rivera does not blame the church directly, but instead points to a larger political problem, of which the church might be a representative participant. Rivera poses his critique in the form of a question and lessens the sting of the accusation, but it is nonetheless there, arrived at through an empowered identification with the abject Lamanite.

As his testimony continues, Rivera's desire to propel a community to action crystallizes in a critique of church hierarchy. Rivera charges that "Spanish conquistadores" and "New World explorers" were "generally" coming to the American continent to exploit its resources. His qualifier "generally" permits him to point out the abuse yet not contradict the church's belief that Christopher Columbus was divinely inspired to reveal the American continent to Joseph Smith's ancestors, thus setting in motion the acts that would lead to the restoration of the church. Rivera then quickly makes the leap to a contemporary situation for Latinos. "I think the condition of colonialism still exists," he says. "While millions of people from other Latin-American countries have come to swell our ranks, we Spanish-speaking people in the United States are still largely disfranchised."[50] It is uncertain if by "our" he is referring to the "ranks" of the Chicano movement, the Lamanite tribe, or the larger church, but the ambiguity allows him to invoke all three.

The state of disenfranchisement that Rivera refers to, he believes, has led to the formation of a Chicano movement which he describes as "a kind of cultural retrenchment . . . as a consequence [of which] we now experience a certain suspicion of anything that is not from our own people."[51] Rivera explicitly counts himself among the members of the Chicano movement while elucidating a distrust of a foreign (non-Chicano) culture that results in disappointing conversion rates among Chicanos. Additionally he offers the Chicano perception that "the policies and practices of Mormonism as a representative practicing American institution must certainly be colonial or racist in nature."[52] Chicanos, himself included, he adds, "lack a certain self-confidence and self-assurance that allows us to be assertive enough to leave our culture or our traditions and to find out what being a convert to Mormonism really means. Thus, as our people look upon Mormonism as an 'American' institution, they do so from the twin vantage of suspicion and insecurity."[53] Because of the psychic toll that internal colonialism has taken on Chicanos, leaving them unsure and "lacking confidence," Chicanos are suspicious of the church and miss out on what the church can offer them—"what being a Mormon convert really means." Rivera seems to imply that what the church offers is akin to the mythology of Chicano nationalism, grounded in claims to indigeneity, though before he elaborates on this offering, Rivera continues to address the custodians.

Rivera critiques past efforts to assimilate converts, a strategy that pairs Lamanite revelation with suppression of cultural particularity. When, under the guise of unifying the church, LDS leaders imply that ethnic and national particularities should be left aside, Rivera tells us, they are communicating an impossible and offensive proposition, one that "prescribes that we 'foreigners' should change culturally but that no such requirement is imposed upon those of the 'central Mormon culture.'"[54] Efforts to assimilate nonwhite Lamanite bodies enact ideological violence on Chicano culture with the help of the very ideological hierarchy that casts white LDS members as the keepers of Lamanites. The racism in the preference of white dominant culture is not lost on Rivera. He continues his testimony by enumerating the ways in which the church, or rather members of the church, hurt their abilities to recruit Latino members with the racism ensconced in Mormon culture, though for Rivera not in Mormon doctrine. In doing so, Rivera's becomes the testimony of a witness that provides proof of the violence perpetuated against his people. Instead of offering Chicanos a racist abjection, Rivera argues, the LDS church should accept Chicano culture, indeed, instrumentalize it.

Rivera served as bishop to a Spanish-speaking ward, or congregation. Drawing from this experience, he explains that conflict arose over maintaining this ward or combining it with the English-speaking congregation. "Some people began to say that if we were going to be Americans, we ought to *be* Americans. Since English is the language spoken here, we ought to speak English. . . . When we begin to say that 'English is the language spoken here,' we really are expressing a strategy of cultural assimilation that smacks of cultural imperialism. Today, most Chicanos will not accept that strategy."[55] Rivera's critique could not be clearer. The cultural imperialism he identifies comes from creating an in-group and an out-group that must assimilate. The in-group is portrayed as somehow more authentic or fitting to the faith, certainly a problem for a worldwide religion. Rivera sees the in-group as created by a direct lineage to the founders of the church. "For instance," he explains, "you are really 'in' if you are a Mormon with a pioneer heritage. That heritage may have nothing to do with your qualifications for the kingdom, but you are in. Anyone who does not have that heritage seems almost by definition to be a foreigner. This is an ironic stance when you consider that my people had lived here for 250 years before the Mormons came. Pioneer vintage, then, doesn't make very much of an impression on us."[56] While many white LDS members cite their familial connection to early pioneer Saints as a source of pride, for Rivera this is indeed the site of problematic cultural exclusions and also the site where Mormon colonialism aligns with the imperial projects of the nation. In quick retort, Rivera cites the much older Lamanite heritage.

Rivera's testimony reveals what perhaps was an unanticipated result in the crafting of a Lamanite subject: empowerment through abjection, not despite it. Though he shows allegiance to the terms of the Book of Mormon, which hails Chicanos and Latinos as Lamanites—terms that function to cohere white LDS members' understanding of themselves as superior—Rivera also refuses the cultural superiority of white LDS culture. Rivera asks white LDS members for "mutual respect, allowing us to be ourselves, to appreciate and understand and learn of our own history and culture."[57] With this request, Rivera reminds white LDS members that their calling is precisely to facilitate the revelation of their true history to the Lamanites. By embracing the subject position, Rivera is able to argue for Chicano culture as a valuable, contemporary Lamanite culture that needs to be kept intact and to acquire knowledge of the past as documented in the Book of Mormon. In closing, Rivera attempts to bridge any distance he might have created from his audience with a reminder of shared family values so central to modern Mormonism: "Cultural characteristics of our people include family solidarity and family-oriented life-style [where] our tradition is for the father to be the head of the house."[58] Highlighting the gendered role of head of household, Rivera claims the heteronormative nuclear family for Chicanos, which he declares is "iminently [sic] compatible with Mormon values."

Rivera's empowered intervention and deployment of a Chicano Lamanite identity is fueled by a sense of injustice within the church and the resultant failure to attract Lamanite converts so central to its mission.[59] By highlighting a divine Lamanite heritage, he is able to make a claim for the serious inclusion of Latino LDS members and their culture in the church and offers a glorified genealogy alternative to that of the vintage pioneer lineage. His deployment, then, moves away from abjection rather quickly, much quicker than we've seen negotiated by the other cultural producers in this book. Additionally, an accompanying ambivalence is generated by the belief that the Lamanites of the Book of Mormon, through whom Rivera strengthens his claims, require the stability of the racial hierarchy of the church as established by Joseph Smith. The teachings of the church require that Rivera navigate his political struggles and those of the Lamanites with care, not only because of the threat of excommunication but also because Rivera has an investment in maintaining the system within which he is advocating for change. Rivera's relatively white-gloved critique, in which he addresses church members' actions and not church policy, fails to address the Book of Mormon's promise of whitened Lamanite skin and its implications and to extend his critique of an implicit elevation of white members found within the church's teaching. He also ushers the Lamanite away from abject status toward a glorified indigenous sanctity of the kind that fueled the Chicanismo shaped by an exaltation of Aztlán and its indigenous progenitors.

I have personally attended countless church gatherings wherein the congregation gathers for the sole purpose of sharing testimony. Congregants are sublimely moved by the spirit of the Holy Ghost, part of a divine trinity that also includes God and his son Jesus Christ, to bear witness to the positive effects of devout Mormon practice and thereby affirm their commitment and belief in the doctrine. By and large, they speak to an audience of peers who are invited to also perform their spiritual commitment and strengthen each other's testimonies.[60] That Rivera uses this staged moment for affirmation in the faith to level a critique on the dominant LDS culture, with accusations of racism working against God-ordained roles and missionary directives, speaks to me of the contestatory potential of the abject Lamanite and its aesthetic engagement through performative testimony. Ultimately, however, Rivera speaks from a desire to critique but still belong, an ambivalent position. His testimony is a response to the perceived failure of the church to address the needs of LDS Latinos, but he also works within the terms that empower him, out of which emerges his Chicano Lamanite identity. Rivera's recourse to Chicano nationalism weighs down his intervention with some of the same ideological problems for which the movement was criticized.[61] Like the Chicano movement, it is Rivera's reach for the normative in recuperative gestures that reveals the limits of the Lamanite identity. When it remains rooted in abjection, however, Rivera is able to draw lines of solidarity to abjected populations across the Americas and level his most poignant critiques against cultural imperialism. Below I examine a similar politicized deployment of the Lamanite identity that nonetheless shows the limits of an ambivalent embrace of abjection.

Abject Limits: Transformative Conversions, or "My Children Are Turning White"

In 2005 the *Salt Lake City Weekly* featured the testimonies of LDS members Oscar Faria, Abraham Tapia, and Oscar Garcia, who shared analogous experiences.[62] The public nature of these testimonies, appearing in print for a broad readership, imbues them with a proselytizing power that centers a racialized identity. The spiritual performances produce and mobilize a very specific Lamanite subject that in many ways builds on Rivera's interpellative work. Both bring a performative component to the page that is meant to generate a very specific reading experience, one that moves its reader spiritually.

Faria testifies that personal revelation led to his immigration from Venezuela to Utah, a beacon of Mormonism. Once in Utah, Faria says he received spiritual guidance resulting in his introduction to the Book of Mormon, in which he recognized a picture of his ancestors among the brightly colored illustrations, catalyzing his conversion. In the aesthetic elation of testimony, Faria shares that his migration, along with that of other Latin Americans, is "a sign of God's gathering of the Children of Israel."

Abraham Tapia, the son of a Mexican migrant farm laborer, traces his roots back to the Aztec and Yaqui tribes. Like all other male, priesthood-ordained members of the church, Tapia conducts baptisms. In great contrast to other, especially white members, Tapia believes he does so as an Aztec priest. The feathered serpent god Quetzalcoatl of his ancestors, he is sure, was Jesus Christ. Through interpretation of LDS scripture, Tapia believes the entire American continent is promised to the Lamanite descendants of the Book of Mormon and points to Latino government officials as signaling the forthcoming repossession of this continent's indigenous land.

Finally, Oscar Garcia, the first missionary from his Mexico City congregation to serve in the United States, testifies to his belief that the migration of Lamanites will result in a blessed and fortified second generation, speaking of his children with his Brazilian wife. Garcia performs total identification with the people of the Book of Mormon in claiming Lamanite as an identity for himself and other Latinos and Latin Americans. Garcia adds to his testimony by explaining that as his children grow in righteousness, they fulfill a self-interpreted prophecy from the Book of Mormon: "My children are turning white and they are Lamanite descendants. My daughter is a white Mexican."[63]

In the testimonies above, Latino members of the church are hailed as Lamanites by the visual images as much as by the text of the Book of Mormon. In responding to the hail, Latinos' understanding of their ancestry, migration, and role in the church and in the nation changes substantially. They become inheritors of a divine mission with heavenly decreed claims on land and, according to one member's interpretation, to government. This Lamanite hailing also reveals the perseverance of the specter of race throughout the church's history and founding up to the present. Garcia's children are "turning white," a physiognomic change linked to moral behavior. As stated in the opening of this chapter but worth reviewing, the Lamanites are a dark tribe whose darkness occurs as a result of their infidelity. It follows that the initial response to the hailing of the Book of Mormon requires the harnessing of a shameful habitation of one's racialized body in order to identify with the abject Lamanite. Simultaneously, an assertion of whiteness is embedded in LDS doctrine and lived practice that reveals the internalized racism that Latino members of the church navigate in an ambivalent belonging.

The Lamanite ideology embraced by Latino members offers justification for difficult migration where promises are spiritual as well as material: deep spiritual connections to past generations, the promise of an eventual reclaiming of land, and fortification in white skin. For others, however, it is a symbol of a deeply ingrained racism. The LDS church has attempted to move beyond its once-popular teaching that converts can expect a literal whitening of the skin after righteous living by altering scripture wording in republications of the Book of Mormon to read "pure and delightsome" where it once read "white and delightsome." Nevertheless, through these testimonies we see that Latino members retain this idea of whiteness as "delightsome" articulated in the saturated history of the faith, if not the actual scripture, when they encounter it along their route to forging a Lamanite identity. For some, it is a miraculous promise that will afford them, if not physical assimilation, then an elevation in the church's problematic doctrinal racial hierarchy. For others this promise is a reminder of the church's racist history and something to attempt to reconcile when read in context with the rest of the teaching of the Book of Mormon.

Abby Maestas, a former member who left the church after serving a mission in a Spanish-speaking community, believes that the Book of Mormon sends mixed messages in its representations of Lamanites. In a 1994 interview for the *Christian Century*, Maestas shares, "As a child I was taught that if you are good, you will turn white. And that's very confusing for people who are brown. It makes you feel like you're a second-class citizen. No one ever told the white kids that if they weren't good they'd turn dark." Furthermore, Maestas believes "the concept that brown is second class is ingrained [in the Mormon church]." The highest levels of leadership of the church remain largely white, though there are many opportunities for members to lead in their local congregations. Maestas claims that church leadership has not done enough to nurture the cultural heritage of Latinos, creating an environment where there is "diversity but not pluralism."[64]

In the same article, Rivera, whose published testimony as the first Latino bishop is of incredible symbolic value, reemerges, agreeing that "there's some terrible language in [the Book of Mormon]" but "you have to read the whole [book]. There are times when the Lamanites are the good guys." Rivera notes the lack of change in the church's hierarchy, offering that "like most American institutions, [the church] might have a fear of minorities. It may like people who are more like themselves, or who are more compliant" for leadership positions despite the centrality of Lamanites in church teachings and their early conversion in the church's history. Despite his early testimony or critique, Rivera now reports that "[he] ceased a long time ago to try to make suggestions [as it] wasn't appreciated."[65]

Present-day Latino Mormones are, however, finding ways to mobilize the Lamanite identity to concrete ends. The "I am Mormon" campaign shows a number of individuals whose profiles identify them as "Lamanites" and "Lamanita" (Lamanite in Spanish), a ready and proud identification. Lamanite Facebook groups and Twitter accounts indicate a growing desire to form a community that is aware of and engaged with doctrinal promises. Latino members are coming together to challenge politicians and pressure the church to support its immigrant members regardless of documentation status. In doing so they build an allegiance, through abjection, with those most dejected in the dominant political imaginary: the undocumented poor. For example, the group Proyecto Latino de Utah launched a letter campaign to the church's current president and prophet, Thomas S. Monson, asking that he clearly delineate the church's position on immigration in hopes that it would abate the anti-immigrant reputation the church presently enjoys, given that LDS member Arizona senator Russell Pearce (R-Mesa) was the primary sponsor of the controversial SB 1070, later endorsed by presidential hopeful Mitt Romney.[66] In response to this and other pressures, the church issued a statement saying it supports a responsible approach to immigration reform that "[includes] measures that will allow those who are now here illegally to work legally, provide for their families and become better contributing members of our community—but without establishing a path to citizenship or granting amnesty."[67] The church based its position on the principles of "1) The commandment to 'love thy neighbor.' 2) The importance of keeping families intact," and "3) The federal government's obligation to secure its borders."[68] Their response attempts to address Latino members' discontent without alienating their conservative base, a difficult balance that nonetheless acknowledges the Lamanite demand.

Other members cited their Lamanite lineage and teachings of the Book of Mormon to organize voters against presidential candidate Mitt Romney and other anti-immigrant candidates despite a shared faith. Among them, Ignacio Garcia, a history professor at Brigham Young University, told reporters, "We view immigration as a God event. . . . The book says no one comes to the Land unless they are brought by God." Garcia applies the belief of the return of the Lamanites to their land to explain immigration as God-ordained. These beliefs inspired political actions that included "firesides (equivalent to a tent revival) on immigration, [protesting] outside of Romney campaign events and [traveling] across state lines to help defeat other Mormon politicians with similar harsh immigration stances."[69]

The LDS church offers all its members strong eternal families in traditionally gendered households, reaffirming patriarchal values; an emphasis on a clean, healthy lifestyle coupled with a strong work ethic; and the opportunity for local leadership and community building. Extraordinarily normative middle-class values, these offerings have translated to many immigrants as the recipe for a thoroughly American and prosperous white respectability.[70] Thus the Lamanite identity that emerges from the Book of Mormon and its popular interpretations weaves in and out of an embrace of abjection, though mostly out. The initial embrace of abjection gives way to normative longing as church doctrine promises transformation out of abjection. Yet moments of critique and demands for change are achieved through abject solidarity when not attempting to assimilate. The Lamanite identity has created an ambivalent space for Latino members such that, despite institutionalized racism within the church, it enables their reinvention as divine inheritors of the teachings of Christ and the American continent, but more importantly it allows for a position of emboldened critique. The promise to feature prominently in Christ's return grants Latino members an empowered claim in the political arena—a claim that Romney, like the church, can readily cite but should be wary of dismissing, as in the joke above that arguably cost Mitt Romney the presidency.

Arriving at Apostasy

As I recount the spaces of belonging negotiated in the affective oscillation between an embrace of abjection and what we might understand as a cultural nationalist celebration of the Lamanite identity, I find that whatever is left of the Holy Spirit within me stirs in ambivalent frustration. Though moved by what an abject identification with the Lamanite facilitates, I cannot reconcile how this subject position is beholden and undeniably structured by a normative longing that leaves intact the church's racialized ideologies, demanding the eventual purging of the abject. While I can recall with ease many moments of joy from within the church—choir practice, family prayer and home evenings, and even the uplifting feeling of spiritual conviction—I also recall those moments during which I was made aware of my racialized particularity in a way that paralleled minoritizing logics outside the church.

Though I largely attended a Spanish-speaking congregation with families representative of the broad Latino matrix—of Mexican origin but also from El Salvador, Guatemala, Argentina, and other countries—I was uncomfortably aware of our minoritized status at national conferences as I was prompted to listen on headphones to Spanish translations of the entirely white English-speaking leadership. Even before being told explicitly, during a blessing, of my dark tribal lineage, I recall the discomfort spurred by the presence of white church members in my home, usually missionaries who sometimes arrived, it seemed to me, unannounced. Their presence in our Latino working-class community was part of their service, even as they relied on members of the congregation to supplement their meals. Dressed in my modest Sunday best as a young girl, I recall with clarity being asked by an incredulous white missionary if that was hair underneath my synthetic pantyhose. His finger pointed to the dark hair on my youthful legs—dark hair I was not yet allowed to shave that was beginning to hint at puberty, dark hair that differentiated me from the light peach-fuzz-covered children to which he was accustomed. This same missionary would often comment on my resemblance to one of his crushes back home. I was no more than ten—racialized, sexualized.

Combined with a crisis of faith spurred by the material violence that is often the consequence of heteropatriarchy, I found myself irreverently withdrawing from the church late in my teen years—I flirted (back) with those crisply dressed white missionaries the church continued to dispatch among Latino communities, taunting them to break their extreme celibacy vows. I prayed aloud at gatherings to a heavenly mother I was taught existed within a church that preaches of a jealous heavenly father, not out of devout belief, but to make a point that if the church claims we have one, I should be able to pray to her. I knew how performative acts of feminism like this would be regarded.[71] When I moved away for college, I started to be counted among the inactive: a member who doesn't attend church yet remains listed on the meticulous scrolls of membership. Occasionally I would receive unannounced visits from missionaries or from the Relief Society, the women's group within the church, whose checking in was meant to provide me with a route back to the fold. Though irked at their insistence and the seemingly panoptic surveillance of my whereabouts, it was not until the very early stages of the writing of this chapter in its dissertation incarnation that I decided I did not want to be counted in any way among church members.

I completed the paperwork necessary to withdraw my membership from the church, therein invalidating any covenants I had made during my young life as a member, forsaking blessings and sacred ordinances, becoming unsealed from the normative forever-family forged within recognized church templates. I became an apostate, an abject subject who has willfully turned away from the church, one meant to be shunned by active members among whom I still count family and friends, and who will, according to the church's teachings, go unrecognized in the afterlife by the family from whom I became unsealed in my departure from the church. I attempt to inhabit this position in the spirit of the promise of the abject Lamanite, not beholden to the church or its structuring ideologies, but in critique of structured injustice and desirous of imagining a more just beyond.

Abject Embodiment

Within translucent synthetic cocoons, Xandra Ibarra and Sophia Wang writhe their recumbent bodies from opposite diagonal ends, across stage, and toward one another. In what follows of the twenty-five-minute work in progress, *Untitled (skins)* (2015–2016), the two—entirely encased in long sheaths matched in color to their skin—mount each other, link their "skins" through a series of knots, crawl into and out of each other's casings, drag or are dragged by their elastic encasement, and pull away from and are drawn to one another, before finally shedding the fabric that contains them. Largely a horizontal performance during which movement is kept close to the floor, Ibarra and Wang's connected cocoons help create moments of exasperation and frustrated action, as well as conditions for intimacy and suffocating proximity. One can only imagine the fluids and smells exchanged within the cocoons, inside of which the nearly nude performers wear only skin-tone-matching undergarments, moving urgently—

at times seductively, and at others, violently—under flashing stage lights to syncopated dance beats or an amplified animatronic pulse. A few moments of verticality emphasize the sinuous connectivity achieved by the performers' encasements. Coordinated movements are smoothed by shared skin, emphasizing continuity, while incongruous actions stretch the fabric casings to emphasize the limits of movement possibility given connectivity (plate 9).

I turn to this unfinished, in-process work at the end of the book in order to return to argumentative trajectories traced throughout and to gesture to possibilities that extend those contained in this project. Instead of bodily narrative coherence, the reach and wrench between performers in *Untitled (Skins)* tells us something of abjection—of the connective sinews of coalition across minoritized populations as represented by the performers, the queer politics for understanding its offerings, the fecund possibilities of its political implications, and finally the textile limits of the heuristic fabric. The work proceeds from desire's proximity to disgust—that combination of push and pull that signals the abject—and its entanglement with queer erotics, augmented by the sublime evasion of form, even though the work traces recognizable choreographic geometries. As case studies in this book, these cultural producers work through racialized subjectivity, deploying aesthetics of abjection as performative illuminations of ideological processes and alternate modes of social organization. In *Untitled (skins)*, as in the case studies that precede it, relational sociality is tethered to the body on display, the dynamics between the performers, and those that extend to the audience that confirm the permeable bounds of the performance. The disquieting affects triggered by the performance pair's physicality, whose visual identitarian markers are obscured by the thin fabric within which they are encased, nonetheless signal a project marked by racialization—even if circumspect to the performance. A sense of dark hair, gendered bodily figurations, the revelation of surnames in performance announcements, all invite us into the realm of coalitional, comparative abjection. The ultimate shedding of "skin" at the end of the performance reveals subjects, individual bodies, that might be recognized along racial sightlines but whose encased struggle in and through abjection activates productive, though less narratively clear, affective binds.

Untitled (skins) is generative in its incompleteness and open in its promise. Rebecca Schneider has argued that the explicit body in performance, like that on display in *Untitled (skins)*, "is foremost a site of social markings" through which we might glimpse "ghosts of historical meaning, markings delineating social hierarchies of privilege and disprivilege."[1] In Ibarra and Wang's collaboration, as in Ibarra's larger body of work, the ghosts encircle, indeed haunt, those uneasy feelings around the successes of national incorporation or easy assimilation and, ultimately, wail against respectability politics.[2] There is much here to explore of comparative relational aesthetics, affect-activated and animating performers, stages, audiences, and their routes of circulation and display. This incomplete, forward-glancing project encourages a robust comparative framework focused on what is shared by distinct racial formations, where those projects converge, are brought into harmonious intimacy, and where they repel violently. It suggests a consideration of the performative function of the skins we're in, those embodied materially shaped structures within which we navigate identitarian projects relationally, and ends with the open question of the function of shedding, of release from the skin of performance.

In order to approximate a sense of the multifaceted labor of skins in the above performance, I turn to Ibarra's solo work, a practice deeply imbricated in discourses on Latinidad and racialized sexuality. In "Ecdysis: The Molting of a Cucarachica," Xandra Ibarra—also known as La Chica Boom—brings together a series of "photographic performance works" that center the cockroach, a hostile racialized emblem of Latinidad, in all its "abjection, disgust, invisibility, hypervisibility, and infestation."[3] The molting cockroach delivers us into a process of shedding and emergence within the bounds of an abject racial signifier. A short artist statement precedes a set of images in which Ibarra reflects on a similar process of shedding for the Latino subject. "Aren't Latinidad and spichood similarly fucked," Ibarra asks, "the fuckedness of always already being the same or of resemblance in repetition?"[4] In doing so, Ibarra homes in on a chain of signification within U.S. racializing schemas wherein Latinidad is always linked to abjection, to "spichood." The accompanying images in the series elaborate on the links in this chain of signification to illuminate a Sisyphean repetition wherein the shedding of skin, the attempt at transformative escape into the respectable, is doomed to return to a similar or identical embodied formation, always circumscribed by abjection.

In *Triptych* (2015) from the *Ecdysis* series, for example, Ibarra lies next to a textile iridescent bronze cockroach skin, the approximate length of her own body, within an emptied pool (plate 10). She wears a dark bikini bottom and pasties over her nipples. A pair of platform peep-toed heels rests diagonal to her feet immediately under the twin skin—the footwear donned by Ibarra as roach before the shedding that she proposes ultimately reveals "fucked . . . resemblance." From the same series, *Molting Showgirl* (2015) and *Molting Tortillera* (2015) show Ibarra lying in a bikini bottom and pasties next to elaborate jewel-toned, ruffled costumes anchored by impossibly high heels, while *Carcass* (2015) simply shows heels, a cape, wig, and headpiece horizontally arranged in a row in the sand off a littered desert highway evocative of the border region of the Southwest—the detritus of performance. In these photographs, the skins range from cockroach shape to those of eroticized Latina performance, costumes donned on the burlesque stage and shed during striptease. The visual-scape of this series brings to the fore the gendered and sexualized vectors of the abject roach as well as its queer otherness (*tortillera*). Within this doomed shedding cycle, however, Ibarra also equates the ruffles and heels that characterize the ideal, exotic "good neighbor"—as embodied by Carmen Miranda with exaggerated hand gestures, wandering eyes, and tutti-frutti hat[5]—to the emblem for the worst of/from our neighboring country who scurry across the border to sully our nation. While revealing the insistent, externally imposed taint of abjection, regardless of the shape of exterior presentation, of skin, Ibarra reframes abjection's potentiality. At opposite ends of interpellative mappings that situate Latinidad in relation to the nation, both of these skins shed to reveal the same Ibarra: exposed flesh, sparkling nipples glistening with queer agential intensity. With the citation of burlesque in each image through her pasties, Ibarra, too, calls forth those spaces of *suciedad*, within which Deb Vargas has located the "persistent sustainability" of queer world making.[6] This persistent and productive survival is brought to bear on sites of racialized crossing toward abject incorporation into the nation like the U.S./Mexico border invoked by the landscape backdrops in *Ecdysis*. Ibarra's work then, insists on the queer abjection of Latinidad, of the immigrant, of the possibilities of the agential performer working with and through abjection.

"Ecdysis: The Molting of a Cucarachica" reveals an abject chain of signification on which *Untitled (skins)* builds, that coalesces unsanctioned points of crossing, the erotic, and agential femme performance. Recently emboldened public performances of racialized insult, particularly from the conservative right within the political arena, have led to recuperative performances of model participation in the life of the nation.[7] We are not her, these performances would suggest, this molting abject queer figure.

The case studies throughout this book might serve as models through which we can construct alternative responses to racialized hostility. The profiled cultural producers often mobilize queer femme erotics toward the uncomfortable inclusion of those not easily respected figures of our community. They show us how performances can beckon communities attentive to shared violence but also insist on recognizing violence originating within us, in our specifically marked bodies, altered and transformed by time and location.

As a strategy, abjection asks for a difficult embodied performance, one that embraces affects counterintuitive to those we have been taught to regard as politically helpful. Embodied performance cautions against majoritarian incorporation, asking us what it might look like to perform failure, but also illuminates those communal articulations that might uncover unknown routes to world making, routes not yet here and of the beyond. The performers that I have followed in this book offer interventions in art institutions, television programming, faith-based organizations, and ultimately our political movements. It is my hope that they have also illuminated interventions for how we ask questions of and in our fields of study. I have sought, here, to build productively on scholarly and creative legacies of thinking about the performative in relationship to subjectivity. I have offered new views of social processes and locations that challenge the sites of political success we have imagined by centering the racialized, embodied particularity of Latinidad. In doing so, I privilege the unreliable body, exploiting the otherness, the queerness that attaches to Latinidad in rejection of easy incorporation.

Following the narrative thread laid out in these chapters, Ana Mendieta's relational and comparative racialization shows us there is no proper subject of Latino studies. Rather, through her cultural production, she asks for attention to the shifting terrains that bring subjects into focus—a project embedded in a long genealogy of women of color feminist theorizing that I linked to the heuristic of subjectless critique proffered by Kandice Chuh's Asian Americanist project. A growing transnational frame for the field of Latino studies requires attention to distinct geospecific racial ideologies, regional dynamics, and the hierarchized and slippery allocation of privilege. This optic can then structure a carefully approached collectivity that, through Asco as affect, we might understand as coalescing in critique of the normative through an aesthetic beyond ethno-nationalist celebration. Asco's production indeed reveals the value of contentious affects for collectivities to decenter the homogeneity of unity in favor of dissensus and uncivic comportment.[8] With the successful incorporation and instrumentalization of ethnonationalism for neoliberal multicultural celebration that offers us a mode of proper minority comportment, abjection, through Nao Bustamante, leads us to a brash embrace of queer failure. Abjection highlights affinity to and with the degraded, with a project of anti-identitarian embodiment whose affective charge is one of refusal of the terms of incorporation. In a moment of self-reflection, I offer that abject performances of Mormon apostasy, or as required by religious submission, respond to logics that structure our everyday with the ability to transform what we imagine of our past and future.

The difficulty of the sustained performance of abjection structures the residual traces that linger long past the body's ability to perform, steeping visual and textual documentation in the affective possibility gestured at throughout this book. I have not offered concrete paths that might amend the manifestos of those policy-oriented social movements with specific dictates and regulations. This is not my way. Instead, through the cultural producers of this book, whom I follow in abjection, I hope to have gestured at an affective terrain capable of reorienting our quotidian commitments, toward willful otherness, displaced phantoms, queer failure, and apostasy that guide us away from currently imagined politicized subjectivities to those we don't yet fully know but around which we might build across communities toward a dismantling of the present.

Notes

INTRODUCTION

1 Hennessy-Fiske, "'Dreamers' Stage Action in Laredo."

2 Nicholls, *The DREAMers*, 147.

3 DREAMers take their name from the policy they promote: the Development, Relief, and Education for Alien Minors Act.

4 In his study, *The DREAMers*, Nicholls credits these overlaps to the prevalence of LGTBQ-identifying leadership in the movement that has also made use of the queer symbology of the butterfly. The most visible artists of what some now call the undocu-queer movement include Faviana Rodriguez and Julio Salgado. The modality of queerness in their works is deserving of its own essay.

5 Rosaldo, "Cultural Citizenship and Educational Democracy," 402.

6 Bogado, "Here's How DACA Will Be Expanded under Obama"; Bogado, "The Executive Action Learning Curve"; and Bogado, "Obama Introduces Deferred Action for Parents."

7 Huntington, "The Hispanic Challenge."

8 Gómez-Barris, "Regarding the Central American Child's Pain." In her "Regarding 'the Mother of Anchor-Children,'" Vera-Rosas argues that this figure "[has] been historically imagined as violable, impure, and unable to achieve familial normalcy, a precondition to being an upstanding female and U.S. citizen." One might think of Moynihan's pathologized black mother as a symbolic cognate.

9 For more on Latina mothers and the culture of poverty see Cruz-Malavé, *Queer Latino Testimonio*; and Vargas, "Rumination on Lo Sucio."

10 On anti-immigrant legislation, Vera-Rosas specifically cites the Birthright Citizenship Act of 2009 and 2013. In her article "Regarding 'the Mother of Anchor-Children,'" she offers a glimpse into what this strategy might look like through an analysis of Jesus Barraza's poster art. She ultimately argues that centering this specific figure allows us "to formulate a dream of alternative futures of freedom from race, class, sex, and citizenship boundaries, while establishing a continuation between the past and present policing of racialized maternity." Here I am interested in what this abject figure foregrounds and the deployment of abjection as an aesthetic strategy.

11 Much has been written about the incoherence of the category "Latino." I draw inspiration from, among others, the work of Viego, *Dead Subjects*; Beltrán, *The Trouble with Unity*; and the recent special issue of *Women and Performance*, "Lingering in Latinidad: Theory, Aesthetics, and Performance in Latino/a Studies," edited by Guzmán and León.

12 Muñoz, "Feeling Brown," 68.

13 This is not a project that is invested in teasing out the differences between affect and feelings. Significant works that address affect and feelings include Cvetkovich, *An Archive of Feelings*; Highmore, "Bitter after Taste"; Muñoz, "Feeling Brown, Feeling Down" (among others); Ngai, *Ugly Feelings*; Doyle, *Hold It against Me*; and Rodríguez, *Sexual Futures*.

14 Working to elaborate a notion of queer temporality and noting the symbolic significance of the child to normative markers of time, Edelman argues that queerness charts an alternate mode of being in the world not beholden to those future symbolic inheritors, around whom heteronormative plans are structured, in favor of focusing on a present structured through the death drive (Edelman, *No Future*).

15 Muñoz, "Gimme Gimme This," 98, 96. In two of his final published essays, Muñoz emphasizes the reparative project he has been elaborating after his mentor Eve Kosofky Sedgwick. See Muñoz, "Gimme Gimme This"; and Muñoz, "Race, Sex and the Incommensurate."

16 Muñoz, *Cruising Utopia*.

17 This formation has been theorized as brownness by Latino studies scholars thinking beyond the models proffered by cultural nationalist ideologies including Muñoz, "Feeling Brown," "Feeling Brown, Feeling Down," "Vitalism's AfterBurn," and "Wise Latinas" (among others); Vargas, *Dissonant Divas in Chicana Music*; and Rodriguez, *Brown Gumshoes*.

18 Cvetkovich, "Public Feelings," 460. See also Love, *Feeling Backward*, who argues for the "need to pursue a fuller engagement with negative affects and with the intransigent difficulties of making feelings the basis of politics" (14).

19 Kant, *The Critique of Judgment* and *Observations on the Feeling of the Beautiful and Sublime*; Gikandi, *Slavery and the Culture of Taste*. See also Lloyd, "Race under Representation"; Jones, *Seeing Differently*; and Brown, *The Repeating Body*.

20 Highmore, "Bitter after Taste"; Rancière, *The Politics of Aesthetics*.

21 See Scott, *Extravagant Abjection*, 15. For links on abjection and language, see Kristeva, *Powers of Horror*, 4.

22 Shimakawa, *National Abjection*, 3; Kristeva, *Powers of Horror*, 4.

23 Scott, *Extravagant Abjection*, 17.

24 Census data released 1 July 2014 reveal that in California, Latinos are now the majority population.

25 Viego, *Dead Subjects*.

26 Kristeva's proposition that the mother is always already abject and her general adherence to Lacanian psychoanalysis, specifically what Wilkie-Stibbs calls a "reliance on the Oedipal paradigm," has garnered criticism or suspicion, especially from feminist theorists wary of psychoanalysis ("Borderland Children," 317). See Tyler, *Revolting Subjects*; and Bois and Krauss, *Formless*, for some of the critiques of Kristeva and the adoption of Batailles as the root of abject art in the 1990s. Also see Arya, *Abjection and Representation*, for the ways Kristeva both uses and transforms the psychoanalytic apparatus she draws from.

27 Menninghaus, *Disgust*.

28 Butler, *Bodies That Matter*, 3.

29 Georgelou, "Abjection and *Informe*," 27.

30 See especially Halperin, *What Do Gay Men Want?*; Shimakawa, *National Abjection*; and Scott, *Extravagant Abjection*. Halperin traces a queer, not psychoanalytic, genealogy of abjection into which he inserts Kristeva, seeking out a nonpathologizing account of abjection's appeal to gay men. For him, abjection reflects social stratifications, "an effect of the play of social power," that can promisingly congeal in collective "[expressions] of antisocial solidarity" (*What Do Gay Men Want?*, 71, 93). By casting abjection's function as such, he provides a way to move from Kristeva's model of interiority and through Butler's social matrix to a model for thinking about collectivity. For Shimakawa, abjection's collectivity, especially embodied Asian American collectivity, functions to cohere the notion of Americanness as national identity. Her invaluable study reminds us that "abjection is at once a specular and affective process" underscoring the utility of the performative for its study and inviting an engagement with aesthetics through its focus on the theatrical stage and the law (*National Abjection*, 19). Meanwhile, Scott's *Extravagant Abjection* seeks to reframe heroic narratives of overcoming historical legacies of trauma and abjection, instead performing queer readings of novels and essays of the "sexual exploitation or humiliation of black men . . . written by canonical African American authors in the 20th century" in order to render abjection a source of "counterintuitive *power*—indeed, what we can begin to think of as *black* power" (10, 9). Other contributions include Cruz-Malavé, "'What a Tangled Web!'"; Hartman, *Scenes of Subjection*; Nguyen, *A View from the Bottom*; Sharpe, *Monstrous Intimacies*; Stockton, *Beautiful Bottom, Beautiful Shame*; and Wilkie-Stibbs, "Borderland Children," in addition to the work in Latino studies cited below.

31 In his brief meditation on the politicized possibilities of abjection for queer Latino men living with AIDS, Alberto Sandoval-Sánchez narrates "bodies in revolt" as "corporalize[d] difference and heterogeneity with the potential to never cease 'challeng[ing their] master' (2) with a boundary crisis, the instability of meaning, and the disruption of order" ("Politicizing Abjection," 549). Deb Vargas's work on the queer analytic of *suciedad*—dirtiness—shows us there is much to be gained from pairing the study of Latinidad and the abject realm. Vargas offers us a study of *lo sucio*, suciedad, and *sucias* that spells out the characteristics of the discursive parameters through and in which the abject can occur that underscores the queerness at the core of Latinidad, amplifying Viego's claim of Latinidad's queer ethno-racial disruption. Within those social spaces marked by suciedad, Vargas locates a mode of queer sociality she terms *socia*-dad—a play on the phonic proximity between *sucia* (dirty) and *socia* (partner/colleague) (see Vargas, "Ruminations on Lo Sucio as a Latino Queer Analytic"; and Vargas, "Sucia Love").

32 Rodríguez, *Sexual Futures*, 21.

33 It is not my intention to position my own intervention against the decolonial project to which Rodríguez's points refer. A growing body of scholarship in many ways emerging from Latin American subaltern studies, the decolonial reframing of aesthetics within "global-local histories entangled with the local imperial history of Euro-American modernity, postmodernity, and altermodernity" is a project that renders visible many of the dynamics at play in my own study (Mignolo and Vázquez, "Decolonial AestheSis"). Indeed, in their "Decolonial AestheSis," Walter D. Mignolo and Rolando Vázquez's understanding of aesthetics as having played "a key role in configuring a canon, a normativity that enabled the disdain and the rejection of other forms of aesthetic practices, or, more precisely, other forms of aestheSis, of sensing and perceiving," outlines a social organization linked to aesthetic discourses that underscores the importance of its study. While scholarship focused on decoloniality stresses alternate origins and parallel understandings of sense and perception that Mignolo and Vázquez term aestheSis, I share with Rodríguez a desire to ruminate in the "taint of racialized abjection," situating it within one of the traditionally privileged categories of aesthetics, the sublime, with the hope of reorienting this dominant ideology instead of elaborating or exploring parallel practices. I do this with the understanding of Latinidad as a racial formation that emerged from and through these dominant discourses. On the decolonial, see also See, *The Decolonized Eye*; Hanna, Vargas, and Saldívar, *Junot Díaz and the Decolonial Imagination*; and Lane, Godoy-Anativa, and

Gómez-Barris, "What Decolonial Gesture Is." Another project with a similar political impulse worth noting is Imogen Tyler's *Revolting Subjects*. Her study elaborates a distinct methodology that centers an "empirical archive" over the affective and aesthetic archive that is the focus of this study.

34 I want to make note of a not-unrelated literature on Latino shame and gay shame in particular by Cruz-Malavé, "What a Tangled Web!"; Pérez, "You Can Have My Brown Body and Eat It, Too!"; La Fountain-Stokes, "Gay Shame, Latina- and Latino-Style"; and Muñoz, "Race, Sex and the Incommensurate." These were largely a response to white gay scholarship on the topic, particularly as it emerged from the Gay Shame conference held at the University of Michigan in 2003. For more about the conference, see Halperin and Traub, *Gay Shame*.

35 Ernst Bloch posits artwork as performing a productive presentiment that can incite a longing look forward, an anticipatory illumination that "provides *a connection to knowledge* at the very least, and it provides a connection to the *material of grasped hope* at the very most" ("The Wish-Landscape Perspective in Aesthetics," 74, emphasis in original). As José E. Muñoz interpreted and applied him in his study of queer utopias, "the anticipatory illumination of certain objects is a kind of potentiality that is open, indeterminate, like the affective contours of hope itself" (*Cruising Utopia*, 7). Engagement with negative affect is a sentiment also echoed in Juana María Rodríguez's work when she writes, "While the types of negation, refusal, masochism, and failure that Halberstam points to are indeed part of the everyday forms of social survival that I also wish to signal, I would argue that refusal, destruction, failure, masochism, and negativity are not the absence of sociality. Instead, they signal the active critical work of engagement and critique that is always already relational" (*Sexual Futures*, 12).

36 Starkman, "Episode 4."

37 Kant, *The Critique of Judgment*, 121.

38 For more on the "visual turn," see Mitchell, *Picture Theory*; and on the development of visual culture see Mirzoeff, *The Visual Culture Reader*.

39 Doyle, *Hold It against Me*, 4–5; Jones and Stephenson, *The Performing Body/The Performing Text*, 3.

40 Kant, *The Critique of Judgment*, 31, 39.

41 In his *Observations on the Feeling of the Beautiful and Sublime*, Kant makes the classed, sexed, gendered and racialized parameters for judgment extraordinarily clear in his dedicated sections on the differences between the genders and nations. Of special note is the appearance of colonization and slavery at the periphery of his study in his brief mention of slaves and noble savages. See also Ngai, *Our Aesthetic Categories*, 22.

42 Habermas, "Modernity versus Postmodernity."

43 Gikandi, *Slavery and the Culture of Taste*, 5.

44 Gikandi, *Slavery and the Culture of Taste*, xii.

45 Gikandi, *Slavery and the Culture of Taste*, 29.

46 Morley, *The Sublime*, 15–16.

47 See Gasché, *The Idea of Form*, 119. Rancière argues similarly, stating, "The rein-terpretation of the Kantian analysis of the sublime introduced into the field of art a concept that Kant had located beyond it. It did this in order to more effectively make art a witness to an encounter with the unrepresentable that cripples all thought, and thereby a witness for the prosecution against the arrogance of the grand aesthetico-political endeavor to have 'thought' become 'world'" (*The Politics of Aesthetics*, 10). Ngai, *Ugly Feelings*, 265.

48 Derrida, "Parergon," 41.

49 Morley, *The Sublime*, 12–13.

50 Brett Farmer has labeled the sublime "queer" as it can signal "radical disconti-nuity in sensory experience through which the quotidian is ruptured and trans-posed" ("The Fabulous Sublimity of Gay Diva Worship," 173).

51 For some, Bustamante's appearance on Bravo is itself a performance (Doyle, "Guest Stars"), and for others this is an experience that would lead to the de-velopment of her Soldadera project (Muñoz, "Wise Latinas"). I certainly read her participation in the series as a performance that possibly extended after her dismissal from the show into her viewing parties. I situate it, above, within the bounds of her earlier interventions.

52 Doyle differentiates between the acceptable difficulty within the art world, that of "the illegibility of nonfigurative and nonrepresentational work; the austerity of abstraction and minimalism; the rigor of institution critique," and the difficulty of audience engagement and discomfort (*Hold It against Me*, xvii).

53 Doyle, *Hold It against Me*, 146.

54 Ngai, *Our Aesthetic Categories*, 19. Elsewhere she writes that sublime encounter "ends by reversing these initial challenges to the self's autonomy, culminating in 'inspiriting satisfaction' rather than unpleasure" (*Ugly Feelings*, 265–266).

55 Morley, *The Sublime*, 16.

56 Butler, "Imitations and Gender Insubordination," 311.

57 Muñoz, "The Sense of Watching Tony Sleep," 550.

58 Both exhibits, for example, produced voluminous catalogues of the same title with scholarly essays, images, and, in the case of the later exhibition, the repro-duction of primary sources. In her "Lost Bodies: Early 1970s Los Angeles Perfor-mance Art in Art History" for the catalogue *Live Art LA: Performance in California, 1970–1983*, Amelia Jones delineates what can be considered the institutional archive of Asco. She writes, "For the past twenty years accounts of histories of Los Angeles and/or Chicano/a art have included the work of Asco—for example, the historically ground-breaking CARA: *Chicano Art: Resistance and Affirmation 1965–1985* at the UCLA Wight Art Gallery in Los Angeles in 1990; the 2008 *Phan-tom Sightings: Art After the Chicano Movement* show and the 2011 retrospective, part of the same Pacific Standard Time initiative supporting the book, *Asco Elite of the Obscure, A Retrospective 1972–1987*, the latter two both at LACMA, an insti-tution that has worked hard to redress its 1970s exclusion of Chicano art. And scholars such as David James, Chon Noriega, and C. Ondine Chavoya, Shifra

Goldman, and Marcos Sanches-Tranquillino have contributed important essays and books addressing Asco's history and practice. Perhaps most importantly, in 1998 Gamboa published his own collection of writings (edited by Noriega and entitled *Urban Exile*) which gives one side of the story, and the UCLA César E. Chavéz Center for Chicana and Chicano Studies acquired the archives of Gronk, among other key materials relating to Asco, in 2005–2007. The Center has also published a 2007 book by Max Benavidez on Gronk" (*Seeing Differently*, 133).

59 Rodriguez, *Brown Gumshoes.*

60 Melamed, *Represent and Destroy.*

61 Saldaña-Portillo, *The Revolutionary Imagination*, 156.

62 Beltrán, "Racial Presence versus Racial Justice," 138.

63 A list for this inspiring literature is long. A very short sampling includes Doyle, *Hold It against Me*; Nash, *The Black Body in Ecstasy*; Sharpe, *Monstrous Intimacies*; English, *How to See a Work of Art in Total Darkness*; Fusco and Wallis, *Only Skin Deep*. Many, many more can be found in the footnotes throughout this book.

CHAPTER 1. OTHER DESIRES

1 Mendieta, *Dialectics of Isolations: An Exhibition of Third World Women Artists of the United States.* Catalogue. 1980; The A.I.R. Gallery Archive; MSS 184; 11; 440 Fales Library and Special Collections, New York University Libraries.

2 Ricky, "The Passion of Ana," 75.

3 Quote taken from the earliest mission statement found in the collective's archives from 1987. Mission statements, 1987–1991, The A.I.R. Gallery Archive; MSS 184, Series 1, Subseries B, 2:61, Fales Library and Special Collections, New York University Libraries.

4 As José E. Muñoz explains, "Raymond Williams coined the term 'structure of feeling' to discuss the connections and points of solidarity between working-class groups and social experience that can be described as 'in process' yet nonetheless historically situated" ("Feeling Brown," 68). Further, Williams explains, "An alternative definition would be structures of experience: in one sense the better and wider word, but with the difficulty that one of its senses has that past tense which is the most important obstacle to recognition of the area of social experience which is being defined . . . not feeling against thought but thought as felt and feelings as thought: practical consciousness of a present kind, in a living and interelating continuity. We are then defining these elements as a 'structure': as a set, with specific internal relations, at once interlocking and in tension" ("Structure of Feeling," 132).

5 Hong and Ferguson, *Strange Affinities*, 9.

6 Carl Andre, famous minimalist sculptor and husband to Ana Mendieta, was tried and acquitted after being charged with pushing his wife, naked, out of their apartment window, thirty-four stories high, to her death in 1985. Her body left an indentation in the roof of the deli below their window that many found resembled her Siluetas, especially those that made use of blood or red pigment.

7 Kwon, "Bloody Valentines," 166.

8 Baum, "Shapely Shapelessness," 81; Quiroga, *Cuban Palimpsest*; Muñoz, "Vitalism's After-Burn."

9 A few notable exceptions include Baum, "Shapely Shapelessness"; Herzberg, whose early dissertation ("Ana Mendieta, the Iowa Years") and subsequent related publications were the first to center Mendieta's Iowa years; and Viso's *Unseen Mendieta*. These works address biographical oversights and contribute to an expanded art historical mapping.

10 Hong and Ferguson, *Strange Affinities*, 1, 9.

11 For critiques of intersectionality, see Pérez, *The Decolonial Imaginary*; Nash, "Rethinking Intersectionality"; Jasbir Puar, "Queer Times"; and Wiegman, *Object Lessons*.

12 Muñoz, "Vitalism's After-Burn," 192.

13 This critique participates in a critical Latino whiteness studies that has yet to be applied to revered figures like Mendieta. For more on critical Latino whiteness see López, "Cosa de Blancos."

14 Muñoz, "Feeling Brown," 68.

15 Organized by the Catholic Welfare Bureau with the help and cooperation of the federal government, the 1960–1962 Operación Pedro Pan helped "Cuban parents send their children unaccompanied to the U.S. to avoid Communist indoctrination" (Herzberg, "Ana Mendieta, the Iowa Years," 19). Operación Pedro Pan and the Cuba Children's Program, also organized by the Catholic Welfare Bureau, were responsible for the visa waivers and the relocation and placement of 14,000 unaccompanied minors, including the Mendieta sisters, who arrived in the United States in 1961 (Roulet, "'Ana Mendieta'").

16 The Mendieta sisters would eventually be reunited with their nuclear family, first their mother and younger brother and eventually their father. For more biographic information, see Viso, *Ana Mendieta*, 36–40; and Herzberg, "Ana Mendieta, the Iowa Years," 22–24.

17 Quiroga, *Cuban Palimpsest*, 177.

18 Butler, *Bodies That Matter*, 3.

19 Roulet, "'Ana Mendieta,'" 227.

20 Quoted in Blocker, *Where Is Ana Mendieta?*, 53.

21 The first master's thesis Mendieta submitted consisted of paintings—self-portraits now available only as photographs; see Herzberg, "Ana Mendieta, the Iowa Years," 55. Herzberg is a notable exception. I am indebted to her for illuminating this work.

22 Herzberg, "Ana Mendieta, the Iowa Years," 54.

23 For example, "Mendieta often told her sister Raquelín, who was also studying painting, that she was uninterested in conventional standards of beauty" (Herzberg, "Ana Mendieta, the Iowa Years," 57).

24 Herzberg, "Ana Mendieta, the Iowa Years," 77.

25 Herzberg, "Ana Mendieta, the Iowa Years," 54.

26 See Herzberg, "Ana Mendieta, the Iowa Years," for a reading focused on the influence of coursework.

27 Herzberg, "Ana Mendieta, the Iowa Years," 60.

28 Lane, *Blackface Cuba*, 16.

29 López, "Cosa de Blancos," 224.

30 "'La Montra': Rita Indiana Hernandez and The Politics of Performing Dominicaness" was presented at the inaugural Latino Studies Association conference, "Imagining Latina/o Studies: Past, Present, and Future: An International Latina/o Studies Conference," Chicago, 17–19 July 2014. Jaime draws from Eric Lott's influential study of the antebellum minstrel show in which he argued that blackface minstrelsy transgressed the color line while it remained centrally racist (Lott, *Love and Theft*).

31 Román and Flores, "Introduction," in *The Afro-Latin@ Reader*, 2.

32 Mendieta was known to refuse the labels feminist, Latina, modern, and postmodern, among others. In an interview with curator Olga Viso, a friend of Mendieta's, Liliana Porter, shared that "Ana liked Rome [where she was awarded a residency] because there she could be a 'Latina' without all that 'Hispanic bullshit' that was prevalent in the U.S." Porter shares what we might understand as Mendieta's deep frustration with U.S.-reified scripts for racial legibility. See "Interview with Liliana Porter conducted by Olga Viso." Smithsonian Institution Archives, Accession 08–096, Hirshhorn Museum and Sculpture Garden, Office of the Deputy Director, Exhibition Records.

33 Muñoz, *Cruising Utopia*.

34 Hull, Scott, and Smith, *All the Women Are White*; Moraga and Anzaldúa, *This Bridge Called My Back*.

35 Anzaldúa, "La Prieta," 220–221.

36 Breder, "Intermedia," 115.

37 Jones and Stephenson, "Introduction," in *The Performing Body*, 1.

38 Kristeva, *Powers of Horror*, 1.

39 For a reading of this work focused on gendered violence, see, among others, Agustí, "'I Carve Myself into My Hands'"; and Baum, "Shapely Shapelessness"; Cabañas, "Ana Mendieta."

40 Guterl, *Seeing Race in Modern America*.

41 Butler, "Imitation and Gender Insubordination."

42 Butler, "Imitation and Gender Insubordination," 308.

43 Butler, "Imitation and Gender Insubordination," 311.

44 Butler, "Imitation and Gender Insubordination," 308–311.

45 Smith, *Conquest*, 153.

46 Hong, *The Ruptures of American Capital*, xxx.

47 Anzaldúa, *Borderlands/La Frontera*, 102.

48 Sandoval, *Methodology of the Oppressed*, 547.

49 Sandoval-Sánchez, "Politicizing Abjection," 549.

50 In her essay "Memory of History," Olga Viso explains that Mendieta "believed that her works could exist on different levels in the time and place of their creation and in the residues and documentation that live afterwards. She contended her works could be both the 'body earthwork *and* photo'" (70).

51 See Herzberg, "Ana Mendieta, the Iowa Years," 163–164. Though Kelly assisted Mendieta the day of the performance, Herzberg reports that Mendieta rehearsed the scene, specifically the placement of the table on which Mendieta lay as well as the positioning of her body, with another friend, Noble Hendrick, who was unavailable during the actual performance. I imagine that, like a piece performed shortly thereafter, *Dead on the Street*, Mendieta waited until the last of the spectators left to end the scene, though it is unclear who, if anyone, helped her remove the restraints.

52 Ana Mendieta, "Iowa Years Spheres of Influence." Smithsonian Institution Archives, Accession 08–096, Hirshhorn Museum and Sculpture Garden, Office of the Deputy Director, Exhibition Records.

53 Derrida, "Parergon," 41.

54 Ngai, *Ugly Feelings*, 267.

55 Gonzales-Day, *Lynching in the West*, 182.

56 Mendieta, "Mendieta: Writings."

57 Cabañas, "Ana Mendieta."

58 Halperin, *What Do Gay Men Want?*, 94.

59 Halperin, *What Do Gay Men Want?*, 87.

60 *Untitled* (Silueta Series, Mexico) has previously been known as *Imagen de Yagul* in scholarly literature.

61 Lucy Lippard, "Foreword," in Redfern, *Who Is Ana Mendieta?*

62 Cabañas, "Ana Mendieta," 16.

63 Cabañas, "Ana Mendieta," 16, 14.

64 Viso, *Ana Mendieta*, 47.

65 Viso, *Ana Mendieta*, 114.

66 See García, *Havana USA*.

67 It should be noted that this permission was rescinded when Breder's and Mendieta's nude work offended locals. See "Field Notes from Site Visits (Olga and Hans Breder), May 6–10, 2002," Box 8, Folder "Interviews B," Smithsonian Institution Archives, Accession 08–096, Hirshhorn Museum and Sculpture Garden, Office of the Deputy Director, Exhibition Records.

68 In her field notes for the Ana Mendieta retrospective, Olga Viso notes the similarities between local cemetery practices and Mendieta's Siluetas. See "Field Notes from Site Visits (Olga and Hans Breder), May 6–10, 2002." Box 8, Folder "Interviews B," Smithsonian Institution Archives, Accession 08–096, Hirshhorn Museum and Sculpture Garden, Office of the Deputy Director, Exhibition Records.

69 "Ana Mendieta/Narrative Account of Career," Box 6, Folder "1979," Smithsonian Institution Archives, Accession 08-096, Hirshhorn Museum and Sculpture Garden, Office of the Deputy Director, Exhibition Records.

70 Herzberg, "Ana Mendieta, the Iowa Years," 173.

71 Brett, "One Energy," 181.

72 Kristeva, *Powers of Horror*, 4.

73 Wilkie-Stibbs, "Borderland Children," 319.

74 Eng, Halberstam, and Muñoz, "What's Queer about Queer Studies Now?," 3.

75 Eng, Halberstam, and Muñoz, "What's Queer about Queer Studies Now?," 4. In her "Queer Theory and Native Studies," Andrea Smith argues for the value of subjectless critique for native studies and the reciprocal need for native studies to augment queer theory. She argues that even when informed by queer of color critique, queer theory "disguises the fact that the queer postcolonial, or environmentally conscious subject is simultaneously a settler subject" (52).

76 Eng, Halberstam, and Muñoz, "What's Queer about Queer Studies Now?," 3.

77 Mendieta, *Dialectics of Isolation*, emphasis added.

78 For example, in Harmony's resignation letter, she writes, "I just wanted to be in touch and to tell you that I have no 'weird' feelings between you and I—despite the recent upheaval between the Native American womens exhibition and A.I.R. . . . Frankly, I also found some of the racist attitudes coming from some A.I.R. members rather appalling. Its too bad. I think it would have been nice for the exhibit to be at A.I.R, a womens gallery—and I think it would have been good for A.I.R. too" ("Harmony, Letter," 1 March 1985. The A.I.R. Gallery Archive; mss 184; 2; 93; Fales Library and Special Collections, New York University Libraries). Additionally, when responding to a survey/questionnaire, in answer to "what issues would you like to see addressed in any subsequent discussions?" Howardena Pindell, a contributing artist to *Dialectics*, answered, "Issues of Racism within the Women's Movement and Solutions" ("Members—surveys/questionnaires re: 'Feminist Art and Practice,' 1981–1992." The A.I.R. Gallery Archive; mss 184; 2; 99; Fales Library and Special Collections, New York University Libraries). Relatedly, as Griefen points out, Mendieta's name was "misspelled in at least five different ways by fellows artists and outside critics, suggesting a range of alternate nationalities" ("Ana Mendieta at A.I.R. Gallery," 180).

79 Griefen, "Ana Mendieta at A.I.R. Gallery," 174; "Current Issues/Monday Evening programs, 1973–1987," The A.I.R. Gallery Archive, MSS 184, 3; 21; Fales Library and Special Collections, New York University Libraries.

80 In a copy of a letter asking for funding written by Sally Webster to Phillip Morris, Mobil Oil, and Con Ed (known for their "support of minority groups"), she writes, "It is being curated by two members of A.I.R., the Cuban-American sculptor, Ana Mendieta, and the Japanese-American sculptor, Kazuko (biographies enclosed) and it will showcase the work of eight extraordinary young American artists. . . . The eight artists chose[n] for this exhibition are: Judith Baca, a street muralist from Los Angeles; Lydia Okumura, a Brazilian-born painter of Japanese descent now living in New York; Zarina, a cast-paper sculptor born in India and who now lives in New York; Beverly Buchanan, a black sculptor from Macon, Georgia; Janet Henry, a black mixed-media artist from Jamaica,

New York; Howardena Pindell, a black New Yorker painter and video artist; Selina Whitefeather, an American Indian, half-black environmental artist living in New York; and Senga Negudi, an Afro-American sculptor from Los Angeles." Webster, Ally. Letter. 1980. The A.I.R. Gallery Archive; mss 184; 11; 440; Fales Library and Special Collections, New York University Libraries.

81 Muñoz, *Cruising Utopia*, 1.

82 Williams, "Structure of Feelings," 132.

83 Herzberg implies Mendieta did not become a feminist until after she relocated to New York, stating, "Mendieta's evolving consciousness as a feminist artist occurred over a period of time. Suffice it to say that, prior to spring of 1975, she seemed to debunk the notion of a feminist art or feminist issues. She did not belong to any university women's group that existed during those years. Although she evidently felt passionate rage over the 1973 murder of Sara Jane Oten, which was expressed through a series of rape pieces, Mendieta never joined the Rape hotline that was established to help women who were victims of abuse in Iowa City. From all the evidence at hand, it seems that Mendieta strongly defended her right to succeed in art because she was a person, not because she was a woman" ("Ana Mendieta, the Iowa Years," 258). Additionally, in an interview conducted by Herzberg for the Smithsonian, when asked about the connection between Mendieta's work and exile/race, Dotty Attie replied, "I didn't think of her work at all as political. Not at all" (Attie, "Interview with Dotty Attie 3/2/94," Current Issues/Monday Evening programs, 1973–1987," The A.I.R. Gallery Archive; mss 184, 3; 21; Fales Library and Special Collections, New York University Libraries). In the case of A.I.R. Gallery members, this may have in fact reflected a desire not to see race as an issue among members despite letters written to the collective on "racist attitudes coming from some A.I.R. members." See "Harmony, letter," 1 March 1985. The A.I.R. Gallery Archive; mss 184; 2; 93; Fales Library and Special Collections, New York University Libraries.

84 Sandoval, *Methodology of the Oppressed*, 184.

CHAPTER 2. PHANTOM ASSHOLES

1 Chavoya, "Internal Exiles."

2 Barthes, *Camera Lucida*.

3 Chavoya and Gonzalez, "Asco and the Politics of Revulsion," 53. In her essay "'Traitor Prophets': Asco's Art as a Politics of the In-Between," Amelia Jones shares that research reveals the actual site of the photograph was Malibu, well beyond their fictive municipality of East Los Angeles, but nonetheless rendered within its affective parameters by the performance (111–114).

4 Gamboa would not provide permission to publish this image, stating simply in e-mail correspondence that it was not his "approved image for the work." This phantom document can be seen in Chavoya, "Internal Exiles"; and Romo, *Patssi Valdez*.

5 Chon A. Noriega, e-mail message to CSRC Press, 1 July 2015. *Ascozilla* was a solo

exhibition held at California State University, Los Angeles. Some authors have identified the flyer as a No Movie; see, for example, Milch, "Dead Girls, Monsters and Assholes," 9–10.

6   The dates I use here are the ones most used by art historians and those provided by Gamboa in *Urban Exile*.

7   Muñoz, "Feeling Brown," 68.

8   For Asco's connections to the punk scene, see Gunckel, "Vexing Questions"; and on the East Los Angeles punk scene preceding the date cited by Gunckel (1977), see Bag, *Violence Girl*. In his manifesto-like "Rasquachismo: A Chicano Sensibility," published in the catalogue for *Chicano Aesthetics: Rasquachismo*, Tómas Ybarra-Frausto describes the now widely used term *rasquache* as "an underdog perspective—a view from *los de abajo*. An attitude rooted in resourcefulness and adaptability yet mindful of stance and style." The manifesto is expansive and explains that "to be *rasquache* is to be down but not out (*fregado pero no jodido*)" in addition to providing a list of "low" and "high" rasquache examples, among which are "the 'No Movies' of ASCO" (Ybarra-Frausto, "Rasquachismo," 5–7).

9   Rodríquez, *Next of Kin*, 21. Rodríguez argues that while it is now common practice to malign cultural nationalism, he believes in a generative engagement with Chicano family. In a way, Asco joins Rodríguez in seeking out a sense of kin beyond an essentialist versus antiessentialist binary.

10   See, among many others, Moraga and Anzaldúa, *This Bridge Called My Back*; Alarcón, "Traddutora, Traditora"; Morales, *Chicana*; Rodríguez, *Next of Kin*.

11   Viego, *Dead Subjects*, 24.

12   To be clear, I am not discounting the radical force of a call for self-determination and the construction of a mestizo nation verbalized in manifestos of the movement like "El Plan Espiritual de Aztlán." Rather, what I am pointing to is how this impetus becomes institutionalized in large part because of the way the mestizo nation is constructed through the reproduction of liberal ideologies.

13   In an interview with Gamboa, who was also a journalist, Gronk expresses a desire to have the audience "get sick" over their No Movies. See "Gronk and Herrón: Muralists" in Gamboa, *Urban Exile*.

14   Hernandez, "Performing the Archival Body," 115. See especially Chavoya, "Internal Exiles," on abjection; and Chavoya and Gonzalez, "Asco and the Politics of Revulsion," on revulsion.

15   Viego, *Dead Subjects*, 6.

16   Viego, *Dead Subjects*, 6; Beltrán, *The Trouble with Unity*.

17   Muñoz, "'Gimme Gimme This,'" 96.

18   See Gonzalez, "Frida, Homeboys, and the Butch Gardens School of Fine Art"; Jones, "'Traitor Prophets'"; Hernandez, *The Fire of Life*; Hernandez, "Drawing Offensive/Offensive Drawing"; Flores-Sternad and Legoretta, "Cyclona and Early Chicano Performance Art."

19   Cvetkovich, *An Archive of Feelings*, 7.

20   Hernandez, "The Art Outlaws of East L.A."

21 While I refer to this grouping throughout this chapter as Asco, I do not mean to reify the grouping—though I understand this to be a natural consequence. Instead, with Asco I refer to the structure of feeling brought into focus through them but which exceeds particular participants. It is useful to again underscore that their moniker was adopted retroactively, well after most of the early performances featured in this chapter. At all stages, many performances included individuals with their own performative artistic practices.

22 While additional voices and archival collections supplement Gamboa's account, such as Gronk's and Cyclona/Robert Legorreta's papers at UCLA's Chicano Studies Research Center, Gamboa's still dominates accounts of the collective.

23 Hinch, "Walking Mural."

24 Derrida, *Archive Fever*, 55.

25 Hernandez, "The Art Outlaws of East L.A."

26 Hernandez, "Drawing Offensive/Offensive Drawing," 125.

27 Hernandez, "Drawing Offensive/Offensive Drawing," 127.

28 Hernandez, "Drawing Offensive/Offensive Drawing," 125.

29 Hernandez writes, "Thus, mariconógraphy retrieves these artistic interventions from archival obscurity and redefines the place of maricones in the formative visual language of gay and lesbian liberation and, in particular, the Chicana/o art movement" ("Drawing Offensive/Offensive Drawing," 146).

30 See Jones, "'Traitor Prophets'"; and, more recently, McMahon, "Self-Fashioning through Glamour and Punk."

31 See Tyler, *Revolting Subjects*, for more on "revolt" as both disgusting and social unrest.

32 See Chavoya, "Internal Exiles," 191.

33 See Kosiba-Vargas, *Harry Gamboa and Asco*, 13; Ontiveros, "Retheorizing Activism," 56–57.

34 See Limón, *Mexican Ballads*.

35 The message of "Yo soy Joaquín" was amended by feminists in texts like *Chicana*, a 1979 film directed by Sylvia Morales that directly responded to Luis Valdez's film as well as texts written by Cherríe Moraga ("Queer Aztlán") and Gloria Anzaldúa (*Borderlands*). Critique of the vision put forth in these texts continues into the present with works like Rodríguez, *Next of Kin*; and Saldaña-Portillo, "Who's the Indian in Aztlán?"

36 Rodríguez, *Next of Kin*, 29, 21.

37 Beltrán, "Racial Presence versus Racial Justice," 138.

38 Rodríguez, *Next of Kin*, 141. I should note that while Rodríguez critiques this tendency, he goes on to explore carnalismo as a stage of desire between gay men.

39 Rodríguez, *Next of Kin*, 20.

40 Rodríguez, *Next of Kin*, 3.

41 Sedgwick, *Between Men*.

42 Lewis, *Children of Sanchez*; Cruz-Malavé, *Queer Latino Testimonio*; Vargas, "Ruminations on Lo Sucio."

43 See Chavoya, "Internal Exiles," 191. Gamboa was closely monitored by the Federal Bureau of Investigation as part of its domestic surveillance program to identify anti-American subversives, COINTELPRO (Kosiba-Vargas, *Harry Gamboa and Asco*, 23). Gamboa's appearance on the list was linked with efforts to defund federal funding for programs serving minorities. As Gamboa reports, "I was used as an example as someone that was receiving federal funds under the EOP program and that if someone like me were to receive a college education, that I would really become a danger to society and really pose a risk and a threat. And you saw that list. So you know there's a lot of recognizable names. . . . And the thing was there was no trial. There was nothing. But again, it was sort of like it's a pronouncement of guilt in this very official-looking document. And suddenly, you're an enemy. And you're an enemy" (Gamboa, Oral history interview with Harry Gamboa Jr).

44 Gamboa, "In the City of Angels," in *Urban Exile*, 75; and Chavoya, *Internal Exiles*, 191. Gronk also performed more unconventional acts of protest, allegedly shaving his head when he was drafted and living in a tent on the roof of a college building as a form of protest.

45 Valdez, Oral history interview with Patssi Valdez; Herrón, Oral history interview with Willie Herrón.

46 Gamboa, *Urban Exile*, 72–75.

47 Anzaldúa, *Borderlands*, 106–107. In her famed *Borderlands/La Frontera*, Gloria Anzaldúa insists on the vital inclusion of jotería, or queerness, in oppositional movements for social justice. I attempt to bring the jotería to the following section.

48 Gronk also did stage sets, costumes, and Cyclona's makeup.

49 My description of this performance draws from oral history interviews with Cyclona by Jennifer Flores-Sternad and of Gronk by Jeffrey Rangel for the Smithsonian Institution Archives of American Art as well as by reading the visual resources from The Fire of Life: The Robert Legorreta/Cyclona Collection at the Chicano Studies Research Center, UCLA.

50 The white face and dark lids and lips would become both Cyclona's and Valdez's signature makeup. Both were initially made up by Gronk, but owned and transformed their painted faces in performance.

51 Legoretta refused the label "drag queen" to describe his performance persona as well as the term "gay" to describe his sexual practice/identity. I have retained use of the masculine pronoun when describing Cyclona as he has done in interviews.

52 In Cyclona's own narration of the performance, he claims this scene as "a protest against gerontocracy, a society ruled by men" (Flores-Sternad and Legoretta, "Cyclona and Early Chicano Performance Art," 482).

53 It is unclear how the audience members acquired these, but this is how Cyclona recalls the event: "The audience went totally berserk: they started throwing eggs, they set the place on fire, and they called the police. The police started banging on the stage to stop the play. We literally had to run for our lives. We all took off

running and laughing and left everything from the play there" (Flores-Sternad and Legoretta, "Cyclona and Early Chicano Performance Art," 482). In an interview for the Smithsonian, Gronk provides a similar account, though it is unclear if it is the audience or the performers manipulating the eggs: "There were like all these kids running around on that stage, somebody banging a drum and somebody getting a coke bottle and crushing eggs underneath somebody's serape and all this activity going on this stage. And then somebody got these fried eggs and threw it on somebody's back and it burned the kid" (Gronk, Oral history interview with Gronk).

54 Flores-Sternad and Legoretta, "Cyclona and Early Chicano Performance Art," 482.

55 Gronk, Oral history interview with Gronk. In other versions of this performance, Gronk describes this actor as a "high school guy and he's wearing a poncho and he's going to have these raw eggs in a Coke bottle underneath him," and Cyclona was to "pull and you squeeze the eggs and crush 'em, and then you lick it and then you get the bottle and you throw it at the audience."

56 Gamboa, *Urban Exile*, 64.

57 Sandoval-Sánchez, "Politicizing Abjection," 549.

58 Gronk, Oral history interview with Gronk.

59 Gronk, Oral history interview with Gronk.

60 Gronk, Cyclona, and Mundo Meza formed part of a queer trio that regularly paraded through East Los Angeles outrageously clad and making "a scene." In 1972 Gronk was drafted and Legorreta moved to live with his mother in Lakewood, Colorado. As Hernandez writes, "Gronk no longer had a cohort of confrontational, gender-bending 'glitter queens'" (*The Fire of Life*, 15); instead he reports redirecting that energy to Asco. Both Legoretta and Meza would participate in Asco performances after 1975.

61 Gronk, Oral history interview with Gronk.

62 Herrón, Oral history interview with Willie Herrón.

63 It is unclear from the archives whether this was the name the artists collectively went by or if this was the name given to the series of pieces, since these are often retroactively narrated as Asco pieces, even by Asco members, though they had yet to adopt the moniker. For example, when asked by Smithsonian interviewer Jeffrey Rangel whether these actions were "you and Willie? Or is this all ASCO?" Gronk responds, "This was all ASCO" (Gronk, Oral history interview with Gronk).

64 Gronk, Oral history interview with Gronk.

65 Gronk, Oral history interview with Gronk.

66 Hinch, "Walking Mural."

67 Gamboa, *Urban Exile*, 74.

68 These alternate views were included in the museum catalogue for *Asco: Elite of the Obscure, a Retrospective, 1972–1987*.

69 Interestingly, Gamboa has referred to Valdez as "the tail of the comet ASCO," a

flashy residue following the substance of the comet (Kosiba-Vargas, *Harry Gamboa and Asco*, 88).

70 Noriega, "Conceptual Graffiti and the Public Art Museum"; Ontiveros, "Retheorizing Activism."

71 Noriega, "Conceptual Graffiti and the Public Art Museum," 260.

72 Beltrán, *The Problem with Unity*, 37.

73 While, as Jones points out, Valdez was largely left out of the flourishing LA feminist art scene (*Seeing Differently*, 138), her profile here might make the contemporary viewer think of Barbara Kruger's *Untitled (Your Gaze Hits the Side of My Face)* from 1981–1983, showing not only Valdez's salience for the avant-garde but also for feminist postmodern strategies.

74 The negative affect invoked throughout this chapter was tapped into for other collaborations, notably those between Gronk and Jerry Dreva, and Patssi Valdez with Cyclona.

75 Muñoz, "Gimme Gimme This," 109.

76 Gamboa, *Urban Exile*, 75–76.

77 Chavoya, "Internal Exiles," 197.

78 Valdez, Oral history interview with Patssi Valdez.

79 Viego, *Dead Subjects*, 6.

80 Valdez, Oral history interview with Patssi Valdez.

81 Description of event culled from photographs by Seymore Rosen. Prints of the photographs were accessed in the Tómas Ybarra-Frausto Research Material on Chicano Art in the Smithsonian Institution Archives.

82 Gamboa, *Urban Exile*, 76–77.

83 Pontius Pilate is best known as the man who sent Christ to his execution. In the biblical account, Pilate finds no sin in Christ and presents him to the Jews of Jerusalem, who then advocate for his execution. Pilate washes his hands in their presence to show his reluctance to send Christ to his death. Pontius Pilate, also called Popcorn, would become a recurring character in future performances.

84 Gamboa, *Urban Exile*, 76–77.

85 Ontiveros, "Retheorizing Activism," 80.

86 Indeed, both Gronk and Herrón would be drafted but would successfully evade deployment.

87 Chavoya, "Internal Exiles," 193.

88 Legoretta was preparing for a move from East Los Angeles to Lakewood, Colorado, to live with his mother (Hernandez, *The Fire of Life*).

89 Gamboa, *Urban Exile*, 75.

90 Burnham, "Asco," 408.

91 "Cruel Profit" is a fiction piece written by Gamboa, distinct from a performance by Asco of the same title. On Chicano muralists, see, for example, the hilarious "Gronk and Herrón: Muralists" from 1976 in Gamboa, *Urban Exile*.

92 Gamboa, *Urban Exile*, 365–366.

93 Gamboa, *Urban Exile*, 79.

94 Chavoya briefly mentions absence in his essay "Internal Exiles" when he writes, "*Asshole Mural* is a performative, active invention of monuments, and in the process marks an absence. Asco's aesthetic strategies and interventionist tactics are a project of cultural invention emanating from neither the fragment nor the ruin, but from the absence. This is perhaps the crucial difference and theoretical site of resistance between Asco and the more traditionally defined Chicano art movement" (199).

95 Ngai, *Ugly Feelings*, 5.

96 Jones, "'Traitor Prophets,'" 123.

97 Viego, *Dead Subjects*, 15.

98 Viego, *Dead Subjects*, 29.

CHAPTER 3. OF BETTIES DECOROUS AND ABJECT

1 *Work of Art: The Next Great Artist*'s executive producers are Dan Cutforth and Sarah Jessica Parker, with China Chow as host, joined by Bill Powers (gallery owner), Jeanne Greenberg Rohatyn (curator, gallery owner), and Jerry Saltz (art critic for *New York* magazine). Simon de Pury, an auctioneer, serves as the participants' advisor. The show borrows its format from Bravo's successful program *Project Runway*, in which competitors create work in response to a per-episode challenge for which they are judged. The top and bottom three works are discussed before a winner is selected, and the artist that created the weakest piece is sent home.

2 The plastic flower was not actually covered in excrement but was largely read as scatological.

3 Wolff, "*Work of Art* Exit Interview." The entire quote from her exit interview with *New York Magazine* reads, "Instead of the art world intervening in the mainstream, I think the mainstream is intervening in the art world."

4 See Muñoz, "Wise Latinas."

5 In her book *Represent and Destroy*, Jodi Melamed theorizes multiple phases of racial hegemony in the United States, which she argues frequently incorporate "antiracist terms of value," prompting the emergence of new terms of "racialized privilege" and "racialized stigma" (2). What she calls the liberal multiculturalism of the 1980s and 1990s, the backdrop for Bustamante's *America, the Beautiful*, she argues, "provided weak terms of social solidarity, enjoining Americans to affirm a positive cultural pluralism" that augmented a previous project of white unification by emphasizing the immigrant narrative through which the nation was forged. "With the inclusion of people of color" in this project, she tells us, "the thesis could then be reworked to describe the United States as an internalized model of global diversity" in which neoliberal multiculturalism becomes an attribute of "global capitalism itself" (35, 42). For more on the history of Latinization of the U.S. and Latino markets, see Dávila, *Latinos, Inc.*; and Negrón-Muntaner, *Boricua Pop*.

6 The Colombian *Yo Soy Betty, la fea* (1999–2001) was adapted in 2006 for Mexico as *La fea más bella* (2006–2007) (Benavidez, *Drugs, Thugs and Divas*).

7 *Ugly Betty* won fifty-five of the 128 awards for which it was nominated, including eight ALMA Awards, five NAACP Awards, three Emmy Awards, and two Golden Globes (Esposito, "Is Ugly Betty a Real Woman?," 328).

8 Esposito, "Is Ugly Betty a Real Woman?," 330. Different roles often serve as vehicles for the archetypes; for example, a "maid" may double as a clown, providing comic relief in addition to theatrical domestic service.

9 Macías, "Femininity Ain't Pretty"; and Paredez, "All about My (Absent) Mother."

10 For excellent work on Justin, see Pérez, "Homo-Narrative Capture, Racial Proximity, and the Queer Latino Child."

11 Paredez, "All about My (Absent) Mother," 131.

12 While Ferrera is striking, I am not diminishing the problematic nature of her limited casting options. She is, after all, not the dominant type in either body shape or color, represented on the show by the many models of *Mode* but also by the character Amanda.

13 Honduran American America Ferrera plays Betty; her father is played by Cuban actor Tony Plana; her sister is played by mixed Puerto Rican Irish Ana Ortiz; and her nephew is played by mixed Puerto Rican Italian Mark Indelicato.

14 Ybarra-Frausto, "Rasquachismo."

15 Other forms of Chicano kitsch include but are not limited to tiny rhinestoned sombreros, porcelain saints, flowered oilcloth table linens, and a glitter Virgen de Guadalupe.

16 Paredez, "All about My (Absent) Mother," 139.

17 See Benavidez, *Drugs, Thugs and Divas.*

18 Amaya, "Citizenship, Diversity, Law and *Ugly Betty*," 804, 815.

19 Transcribed from the program by author.

20 Horta and Hayek, "Swag," *Ugly Betty* (2007).

21 Horta and Hayek, "The Passion of the Betty," *Ugly Betty* (2010). As it turns out, Betty's orthodontist was keeping her braces on as an excuse to see her.

22 The movie *The Devil Wears Prada*, based on the book by the same title, perfectly illustrates makeover conventions.

23 In "The Passion of the Betty," she tells her orthodontist, "Small changes. No bangs. New glasses."

24 Here, I am quoting an insult alternate-world Daniel hurls at alternate-world Betty, whom he belittles.

25 This strategy is used on at least two occasions when Becky Newton, who plays Amanda, appears as Sofia Reyes's (Selma Hayek) "ugly" assistant and when Lucy Liu guest stars as a stunning lawyer, whom Daniel stood up in their college years when she was significantly "Betty"-er.

26 Melamed, *Represent and Destroy*, 41, 42.

27 Paredez, "All about My (Absent) Mother," 64.

28 President Obama was elected midway through the run of the show. Indeed, Ignacio, as a newly designated citizen, would vote in that particular election.

29 Chow, *The Protestant Ethnic*, 47.

30 Chow, *The Protestant Ethnic*, 32.

31 Bustamante, "*America, the Beautiful*," in *Mega Compilation*.

32 Bustamante, *Interview with Nao Bustamante*. For my reading, I use her 2002 performance at the Hemispheric Institute Encuentro, available on video in their digital archive and as part of Bustamante's *Mega Compilation*.

33 Bustamante, *Interview with Nao Bustamante*.

34 Bustamante, *Interview with Nao Bustamante*.

35 Proposition 187 was eventually deemed unconstitutional, though the other two still stand.

36 Goldman, "La Princesa Plástica."

37 Muñoz, "The Vulnerability Artist," 199.

38 Mendible, "Introduction," in *From Bananas to Buttocks*, 13.

39 Bustamante, *Interview with Nao Bustamante*.

40 Archibold, "Arizona Enacts Stringent Law on Immigration." I elaborate more on these propositions in chapter 4.

41 These included Arizona's SB 1070, Alabama's HB 56, and similar laws in Indiana, Georgia, South Carolina, and Utah. Beard and Neighbor, "National Council of La Raza Calls Off Boycott."

42 Doyle, "Guest Stars."

43 This moment is also marked by increased deregulation, privatization, and surveillance and the discursive construction of a public interest through which politicians/lobbyists no longer had to represent an actual public interest at a moment of intense homophobia in the face of the AIDS epidemic and xenophobia.

44 Doyle, "Guest Stars"; and Muñoz, "Wise Latinas." This substance is described by Doyle as art world detritus and by Muñoz as "primal-looking brown fluids."

45 It is surprising that they would expect her to provide a narrative of her work, given Bustamante's often played-back proclamation during an earlier episode's bottom three critique that she is "not responsible for [their] experience of [her] work."

46 Interestingly, Doyle shares that truly shocking art actually disgusts, repels—precisely the judges' response (Doyle, "Guest Stars").

47 Wolff, "*Work of Art* Exit Interview." For me the piece recalls the character of Bustamante's *Given Over to Want* (2007), a work about succumbing to base desires and overconsumption, an interesting character to bring to a show on the popular commodification of art consumption. Doyle makes a similar comparison in her "Guest Stars."

48 For more on Bustamante and failure, see Chambers-Letson, "The Politics of Failure."

49 At an artist talk, Bustamante shared that at this point in the show she wanted to be kicked off. Bustamante claims she was actively pursuing failure. She was thus not only embracing failure in performance but also seeking it as an outcome (Bustamante, "Artist Talk").

50 Halberstam, *The Queer Art of Failure*, 88.

1 Sacred LDS texts include the Book of Mormon, the Bible, the Pearl of Great Price, and Doctrine and Covenants—where modern-day revelation to the church's prophet is recorded. I am referring here to the 1981 and 2013 editions of the Book of Mormon. The church released a digital format in 2013 that also includes these images. See Book of Mormon, "Illustrations," Church of Jesus Christ of Latter-Day Saints, accessed 27 June 2017, https://www.lds.org/scriptures/bofm/illustrations?lang=eng.

2 Morgan and Promey, "Introduction," in *The Visual Culture of American Religions*, 6.

3 On the problematic valences of this claim and a critique of claims to indigeneity, see chapter 2; and Saldaña-Portillo, *Indian Given*.

4 New scholarship by Jared Hickman reads this narrative as an apocalyptic warning to U.S. imperial prosperity (Hickman, "*The Book of Mormon* as Amerindian Apocalypse").

5 Hansen, *Mormonism and the American Experience*.

6 See chapter 2 for an elaboration of the ideological function of Aztlán.

7 Stevenson, *Sensational Devotion*.

8 In the LDS church, a worthy married priesthood holder is called to serve as bishop for four to seven years from among the local congregation or ward. He presides over weekly gatherings and other lay appointments as well as the spiritual well-being of his congregation. His time, as with other lay appointments, is volunteered. I also received a blessing during which my ancestral tribe was revealed to me, indeed linking me to the Lamanite lineage.

9 Griffith, *God's Daughters*, 14.

10 According to the Pew Research Center's "A Portrait of Mormons in the U.S.," "Converts are more likely than lifelong members to come from minority racial and ethnic groups. One-in-ten converts to Mormonism are black, and nearly all black Mormons are converts. An additional one-in-ten Mormon converts are Hispanic, and just 72% are white; by contrast, 91% of lifelong Mormons are white. Converts are also more than three times as likely as lifelong members to be immigrants to the U.S. (14% vs. 4%)."

11 Megli, "Growth of Latino Membership."

12 Watson, "Statistical Report, 2006"; Gurnon, "Minority Mormons." Additionally, Megli notes significant growth in the faith—a "45.5 percent increase to more than 14 million members worldwide between 2000 and 2010" (Megli, "Growth of Latino Membership"). According to the Pew Research Center on Religion and Life, these numbers make the church comparable in size to the U.S. Jewish population (Pew Research Center, "A Portrait of Mormons in the U.S."). In his "Mormonism," Solórzano writes, "In the United States, Mormonism represents the fourth largest denomination with 5.5 million members representing 1.93 percent of the total US population."

13 Reeve, *Religion of a Different Color*, 3.

14 Stevenson, *Sensational Devotion*, 15. Stevenson elaborates a theory of evangelical dramaturgy as an embodied aesthetic with both affirming and interpellative functions. Mormons are by no means considered evangelical, though they do share some of the characteristics that Stevenson identifies. These are (citing Randall Balmer's general characteristics of a diverse range of practitioners) "an embrace of the Holy Bible as inspired and God's revelation to humanity, a belief in the centrality of the conversion or 'born again' experience, and the impulse to evangelize or bring others to the faith" (4).

15 Saldaña-Portillo, *The Revolutionary Imagination*, 154, 156.

16 While women also serve missions, they are less visible in popular culture parodies. Interested women serve missions at an older age than their counterparts, and only if marriage is not in their immediate future.

17 I recall setting these goals as a young woman with the guidance of church leaders.

18 Erzen, *Straight to Jesus*, 11.

19 Ghassem-Fachandi, "About Prayer," 225.

20 Schlep Labs, "Easier as a Latino?"

21 Mirzoeff, "In Besieged Mormon Colony."

22 For more on the links between colonization and empire, see Chidester, *Empire of Religion*; and Aikau, *A Chosen People*, in which she presents the Mormon church as a "colonial agent of U.S. imperialism" (13).

23 For research on Lamanites in Native communities, see Murphy, "From Racist Stereotypes to Ethnic Identity"; Murphy, *Imagining Lamanites*; Mauss, *All Abraham's Children*; Reeve, *Religion of a Different Color*; and Hickman, "*The Book of Mormon* as Amerindian Apocalypse." Proselytizing to Native communities in North America emphasized assimilation by placing Native children in white Mormon foster homes (Mauss, *All Abraham's Children*). New scholarship on DNA findings has led the church to revise statements on Lamanites as only one possible genealogical antecedent to Native and indigenous populations of the Americas (Murphy, "Lamanite Genesis, Genealogy, and Genetics").

24 Aikau, *A Chosen People*. Given the vast application of the term "Lamanite," I use "native" and "indigenous" almost interchangeably throughout to note the claims derived from the Book of Mormon and doctrinal teachings and not to signal socially and politically situated identity.

25 Mauss, *All Abraham's Children*; Reeve, *Religion of a Difference Color*; and Bringhurst, *Saints, Slaves and Blacks*.

26 Mauss, *All Abraham's Children*, 2; and Aikau, *A Chosen People*, 52.

27 In an *L.A. Times* report of the rise of Latino members in the church over twenty years ago, Drummond reported that the LDS church had been accused of luring converts through coercive measures by Catholic bishops in California, who are seeing a rapid conversion of their parishes to this and other denominations (Drummond, "Mormons Reach Out for Latino Converts"). Similar claims were leveled against Seventh-Day Adventists and Jehovah's Witnesses. Emily Gurnon

wrote for the *Christian Century* that the church's bountiful welfare program has been cited as a major lure for the conversion of new immigrants of limited means (Gurnon, "Minority Mormons"). In fact, the church itself cites its outreach and welfare programs as proof of its interest in nonwhite membership. Though the church is very protective of its economic statistics, an estimate of tens of millions of dollars of total yearly assistance was given worldwide in cash and commodities through the Mormons' vast welfare program.

28 Two scripts became readily apparent when listening to the actors share their testimonies with members of the audience: when speaking to members, they asked for and collected the information of anyone who might welcome a visit from missionaries; nonmembers were asked to share their personal information so that they might receive a visit from missionaries in the near future. I want to note that there were two missionary-staffed information booths on the green that evening identified with bold lettering, one of the two "en español."

29 A "singles ward" is a congregation composed of unmarried adults. Though I had told these young women that I was a member, hoping to steer the conversation away from conversion strategies and more toward sharing of their everyday lives, as the evening progressed and more of the actors asked if I was a member, I simply stated that I had grown up in the church.

30 No mention of skin color was made during the performance, nor in the conversations I had with multiple actors before the performance.

31 Seed, *American Pentimento*, 46. Some of these theological questions included "infant baptism, ordination, the trinity . . . and even the question of free masonry, republican government and the rights of man" (Alexander Campbell quoted in Hansen, *Mormonism and the American Experience*, 14). For more on racial context of the early church, see Reeve, *Religion of a Different Color*; and Mauss, *All Abraham's Children*.

32 While Seed's *American Pentimento*, presents different strategies for Spanish and Portuguese colonization, the British model is most relevant as it structures the North American ideologies from which Mormonism would draw.

33 Book of Mormon, 1 Nephi 12:23.

34 Lamanites were proclaimed the descendants of Manasseh while white LDS members were descendants of Ephraim. In the biblical narrative, Manasseh and Ephraim are brothers whose father, Joseph, belonged to the favored tribe of Israel, Judah. Ephraim's descendants are believed to be the Anglo-Saxon and Germanic peoples dispersed throughout western Europe. Manasseh's descendants are believed to have migrated to the Americas (see Hansen, *Mormonism and the American Experience*, 190–191).

35 Deloria, *Playing Indian*, 20.

36 Deloria, *Playing Indian*, 3.

37 Initial publications of the Book of Mormon claimed that after living righteously the Lamanites will once again become a "white and delightsome" people as they were before God placed a curse of "a skin of blackness to come upon them" for their iniquity (2 Nephi 5:21). Modern reprintings of the book have changed the passage to read "pure and delightsome," though they have not changed numerous passages throughout the Book of Mormon that reflect a similar conflation of skin color and morality.

38 Mauss, *All Abraham's Children*; Reeve, *Religion of a Different Color*; Murphy, *Imagining Lamanites*; and Murphy, "From Racist Stereotypes to Ethnic Identity."

39 Heinerman and Shupe, *The Mormon Corporate Empire*.

40 Embry, *"In His Own Language,"* 27.

41 For example, according to Jessie L. Embry in his work on Spanish-speaking congregations, "From 1945 to 1967, the Church sponsored an annual 'Lamanite Conference' in Mesa at which Spanish-speaking members from the United States and Mexico attended the temple and received instructions from Church leaders. (Despite the conferences' name, Native Americans such as nearby Navajos apparently were not invited unless they spoke Spanish.)" (Embry, *"In His Own Language,"* 27).

42 The same can be said of Lamanite identity for Native communities in the United States. For more see Murphy, *Imagining Lamanites*; and Murphy, "From Racist Stereotypes to Ethnic Identity."

43 Parry, "Joseph Smith and the Clash of Sacred Cultures," 66.

44 Though, as Reeve argues, the racial status of the church has not always been the same, the centrality and superiority of whiteness undergird its doctrine.

45 It should be noted that while Rivera was the first bishop, a convert from the early successful missionary efforts of the Mexican mission, Margarito Bautista, served as a branch president of the first Mexican congregation in Utah. His conversion testimony, "M. Bautista, a Descendant of father Lehi," published in 1920 in *Improvement Era*, a Mormon publication, was a precursor to his larger tome, *La evolución de Mexico: Sus Verdaderos Progenitores y su Origen, El Destino de America y Europa* (1935). In both he displays full interpellation by the historical claims of the Book of Mormon, believing himself a Lamanite to whom "glorious" things are promised after the restoration of his true history. With the Lamanites at their center, the texts weave together the Bible, the Book of Mormon, and Mexican history with a strong pro-Mexican and anti–United States message that the church disapproved of, leading to an official censure and Bautista's excommunication. His text was met by a receptive audience of converts in Mexico whose embrace of the Lamanite identity led them to make demands on unimpressed church leaders. When Bautista was excommunicated, a third of the Mexican Branch members—about eight hundred in 1936—left the church to found their own "Third Convention" organized around Bautista's radical interpretation of the Book of Mormon. For more on Bautista, see Murphy, *Imagining Lamanites*.

46 Tullis, *Mormonism*, viii.

47 Tullis, *Mormonism*, ix

48 Rivera, "Mormonism and the Chicano," 116.

49 Rivera, "Mormonism and the Chicano," 118. Here too Rivera seems to echo the movement, specifically "El Plan Espiritual de Aztlán," which explicitly states that "a nation, autonomous and free—culturally, socially, economically, and politically—will make its own decisions on the usage of our lands, the taxation of our goods, the utilization of our bodies for war, the determination of justice (reward and punishment), and the profit of our sweat."

50 Rivera, "Mormonism and the Chicano," 120.

51 Rivera, "Mormonism and the Chicano," 120.

52 Rivera, "Mormonism and the Chicano," 122.

53 Rivera, "Mormonism and the Chicano," 121.

54 Rivera, "Mormonism and the Chicano," 123.

55 Rivera, "Mormonism and the Chicano," 124.

56 Rivera, "Mormonism and the Chicano," 123.

57 Rivera, "Mormonism and the Chicano," 124.

58 Rivera, "Mormonism and the Chicano," 124.

59 In addition to this published testimony, Rivera participated in the creation of the Spanish Speaking Organization for Community Integrity and Opportunity, socio—a cross-class, pan-ethnic, interfaith organization that created cultural programs and addressed the needs of Latino communities in Utah. Also, socio provided job training, English classes, and other skill development courses as well as negotiating the creation of affirmative action and recruitment programs, educational reforms, and college scholarship and financial aid packages. Rivera and socio drew on church teachings to validate a strong Chicano presence and focused on negotiation and cooperation, in great contrast to the militancy displayed by Chicano nationalists, such as Corky Gonzales and Reies López Tijerina, who visited Utah in the 1970s. The organization, however, also served to temper the more radical leanings of Chicano students in Utah, offering instead ways to work within the system. As quoted in the *Salt Lake Tribune*, socio's leaders believed "[the] Negroes have gained attention through their riots. But we do not want that, we think there is a better way" (Iber, *Hispanics in the Mormon Zion*, 93).

60 Testimony meetings occur monthly within local wards. The ward you attend is determined by where you live and sometimes the language you speak. This is the case if there happens to be a Spanish-speaking ward that covers the same area as an English-speaking ward such that for the most part you worship alongside socioeconomic peers.

61 For some of these critiques, see chapter 2.

62 Zeveloff, "Immigration and Revelation."

63 Garcia is interpreting the Book of Mormon scripture 2 Nephi 30:6, which ends with "and they shall be a white and delightsome people." The same Salt Lake paper includes quote from church official Bennett, stating, "The understanding of the scripture of the Book of Mormon is as the Lamanites increase in righteousness, they will become 'white' in the sense of having their sins perfectly cleaned out of them. They become purified as a white and delightsome people but not in

the connotation of pigmentation or racial expression. [. . .] Righteousness isn't a matter of color, it's a matter of heart" (Zeveloff, "Immigration and Revelation").

64 Gurnon, "Minority Mormons."

65 Gurnon, "Minority Mormons."

66 Moulton, "LDS Latinos Amp Up Pressure"; Biggers, "In the 19th Century."

67 Church of Jesus Christ of Latter-Day Saints, "Immigration Response."

68 Church of Jesus Christ of Latter-Day Saints, "Immigration Response."

69 Contreras, "Latino Mormons Speaking Out against Romney."

70 Ong, *Buddha Is Hiding*, 195.

71 While there is now an organized Mormon feminist contingent, the church has made an example of those asking for concrete changes by excommunicating them.

CONCLUSION

1 Schneider, *The Explicit Body in Performance*, 1.

2 See Rodríguez, *Sexual Futures*; and Ramos, "Spic(y) Appropriations," for related arguments on Ibarra's performances.

3 Ibarra, "Ecdysis," 355.

4 Ibarra, "Ecdysis," 355.

5 For more on Carmen Miranda as ambassador of the Good Neighbor Policy, see Mendible, *From Bananas to Buttocks*; and Sandoval-Sánchez, *José, Can You See.*

6 Vargas, "Ruminations on Lo Sucio," 725.

7 As an example of this response, one might think of the Emilio Estefan–produced "We're All Mexican" anthem created in response to presidential candidate Donald Trump's proclamation that Mexican immigrants represent Mexico's criminal element—thieves and rapists. Featuring Pitbull, Eva Longoria, Wyclef, and Thalia, among others, the music video for the song ends with a montage of newly declared U.S. citizens of "Mexica" origin waving American flags, gowned Mexican students tossing their caps, and a Mexican chef and his Mexican staff declaring "Viva America," displaying models of normative success across the Latino matrix.

8 In his *Dissensus*, Rancière broadly defines dissensus as a collective act that challenges the order of preexisting political arrangements. Dispute or dissensus, he tells us, is the essence of politics (38).

Bibliography

Agustí, Clara Escoda. "'I Carve Myself into My Hands': The Body Experienced from Within in Ana Mendieta's Work and Migdalia Cruz's *Miriam's Flowers*." *Hispanic Review* 75, no. 3 (summer 2007): 289–311.

Aikau, Hokulani K. *A Chosen People, a Promised Land: Mormonism and Race in Hawaii*. Minneapolis: University of Minnesota Press, 2012.

Alarcón, Norma. "Traddutora, Traditora: A Paradigmatic Figure of Chicana Feminism." *Cultural Critique* 13 (autumn 1989): 55–87.

Althusser, Louis. "Ideology and Ideological State Apparatuses." In *Lenin and Philosophy, and Other Essays*, 127–186. New York: Monthly Review Press, 1972.

Alvarado, Leticia. "Asco's *asco* and the Queer Affective Resonance of Abjection." *Aztlán: A Journal of Chicano Studies* 40, no. 2 (fall 2015): 63–94.

———. "'. . . Towards a Personal Will to Continue Being Other': Ana Mendieta's Abject Performances." *Journal of Latin American Cultural Studies* 24, no. 1 (2015): 65–85.

———. "'What Comes after Loss?': Ana Mendieta after José." *Small Axe: A Caribbean Journal of Cultural Criticism* 19, no. 2 (July 2015): 104–110.

Amaya, Hector. "Citizenship, Diversity, Law and *Ugly Betty*." *Media, Culture and Society* 32, no. 5 (2010): 801–817.

Anaya, Rudolfo, and Francisco Lomelí, eds. *Aztlán: Essays on the Chicano Homeland.* Albuquerque: University of New Mexico Press, 1989.

———. "El Plan Espiritual de Aztlán." In *Aztlán: Essays on the Chicano Homeland,* ed. Rudolfo A. Anaya and Francisco Lomelí, 1–5. Albuquerque: University of New Mexico Press, 1989.

Anzaldúa, Gloria. *Borderlands/La Frontera: The New Mestiza.* San Francisco, CA: Aunt Lute, 1999.

———. "La Prieta." In *This Bridge Called My Back: Writings by Radical Women of Color,* edited by Cherríe L. Moraga and Gloria Anzaldúa. Women of Color Series. Berkeley, CA: Third Woman Press, 2002.

Archibold, Randal C. "Arizona Enacts Stringent Law on Immigration." *New York Times,* 23 April 2010.

Arya, Rina. *Abjection and Representation: An Exploration of Abjection in the Visual Arts, Film and Literature.* New York: Palgrave Macmillan, 2014.

Bag, Alice. *Violence Girl: East L.A. Rage to Hollywood Stage, a Chicana Punk Story.* Los Angeles, CA: Feral House, 2011.

Barthes, Roland. *Camera Lucida: Reflections on Photography.* New York: Hill and Wang, 1980.

Baum, Kelly. "Shapely Shapelessness: Ana Mendieta's 'Untitled (Glass on Body Imprints–Face),' 1972," *Records67,* 2008, 80–93.

Beard, Betty, and Megan Neighbor. "National Council of La Raza Calls Off Boycott." *Arizona Republic,* 9 September 2011.

Beltrán, Cristina. "Racial Presence versus Racial Justice: The Affective Power of an Aesthetic Condition." *Du Bois Review* 11, no. 1 (2014): 137–158.

———. *The Trouble with Unity: Latino Politics and the Creation of Identity.* New York: Oxford University Press, 2010.

Benavidez, Max. *Gronk.* Los Angeles: UCLA Chicano Studies Research Center Press, 2007.

Benavidez, Max, and Liz Lima Boweman. *Post-Chicano Generation in Art: Breaking Boundaries.* Phoenix, AZ: MARS Artspace, 1990.

Benavidez, O. Hugo. *Drugs, Thugs and Divas: Telenovelas and Narco-Dramas in Latina America.* Austin: University of Texas Press, 2008.

Bhabha, Homi. "Of Mimicry and Man: The Ambivalence of Colonial Discourse." In *The Location of Culture,* 85–92. New York: Routledge, 1990.

Biggers, Jeff. "In the 19th Century, the Romneys Fled the Law." *Salon,* 9 September 2011.

Bloch, Ernst. *The Utopian Function of Art and Literature: Selected Essays.* Cambridge, MA: MIT Press, 1988.

———. "The Wish-Landscape Perspective in Aesthetics: The Order of Arts Materials According to the Dimension of Their Profundity and Hope (1959)." In *The*

Utopian Function of Art and Literature: Selected Essays, translated by Jack Zipes and Frank Mecklenburg. Cambridge, MA: MIT Press, 1988.

Blocker, Jane. *Where Is Ana Mendieta? Identity, Performativity, and Exile.* Durham, NC: Duke University Press, 1999.

Bogado, Aura. "The Executive Action Learning Curve." *Colorlines,* 11 February 2015, 1–5. http://www.colorlines.com/articles/executive-action-learning-curve.

———. "Here's How DACA Will Be Expanded under Obama." *Colorlines,* 21 November 2014, 1–3. http://www.colorlines.com/articles/heres-how-daca-will-be-expanded-under-obama.

———. "Obama Introduced Deferred Action for Parents, or DAP." *Colorlines,* 21 November 2014, 1–3. http://www.colorlines.com/articles/obama-introduces-deferred-action-parents-or-dap.

Bois, Yves-Alain, and Rosalind Krauss. *Formless: A User's Guide.* Cambridge, MA: MIT Press, 1997.

Bonilla Silva, Eduardo. *Racism without Racists: Color-Blind Racism and the Persistence of Racial Inequity in the United States.* New York: Rowman and Littlefield, 2006.

Breder, Hans. "Intermedia: Enacting the Liminal." *Performing Arts Journal* 17, no. 2/3 (May–September 1995): 112–120.

Brett, Guy. "One Energy." In *Ana Mendieta: Earth Body: Sculpture and Performance, 1972–1985,* edited by Olga M. Viso. Washington, DC: Hirshhorn Museum and Sculpture Garden in association with Hatje Cantz, 2004.

Bringhurst, Newell G. *Saints, Slaves and Blacks: The Changing Place of Black People within Mormonism.* Westport, CT: Greenwood, 1981.

Brown, Kimberly Juanita. *The Repeating Body: Slavery's Visual Resonance in the Contemporary.* Durham, NC: Duke University Press, 2015.

Brown, Wendy. *States of Injury: Power and Freedom in Late Modernity.* Princeton, NJ: Princeton University Press, 1995.

Burnham, Linda Frye. "Asco: Camus, Daffy, Duck, and Devil Girls from East L.A." (*LA Weekly,* 1987). In *Asco: Elite of the Obscure, a Retrospective, 1972–1987,* edited by C. Ondine Chavoya and Rita Gonzalez, 406–409. Ostfildern, Germany: Hatje Cantz, 2011.

Bustamante, Nao. *America, the Beautiful.* DVD. Independently produced, 1995.

———. "*America, the Beautiful.*" In *Corpus Delecti: Performance Art of the Americas.* Edited by Coco Fusco, 197. New York: Routledge, 2000.

———. "*America, the Beautiful.*" In *Mega Compilation.* DVD. Independently produced, 2000.

———. "Artist Talk." At "Against Respectability Politics: Conversations on Latina *suciedad.*" Center for the Study of Race and Ethnicity in America, Brown University, November 2015.

———. *Interview with Nao Bustamante.* Hemispheric Institute Digital Video Library, 2002. http://hdl.handle.net/2333.1/5dv41nv8.

Butler, Judith. *Bodies That Matter: On the Discursive Limits of "Sex."* New York: Routledge, 1993.

———. "Imitation and Gender Insubordination." In *The Lesbian and Gay Studies Reader*, edited by Henry Abelove. New York: Routledge, 1993.

———. *Psychic Life of Power: Theories in Subjection.* Stanford, CA: Stanford University Press, 1997.

Cabañas, Kaira M. "Ana Mendieta: 'Pain of Cuba, Body I Am.'" *Women's Art Journal* 20, no. 1 (spring–summer 1999): 12–17.

Chambers-Letson, Joshua. "The Politics of Failure: Nao Bustamante's Hero." *TDR: The Drama Review* 51, no. 3 (fall 2007): 174–181.

Chanter, Tina. *The Picture of Abjection: Film, Fetish and the Nature of Difference.* Bloomington: Indiana University Press, 2008.

Chavoya, C. Ondine. "Internal Exiles: The Interventionist Public and Performance Art of Asco." In *Space, Site, Intervention: Situating Installation Art*, edited by Erika Suderburg, 189–208. Minneapolis: University of Minnesota Press, 2000.

Chavoya, C. Ondine, and Rita Gonzalez, eds. *Asco: Elite of the Obscure, a Retrospective, 1972–1987.* Ostfildern, Germany: Hatje Cantz, 2011.

———. "Asco and the Politics of Revulsion." In *Asco: Elite of the Obscure, a Retrospective, 1972–1987*, 37–85. Ostfildern, Germany: Hatje Cantz, 2011.

———. "Elite of the Obscure: An Introduction." In *Asco: Elite of the Obscure, a Retrospective, 1972–1987*, 18–27. Ostfildern, Germany: Hatje Cantz, 2011.

Chidester, David. *Empire of Religion: Imperialism and Comparative Religion.* Chicago: University of Chicago Press, 2014.

Chow, Rey. *The Protestant Ethnic and the Spirit of Capitalism.* New York: Columbia University Press, 2002.

Chuh, Kandice. *Imagine Otherwise: On Asian Americanist Critique.* Durham, NC: Duke University Press, 2003.

Church of Jesus Christ of Latter-Day Saints. "Immigration Response." *Newsroom*, 22 July 2011. http://www.mormonnewsroom.org/article/immigration -response.

Contreras, Russell. "Latino Mormons Speaking Out against Romney." *Washington Times*, 23 February 2012.

Critical Ethnic Studies Association. "Our Visions." October 2012. http://critical ethnicstudies.org/mission-vision.

Cruz-Malavé, Arnaldo. *Queer Latino Testimonio, Keith Haring, and Juanito Xtravaganza: Hard Tails.* London: Palgrave Macmillan, 2007.

———. "'What a Tangled Web!' Masculinity, Abjection and the Foundations of Puerto Rican Literature in the United States." *Differences: A Journal of Feminist Cultural Studies* 8, no. 1 (1996): 132–151.

Cvetkovich, Ann. *An Archive of Feelings: Trauma, Sexuality and Lesbian Public Cultures.* Durham, NC: Duke University Press, 2003.

———. "Public Feelings." *South Atlantic Quarterly* 106, no. 3 (2007): 459–468.

Dart, John. "Catholic Bishops Upset by Conversion of Latinos Proselytizing: Mormons, Adventists and Other Churches Are Accused of Using Unfair Tactics to Gain New Spanish-Speaking Members." *Los Angeles Times*, 3 March 1990, 15.

Dávila, Arlene. *Latinos, Inc.: The Marketing and Making of a People*. Berkeley: University of California Press, 2001.

Deloria, Philip J. *Playing Indian*. New Haven, CT: Yale University Press, 1998.

Derrida, Jacques. *Archive Fever: A Freudian Impression*. Translated by Eric Prenowitz. Chicago: University of Chicago Press, 1995.

———. "Parergon." In *The Sublime: Documents of Contemporary Art*, edited by Simon Morley. Cambridge, MA: MIT Press, 2010.

Doyle, Jennifer. "Guest Stars." Frieze Blog. *Frieze Magazine*, 22 July 2010.

———. *Hold It against Me: Difficulty and Emotion in Contemporary Art*. Durham, NC: Duke University Press, 2013.

Drummond, Tammerlin. "Mormons Reach Out for Latino Converts: Religion: Spanish-Speaking People Are among the Fastest-Growing Group in the Latter-Day Saints, Church Officials Say." *Los Angeles Times*, 8 March 1992, 3.

Edelman, Lee. *No Future: Queer Theory and the Death Drive*. Durham, NC: Duke University Press, 2004.

Eichhorn, Kate. *The Archival Turn in Feminism: Outrage in Order*. Philadelphia, PA: Temple University Press, 2013.

Embry, Jessie L. *"In His Own Language": Mormon Spanish-Speaking Congregations in the United States*. Provo, UT: Charles Redd Center for Western Studies, Brigham Young University, 1997.

Eng, David L., Judith Halberstam, and José Esteban Muñoz, eds. "What's Queer about Queer Studies Now?" Special issue, *Social Text* 84–85, no. 23 (fall/winter 2005).

English, Darby. *How to See a Work of Art in Total Darkness*. Cambridge, MA: MIT Press, 2007.

Erzen, Tanya. *Straight to Jesus: Sexual and Christian Conversion in the Ex-Gay Movement*. Berkeley: University of California Press, 2006.

Esposito, Jennifer. "Is Ugly Betty a Real Woman? Representations of Chicana Femininity Inscribed as a Site of (Transformative) Difference." In *Performing the US Latina and Latino Borderlands*, edited by Arturo J. Aldama, Chela Sandoval, and Peter Garcia. Bloomington: Indiana University Press, 2012.

Farmer, Brett. "The Fabulous Sublimity of Gay Diva Worship." *Camera Obscura* 20, no. 2 59 (2005): 165–194.

Farnsworth, Dewey. *Book of Mormon Evidences in Ancient America*. Salt Lake City, UT: Deseret, 1953.

Fenton, Elizabeth. "Open Canons: Sacred History and American History in the Book of Mormon." *Journal of Nineteenth-Century Americanists* 1, no. 2 (2013): 339–361.

Ferguson, Roderick. *Aberrations in Black: Toward a Queer of Color Critique*. Minneapolis: University of Minnesota Press, 2004.

Ferreira, Mario Ribero, dir. *Yo Soy Betty, la fea*. RCN Televisión. Columbia, 25 October 1999–8 May 2001.

Flores-Sternad, Jennifer, and Robert Legoretta. "Cyclona and Early Chicano Performance Art: An Interview with Robert Legoretta." *GLQ* 12, no. 3 (2006): 475–490.

Frantz, David, and Mia Locks. *Cruising the Archive: Queer Art and Culture in Los Angeles, 1945–1980*. Los Angeles, CA: ONE National Gay and Lesbian Archives, 2011.

Frueh, Joanna. "The Body through Women's Eyes." In *The Power of Feminist Art: The American Movement of the 1970s, History and Impact*, edited by Norma Broude and Mary D. Garrard. New York: Harry N. Abrams, 1994.

Fusco, Coco, and Brian Wallis, eds. *Only Skin Deep: Changing Visions of the American Self*. New York: International Center of Photography with Harry N. Abrams, 2004.

Gamboa, Harry, Jr. Oral history interview with Harry Gamboa Jr., 1–16 April 1999. Archives of American Art, Smithsonian Institution, Washington, DC.

———. *Urban Exile: Collected Writings of Harry Gamboa Jr.*, edited by Chon Noriega. Minneapolis: University of Minnesota Press, 1998.

García, María Cristina. *Havana USA: Cuban Exiles and Cuban Americans in South Florida, 1959–1994*. Berkeley: University of California Press, 1996.

Garcia, Ramón. "Patssi's Eyes." *Atzlán* 22, no. 2 (fall 1997): 169–180.

Garza, Juan Carlos, dir. *Latino Artists: Pushing the Boundaries*. Perf. Harry Gamboa Jr., Patssi Valdez, Gronk, and Willie Herrón. Films for the Humanities and Sciences Video, 1995.

Gasché, Rodolphe. *The Idea of Form: Rethinking Kant's Aesthetics*. Stanford, CA: Stanford University Press, 2003.

Gaspar de Alba, Alicia. *Chicano Art inside/outside the Master's House: Cultural Politics and the CARA Exhibition*. Austin: University of Texas Press, 1998.

Georgelou, Konstantina. "Abjection and *Informe*: Operations of Debasing." *Performance Research* 19, no. 1 (June 2014): 25–32.

Ghassem-Fachandi, Parvis. "About Prayer: Abjection and Urgency in an American Holiness Church." *Ethnography* 8, no. 3 (September 2007): 235–265.

Gikandi, Simon. *Slavery and the Culture of Taste*. Princeton, NJ: Princeton University Press, 2011.

Goldman, Karen. "La Princesa Plástica: Hegemonic and Oppositional Representations of Latinidad." In *From Bananas to Buttocks: The Latina Body in Popular Film and Culture*, edited by Myra Mendible, 263–278. Austin: University of Texas Press, 2007.

Gómez-Barris, Macarena. "Regarding the Central American Child's Pain." *American Quarterly* 66, no. 3 (September 2014).

Gonzalez, Juan. *Harvest of Empire: A History of Latinos in America*. New York: Penguin, 2001.

Gonzalez, Rita. "Frida, Homeboys, and the Butch Gardens School of Fine Art." In *Asco: Elite of the Obscure, a Retrospective, 1972–1987*, edited by C. Ondine Chavoya and Rita Gonzalez, 318–325. Ostfildern, Germany: Hatje Cantz, 2011.

Gonzalez, Rita, Howard N. Fox, and Chon A. Noriega. *Phantom Sightings: Art after the Chicano Movement*. Los Angeles: University of California Press and Los Angeles County Museum of Art, 2008.

Gonzales-Day, Ken. *Lynching in the West: 1850–1935*. Durham, NC: Duke University Press, 2006.

Gregg, Melissa, and Gregory J. Siegworth, eds. *The Affect Theory Reader*. Durham, NC: Duke University Press, 2010.

Griefen, Kat. "Ana Mendieta at A.I.R. Gallery, 1977–82." *Women and Performance* 21, no. 2 (2011): 171–181.

Griffith, Marie. *God's Daughters: Evangelical Women and the Power of Submission*. Berkeley: University of California Press, 2000.

Gronk. Oral history interview with Gronk, 20–23 January 1997. Archives of American Art, Smithsonian Institution, Washington, DC.

Gunckel, Colin. "Vexing Questions: Rethinking the History of East LA Punk." *Atzlán: A Journal of Chicano Studies* 37, no. 2 (fall 2012): 127–156.

Gurnon, Emily. "Minority Mormons: Latinos and Latter-Day Saints." *Christian Century*, 16 February 1994.

Guterl, Matthew Pratt. *Seeing Race in Modern America*. Chapel Hill: University of North Carolina Press, 2013.

Guzmán, Joshua Javier, and Christina A. León, eds. "Lingering in Latinidad: Theory, Aesthetics, and Performance in Latino/a Studies." *Women and Performance* 25, no. 3 (2016).

Habermas, Jürgen. "Modernity versus Postmodernity." *New German Critique* 22 (1981): 3–14.

Halberstam, Judith. *The Queer Art of Failure*. Durham, NC: Duke University Press Books, 2011.

Halperin, David. *What Do Gay Men Want? An Essay on Sex, Risk, and Subjectivity*. Ann Arbor: University of Michigan Press, 2007.

Halperin, David, and Valerie Traub. *Gay Shame*. Chicago: University of Chicago Press, 2010.

Hammond, Harmony, "Letter from Harmony," 1 March 1985. The A.I.R. Gallery Archive; MSS 184; 2; 93; Fales Library and Special Collections, New York University Libraries.

Hanna, Monica, Jennifer Harford Vargas, and José David Saldívar. *Junot Díaz and the Decolonial Imagination*. Durham, NC: Duke University Press, 2016.

Hansen, Klaus J. *Mormonism and the American Experience*. Chicago: University of Chicago Press, 1981.

Hartman, Saidiya. *Scenes of Subjection: Terror, Slavery, and Self-Making in Nineteenth-Century America*. Oxford: Oxford University Press, 1997.

Heartley, Eleanor. "Rediscovering Ana Mendieta." *Art in America* 92 (2004): 138–143.

Heinerman, John, and Anson Shupe. *The Mormon Corporate Empire*. Boston: Beacon, 1985.

Hennessy-Fiske, Molly. "'Dreamers' Stage Action in Laredo, Texas." *LA Times*, 30 September 2013, 1–2.

Hernandez, Daniel. "The Art Outlaws of East L.A." *L.A. Weekly*, 6 June 2007.

Hernandez, Robb. "Drawing Offensive/Offensive Drawing: Toward a Theory of Mariconógraphy." *MELUS* 39, no. 2 (2014): 121–152.

———. *The Fire of Life: The Robert Legorreta-Cyclona Collection*. Los Angeles: UCLA Chicano Studies Research Center Press, 2009.

———. "Performing the Archival Body in the Robert 'Cyclona' Legorreta Fire of Life/El Fuego de la Vida Collection." *Aztlán: A Journal of Chicano Studies* 31, no. 2 (2006): 113–125.

Herrón, Willie. Oral history interview with Willie Herrón, 5 February–17 March 2000. Archives of American Art, Smithsonian Institution, Washington, DC.

Herzberg, Julia Ann. "Ana Mendieta, the Iowa Years: A Critical Study, 1969 through 1977." PhD diss., City University of New York. Ann Arbor, MI: ProQuest/UMI, 1998.

Hickman, Jared. "*The Book of Mormon* as Amerindian Apocalypse." *American Literature* 86, no. 3 (2014): 429–461.

Highmore, Ben. "Bitter after Taste: Affect, Food, and Social Aesthetics." In *The Affect Theory Reader*, edited by Melissa Gregg and Gregory J. Siegworth. Durham, NC: Duke University Press, 2010.

Hinch, Jim. "Walking Mural: Asco and the Ends of Chicano Art." *Los Angeles Review of Books*, 23 August 2012.

Hong, Grace Kyungwon. *The Ruptures of American Capital: Women of Color, Feminism and the Culture of Immigrant Labor*. Minneapolis: University of Minnesota Press, 2006.

Hong, Grace Kyungwon, and Roderick A. Ferguson, eds. *Strange Affinities: The Gender and Sexual Politics of Comparative Racialization*. Durham, NC: Duke University Press, 2011.

Horkheimer, Max, and Theodor Adorno. "The Culture Industry." In *Dialectic of Enlightenment*, edited by Gunzelin Schmid Noerr. Stanford, CA: Stanford University Press, 2002.

Horta, Silvio, and Salma Hayek, prods. *Ugly Betty*. Touchstone Television. ABC Television Network, 2006–2010.

Houser, Craig, Leslie C. Jones, Simon Taylor, and Jack Ben-Levi. *Abject Art: Repulsion and Desire in American Art*. New York: Whitney Museum of American Art, 1993.

Hull, Akasha Gloria T., Patricia Bell-Scott, and Barbara Smith. *But Some of Us Are Brave: All the Women Are White, All the Blacks Are Men: Black Women's Studies*. New York: The Feminist Press at CUNY, 1993.

Huntington, Samuel. "The Hispanic Challenge." *Foreign Policy*, March/April 2004, 1–16.

Ibarra, Xandra. "Ecdysis: The Molting of a Cucarachica." *Women and Performance* 25, no. 3 (2016): 354–356.

Iber, Jorge. *Hispanics in the Mormon Zion: 1912–1999*. College Station, TX: Texas A&M University Press, 2000.

Jaime, Karen. "'La Montra': Rita Indiana Hernandez and the Politics of Performing Dominicaness." Presentation at inaugural Latino Studies Association Conference, Imagining Latina/o Studies: Past, Present, and Future, an International Latina/o Studies Conference, Chicago, 17–19 July 2014.

James, David E. "Hollywood Extras: One Tradition of 'Avant-Garde' Film in Los Angeles." *October* 90 (autumn 1999): 3–24.

Jones, Amelia. *Seeing Differently: A History and Theory of Identification and the Visual Arts.* New York: Routledge, 2012.

———. "Lost Bodies: Early 1970s Los Angeles Performance Art in Art History." In *Live Art LA: Performance in California, 1970–1983*, 115–184. New York: Routledge, 2012.

———. "'Traitor Prophets': Asco's Art as a Politics of the In-Between." In *Asco: Elite of the Obscure, a Retrospective, 1972–1987*, 107–151. Ostfildern, Germany: Hatje Cantz, 2011.

Jones, Amelia, and Andrew Stephenson. *The Performing Body/The Performing Text.* New York: Routledge, 1999.

Kant, Immanuel. *The Critique of Judgment.* Translated by James Creed Meredith. Stilwell, KS: Digireads.com, 2006.

———. *Observations on the Feeling of the Beautiful and Sublime.* Translated by John T. Goldthwait. California: University of California Press, 2004.

Katz, Robert. *Naked by the Window: The Fatal Marriage of Carl Andre and Ana Mendieta.* New York: Atlantic Monthly Press, 1990.

Kosiba-Vargas, S. Zaneta. *Harry Gamboa and Asco: The Emergence and Development of a Chicano Art Group 1971–1987.* Ann Arbor: University of Michigan Press, 1988.

Kristeva, Julia. *Powers of Horror: An Essay on Abjection.* New York: Columbia University Press, 1982.

Kwon, Miwon. "Bloody Valentines: Afterimages by Ana Mendieta." In *Inside the Visible*, edited by Catherine de Zegher, 165–172. Boston: Institute of Contemporary Art and MIT Press, 1996.

La Fountain-Stokes, Lawrence. "Gay Shame, Latina- and Latino-Style: A Critique of White Queer Performativity." In *Gay Latino Studies: A Critical Reader*, edited by Michael Hames Garcia and Ernesto Javier Martinez. Durham, NC: Duke University Press, 2011.

Lane, Godoy-Anativia, and Gómez-Barris. "What Decolonial Gesture Is." *E-Misférica* 11, no. 1 (2014).

Lane, Jill. *Blackface Cuba, 1840–1895.* Philadelphia: University of Pennsylvania Press, 2005.

Lattin, Don. "New Mormon Melting Pot: Church Transcends Its Racist History." *San Francisco Chronicle*, 10 April 1996, A1.

Lewis, Oscar. *The Children of Sanchez.* New York: Vintage, 1979.

Limón, José E. *Mexican Ballads, Chicano Poems: History and Influence in Mexican-American Social Poetry.* Berkeley: University of California Press, 1992.

Lippard, Lucy. *Mixed Blessings: New Art in a Multicultural America.* New York: New Press, 1990.

Lloyd, David. "Race under Representation." *Oxford Literary Review* 13, no. 1–2 (1991): 62–94.

López, Antonio. "Cosa de Blancos: Cuban-American Whiteness and the Afro-Cuban-Occupied House." *Latino Studies* 8 (2010): 220–243.

López, Yolanda M., and Moira Roth. "Social Protest: Racism and Sexism." In *The Power of Feminist Art: The American Movement of the 1970s, History and Impact*, edited by Norma Broude and Mary D. Garrard. New York: Harry N. Abrams, 1994.

Lott, Eric. *Love and Theft: Blackface Minstrelsy and the American Working Class*. Oxford: Oxford University Press, 2013.

Love, Heather. *Feeling Backward: Loss and the Politics of Queer History*. Cambridge, MA: Harvard University Press, 2007.

Macías, Stacy I. "Femininity Ain't Pretty: Reading Latina Racialized, Queer Femininities in *Ugly Betty*." Presentation at the Annual International Congress of the Latin American Studies Association, San Francisco, 23–26 May 2012.

Mauss, Armand L. *All Abraham's Children: Changing Mormon Conceptions of Race and Lineage*. Urbana: University of Illinois Press, 2003.

McMahon, Marci R. "Self-Fashioning through Glamour and Punk in East Los Angeles: Patssi Valdez in Asco's *Instant Mural* and *A La Mode*." *Aztlán: A Journal of Chicano Studies* 36, no. 2 (fall 2011): 21–49.

Megli, Dawn. "Growth of Latino Membership Shows Mormonism's Surprising Diversity." *Neon Tommy, Annenberg Digital News*, 5 May 2012.

Melamed, Jodi. *Represent and Destroy: Rationalizing Violence in the New Racial Capitalism*. Minneapolis: University of Minnesota Press, 2011.

Mendible, Myra, ed. *From Bananas to Buttocks: The Latina Body in Popular Film and Culture*. Austin: University of Texas Press, 2007.

Mendieta, Ana. Introduction to *Dialectics of Isolation: An Exhibition of Third World Women Artists of the United States*, 2–20 September 1980. The A.I.R. Gallery Archive; MSS 184; 11; 440, Fales Library and Special Collections, New York University Libraries.

Menninghaus, Winfried. *Disgust: Theory and History of a Strong Sensation*. Albany: State University of New York Press, 2003.

Mignolo, Walter D., and Rolando Vázquez. "Decolonial AestheSis: Colonial Wounds/Decolonial Healings." *Social Text: Periscope*, July 2013.

Milch, Ilana Daphne. "Dead Girls, Monsters and Assholes: Marginality in the Practices of Asco and Marnie Weber in Los Angeles." Master's thesis, University of Southern California, 2012.

Mirzoeff, Nicholas. "In Besieged Mormon Colony, Mitt Romney's Mexican Roots." *Washington Post*, 23 July 2011.

———, ed. *The Visual Culture Reader*. London: Routledge, 2002.

Mitchell, W. J. T. *Picture Theory: Essays on Verbal and Visual Representation*. Chicago: University of Chicago Press, 1994.

Moraga, Cherríe. "Queer Aztlán: the Re-formation of Chicago Tribe." In *The Last Generation: Prose and Poetry*. Boston: South End Press, 1993.

Moraga, Cherríe, and Gloria Anzaldúa, eds. *This Bridge Called My Back: Writings by Radical Women of Color*. Berkeley, CA: Third Woman Press, 2002.

Morales, Sylvia, dir. *Chicana*. Perf. Narrator, Carmen Zapata; writer, Anna Nieto-Gomez; music, Carmen Moreno. Women Make Movies (WMM), 1979.

Morgan, David, and Sally Promey, eds. *The Visual Culture of American Religions*. Berkeley: University of California Press, 2001.

Morley, Simon, ed. *The Sublime*. Cambridge, MA: MIT Press, 2010.

Moulton, Kristen. "LDS Latinos Amp Up Pressure on Church on Immigration." *Salt Lake Tribune*, 8 June 2010.

Moya, Paula M. L., and Michael R. Hames-García. *Reclaiming Identity: Realist Theory and the Predicament of Postmodernism*. Berkeley: University of California Press, 2000.

Muñoz, José Esteban. "Brown Theory/Latino Studies." Presentation at the American Studies Association Annual Meeting, Washington, DC, November 2013.

———. *Cruising Utopia: The Then and There of Queer Futurity*. New York: New York University Press, 2009.

———. *Disidentifications: Queers of Color and the Performance of Politics*. Minneapolis: University of Minnesota Press, 1999.

———. "Ephemera as Evidence: Introductory Notes to Queer Acts." *Women and Performance* 8, no. 2 (2008): 5–16.

———. "Feeling Brown: Ethnicity and Affect in Ricardo Bracho's The Sweetest Hangover (and Other STDS)." *Theater Journal* 52, no. 1 (January 2000): 67–79.

———. "Feeling Brown, Feeling Down: Latina Affect, the Performativity of Race, and the Depressive Position." *Signs* 31, no. 3 (2006): 675–688.

———. "From Surface to Depth: Between Psychoanalysis and Affect." *Women and Performance* 12, no. 2 (1996): 123–129.

———. "'Gimme Gimme This . . . Gimme Gimme That': Annihilation and Innovation in the Punk Rock Commons." *Social Text 116* 31, no. 3 (fall 2013): 95–110.

———. "Performing Greater Cuba: Tania Bruguera and the Burden of Guilt." *Women and Performance* 11, no. 2 (2008): 252–253.

———. "Race, Sex and the Incommensurate: Gary Fisher with Eve Kosofsky Sedgwick." In *Queer Futures: Reconsidering Ethics, Activism and the Political*, eds. Elahe Haschemi Yekani et al. Surrey, UK: Ashgate, 2013.

———. "The Sense of Watching Tony Sleep." *South Atlantic Quarterly* 106, no. 3 (summer 2007): 543–551.

———. "Teaching, Minoritarian Knowledge, and Love." *Women and Performance* 14, no. 2 (2005): 117–121.

———. "Towards a Methexic Queer Media." *GLQ* 19, no. 4 (2013): 564.

———. "Vitalism's After-Burn: The Sense of Ana Mendieta." *Women and Performance* 21, no. 2 (2011): 191–198.

———. "The Vulnerability Artist: Nao Bustamante and the Sad Beauty of Reparation." *Women and Performance* 16, no. 2 (2007): 191–200.

———. "Wise Latinas." *Criticism* 56, no. 2 (2014): 249–265.

Muñoz, José Esteban, and Lisa Duggan. "Hope and Hopelessness: A Dialogue."
Women and Performance 19, no. 2 (2009): 275–283.

Murphy, Thomas W. "From Racist Stereotypes to Ethnic Identity: Instrumental
Uses of the Mormon Racial Doctrine." *Ethnohistory* 46, no. 3 (summer 1999):
451–480.

———. "Imagining Lamanites: Native Americans and the Book of Mormon." PhD
diss., University of Washington, 2003.

———. "Lamanite Genesis, Genealogy, and Genetics." In *American Apocrypha:
Essays on the Book of Mormon*, edited by Dan Vogel and Brent Lee Metcalfe. Salt
Lake City, UT: Signature, 2002.

Nash, Jennifer Christine. *The Black Body in Ecstasy: Reading Race, Reading Pornography*. Durham, NC: Duke University Press, 2014.

———. "Rethinking Intersectionality." *Feminist Review* 89 (2008): 1–15.

Negrón-Muntaner, Frances. *Boricua Pop: Puerto Ricans and the Latinization of American Culture*. New York: New York University Press, 2004.

Ngai, Sianne. *Our Aesthetic Categories: Zany, Cute, Interesting*. Cambridge, MA: Harvard University Press, 2012.

———. *Ugly Feelings*. Cambridge, MA: Harvard University Press, 2005.

Nguyen, Tan Hoang. *A View from the Bottom: Asian American Masculinity and Sexual
Representation*. Durham, NC: Duke University Press, 2014.

Nicholls, Walter J. *The DREAMers: How the Undocumented Youth Movement Transformed the Immigrant Rights Debate*. Stanford, CA: Stanford University Press, 2013.

Noriega, Chon A. "Conceptual Graffiti and the Public Art Museum: *Spray Paint
LACMA*." In *Asco: Elite of the Obscure, a Retrospective, 1972–1987*, edited by C. Ondine Chavoya and Rita Gonzalez, 256–261. Ostfildern, Germany: Hatje Cantz, 2011.

———. "The Orphans of Modernism." In *Phantom Sightings: Art after the Chicano
Movement*. Los Angeles: University of California Press and Los Angeles County
Museum of Art, 2008.

———. "U.S. Latinos and the Media: Theory and Practice." *Jump Cut* 39 (June
1994): 57–58.

O'Dell, Kathy. "Ana Mendieta: Hirshhorn Museum and Sculpture Garden, Washington, DC." *Artforum International* 43, no. 7 (March 2005): 232.

Ong, Aihwa. *Buddha Is Hiding: Refugees, Citizenship, the New America*. Berkeley:
University of California Press, 2003.

Ontiveros, Mario. "Retheorizing Activism: The Aesthetics of Social Responsibility in
the Work of Asco, Group Material, Gran Fury, and Félix González-Torres." PhD
diss., University of California, Los Angeles, 2005.

Paredez, Deborah. "All about My (Absent) Mother: Young Latina Aspirations in *Real
Women Have Curves* and *Ugly Betty*." In *Beyond El Barrio: Everyday Life in Latina/o
America*, edited by Gina Perez, Frank Guridy, and Adrian Burgos. New York: NYU
Press, 2010.

Parry, Keith. "Joseph Smith and the Clash of Sacred Cultures." *Dialogue: A Journal of Mormon Thought* 18, no. 4 (winter 1985): 65–78.

Pérez, Emma. *The Decolonial Imaginary: Writing Chicanas into History.* Bloomington: Indiana University Press, 1999.

Pérez, Hiram. "You Can Have My Brown Body and Eat It, Too!" *Social Text* 84–85, no. 23 (fall/winter 2005): 171–191.

Pérez, Roy. "Homo-Narrative Capture, Racial Proximity, and the Queer Latino Child." In *Narrative, Race and Ethnicity in the Americas*, eds. Jim Donahue, Jennifer Ho, and Shaun Morgan. Columbus: Ohio State University Press, 2017.

Pew Research Center, Religion and Public Life. "A Portrait of Mormons in the U.S." 24 July 2009. http://www.pewforum.org/2009/07/24/a-portrait-of-mormons-in-the-us/.

Porter, Liliana. Interview by Olga Viso. Ana Mandieta Herzberg correspondence, 09–103: 1. Smithsonian Institution Archives, Accession 08–096, Hirshhorn Museum and Sculpture Garden, Office of the Deputy Director, Exhibition Records, Washington, DC.

Puar, Jasbir. "Queer Times, Queer Assemblages." *Social Text* 84–85, no. 23 (fall/winter 2005): 171–191.

Pulido, Laura. *Black, Brown, Yellow and Left: Radical Activism in Los Angeles.* Berkeley: University of California Press, 2006.

Quiroga, Jose. *Cuban Palimpsest.* Minneapolis: University of Minnesota Press, 2005.

Ramos, Iván A. "Spic(y) Appropriations: The Gustatory Aesthetics of Xandra Ibarra (aka La Chica Boom)." *Art and Architecture in the Americas* 12 (2016): 1–18.

Rancière, Jacques. *Dissensus: On Politics and Aesthetics.* New York: Bloomsbury Academic, 2015.

———. *The Politics of Aesthetics: The Distribution of the Sensible.* New York: Continuum, 2000.

Redfern, Christine. *Who Is Ana Mendieta?* New York: Feminist Press at CUNY, 2011.

Reeve, W. Paul. *Religion of a Different Color: Race and the Mormon Struggle for Whiteness.* Oxford: Oxford University Press, 2015.

Ricky, Carrie. "The Passion of Ana." *Village Voice*, 10–16 September 1980.

Rivera, Orlando A. "Mormonism and the Chicano." In *Mormonism: A Faith for All Cultures*, edited by F. LaMond Tullis. Provo, UT: Brigham Young University Press, 1978.

Rodríguez, Juana María. *Queer Latinidad: Identity Practices, Discursive Spaces.* New York: New York University Press, 2003.

———. *Sexual Futures, Queer Gestures, and Other Latina Longings.* New York: New York University Press, 2014.

Rodriguez, Ralph E. *Brown Gumshoes: Detective Fiction and the Search for Chicana/o Identity.* Austin: University of Texas Press, 2005.

Rodríguez, Richard T. *Next of Kin: The Family in Chicano/a Cultural Politics.* Durham, NC: Duke University Press, 2010.

Román, Miriam Jiménez, and Juan Flores, eds. *The Afro-Latin@ Project Reader:*

History and Culture in the United States. Durham, NC: Duke University Press, 2010.

Romo, Tere. *Patssi Valdez: A Precarious Comfort, Una comodidad precaria*. San Francisco, CA: Mexican Museum, 1999.

Rosaldo, Renato. "Cultural Citizenship and Educational Democracy." *Cultural Anthropology* 9, no. 3 (1994): 402–411.

Rosenthal, Stephanie, ed. *Traces: Ana Mendieta*. London: Hayward, 2013.

Roulet, Laura. "'Ana Mendieta': A Life Context." In *Ana Mendieta: Earth Body: Sculpture and Performance, 1972–1985*, edited by Olga M. Viso. Washington, DC: Hirshhorn Museum and Sculpture Garden in association with Hatje Cantz, 2004.

Saldaña-Portillo, María Josefina. *Indian Given: Racial Geographies across Mexico and the United States*. Durham, NC: Duke University Press, 2016.

———. *The Revolutionary Imagination in the Americas and the Age of Development*. Durham, NC: Duke University Press, 2003.

———. "Who's the Indian in Aztlan? Re-writing Mestizaje, Indianism, and Chicanismo from the Lacandon." In *The Latin American Subaltern Studies Reader*, edited by Ilcana Rodriguez, 402–423. Durham, NC: Duke University Press, 2001.

Saldívar, Ramón. "Historical Fantasy, Speculative Realism, and Postrace Aesthetics in Contemporary American Fiction." *American Literary History* 23, no. 3 (2011): 574–599.

Sandoval, Chela. *Methodology of the Oppressed*. Minneapolis: University of Minnesota Press, 2000.

Sandoval-Sánchez, Alberto. *José, Can You See: Latinos on and off Broadway*. Madison: University of Wisconsin Press, 1999.

———. "Politicizing Abjection: In the Manner of a Prologue for the Articulation of AIDS Latino Queer Identities." *American Literary History* 17, no. 3 (2005): 542–549.

Schlep Labs. "Easier as a Latino? Actually . . . " YouTube, 14 October 2012. https://www.youtube.com/watch?v=EVIrNxbaols.

Schneider, Rebecca. *The Explicit Body in Performance*. New York: Routledge, 1997.

Schor, Mira. "Backlash and Appropriation." In *The Power of Feminist Art: The American Movement of the 1970s, History and Impact*, edited by Norma Broude and Mary D. Garrard. New York: Harry N. Abrams, 1994.

Schultz, Stacy E. "Latina Identity: Reconciling Ritual, Culture, and Belonging." *Women's Art Journal* 29 (2008): 13–20.

Scott, Darieck. *Extravagant Abjection: Blackness, Power and Sexuality in the African American Literary Imagination*. New York: New York University Press, 2010.

Sedgwick, Eve Kosofsky. *Between Men: English Literature and Male Homosocial Desire*. New York: Columbia University Press, 1985.

See, Sarita. *The Decolonized Eye: Filipino American Art and Performance*. Minnesota: University of Minnesota Press, 2009.

Seed, Patricia. *American Pentimento: The Invention of Indians and the Pursuit of Riches*. Minneapolis: University of Minnesota Press, 2001.

Sharpe, Christina. *Monstrous Intimacies: Making Post-slavery Subjects*. Durham, NC: Duke University Press, 2010.

Shaw, Philip. *The Sublime*. New York: Routledge, 2006.

Shimakawa, Karen. *National Abjection: The Asian American Body Onstage*. Durham, NC: Duke University Press, 2002.

Sillito, Mat. "Don't Call Me a Lamanite." *Young Mormon Feminists Blog*, 3 March 2015. https://youngmormonfeminists.org/2015/03/03/dont-call-me-a-lamanite/.

Smith, Andrea. *Conquest: Sexual Violence and American Indian Genocide*. Durham, NC: Duke University Press, 2015.

———. *Native Americans and the Christian Right: The Gendered Politics of Unlikely Alliances*. Durham, NC: Duke University Press, 2008.

———. "Queer Theory and Native Studies: The Heteronormativity of Settler Colonialism." *GLQ* 16, no. 1–2 (2016): 41–68.

Solórzano, Armando. "Mormonism: Homogeneity, Latino and Latina Mormons, Latinos and Latinas as Lamanites, Familism," 22 July 2011. PDF printout.

Starkman, Paul, dir. "Episode 4: A Shock to the System." In *Work of Art: The Next Great Artist*. Prod. Sarah Jessica Parker et al. Bravo TV, June 30, 2010.

Steedman, Carolyn. *Dust: The Archive and Cultural History*. New Brunswick, NJ: Rutgers University Press, 2002.

Sternad, Jennifer Flores. "Cyclona and Early Chicano Performance Art: An Interview with Robert Legoretta." *GLQ* 12, no. 3 (2006).

Stevenson, Jill. *Sensational Devotion: Evangelical Performance in Twenty-First-Century America*. Ann Arbor: University of Michigan Press, 2013.

Stockton, Kathryn Bond. *Beautiful Bottom, Beautiful Shame: Where "Black" Meets "Queer."* Durham, NC: Duke University Press, 2006.

Taylor, Diana. *The Archive and the Repertoire: Performing Cultural Memory in the Americas*. Durham, NC: Duke University Press, 2003.

Torres, Maria de los Angeles. "Remembering Ana." *Latino Studies* 3 (2005): 428–431.

Tullis, F. LaMond. *Mormonism: A Faith for All Cultures*. Salt Lake City, UT: Brigham Young University Press, 1978.

Tyler, Imogen. *Revolting Subjects: Social Abjection and Resistance in Neoliberal Britain*. London: Zed, 2013.

Valdez, Patssi. Oral history interview with Patssi Valdez, 26 May–2 June 1999, Archives of American Art, Smithsonian Institution Archives, Washington, DC.

Vargas, Deborah R. *Dissonant Divas in Chicana Music: The Limits of La Onda*. Minneapolis: University of Minnesota Press, 2012.

———. "Ruminations on Lo Sucio as a Latino Queer Analytic." *American Quarterly* 66, no. 3 (September 2014): 715–726.

———. "Sucia Love: Losing, Lying, and Leaving in This Is How You Lose Her." In *Junot Díaz and the Decolonial Imagination*, edited by Monica Hanna, Jennifer Harford Vargas, and José David Saldívar. Durham, NC: Duke University Press, 2016.

Vera-Rosas, Gretel H. "Regarding 'the Mother of Anchor-Children': Towards an Ethical Practice of the Flesh." *E-misférica* 11, no. 1 (spring 2014).

Viego, Antonio. *Dead Subjects: Toward a Politics of Loss in Latino Studies.* Durham, NC: Duke University Press, 2007.

Viso, Olga M. *Ana Mendieta: Earth Body (Sculpture and Performance), 1972–1985.* Washington, DC: Hirshhorn Museum and Sculpture Garden in association with Hatje Cantz, 2004.

———. "Memory of History." In *Ana Mendieta: Earth Body (Sculpture and Performance), 1972–1985,* edited by Olga Viso. Washington, DC: Hirshhorn Museum and Sculpture Garden in association with Hatje Cantz, 2004.

———. *Unseen Mendieta: The Unpublished Works of Ana Mendieta.* New York: Prestel USA, 2008.

Vogel, Dan, and Brent Lee Metcalfe, eds. *American Apocrypha: Essays on the Book of Mormon.* Salt Lake City, UT: Signature, 2002.

Watson, Michael F. "Statistical Report, 2006." *Ensign,* May 2007, 7.

Webster, Sally. "Letter by Sally Webster," 1980. The A.I.R. Gallery Archive; MSS 184; 11; 440; Fales Library and Special Collections, New York University Libraries.

Wiegman, Robyn. *Object Lessons.* Durham, NC: Duke University Press, 2012.

Wilkie-Stibbs, Christine. "Borderland Children: Reflections on Narratives of Abjection." *Lion and the Unicorn* 30, no. 3 (2006): 319.

Williams, Raymond. "Structure of Feelings." In *Marxism and Literature.* New York: Oxford University Press, 1987.

Wolff, Rachel. "*Work of Art* Exit Interview No. 1: Episode Four." *New York Magazine,* 1 July 2010, http://nymag.com/author/Rachel%20Wolff/6/.

Ybarra-Frausto, Tómas. "Rasquachismo: A Chicano Sensibility." In *Chicano Aesthetics: Rasquachismo.* Phoenix: MARS Artspace, 1989.

Young, Cynthia. *Soul Power: Culture, Radicalism, and the Making of a U.S. Third World Left.* Durham, NC: Duke University Press, 2006.

Young, Lawrence. "Confronting Turbulent Environments: Issues in the Organizational Growth and Globalization of Mormonism." *Contemporary Mormonism: Social Science Perspectives,* edited by Marie Cornwall, Tim B. Heaton, and Lawrence Young. Urbana: University of Illinois Press, 1994.

Zeveloff, Naomi. "Immigration and Revelation: Some of Utah's LDS Latinos Believe Their Presence Is Part of Heavenly Father's Master Plan." *Salt Lake City Weekly,* 21 July 2005, 22.

Index